LOUIS I. KAHN

Writings, Lectures, Interviews

Louis I. Kahn, high school graduation portrait, 1920.

LOUIS I. KAHN

Writings, Lectures, Interviews

Introduction and edited by Alessandra Latour

RIZZOLI
NEW YORK

A mia madre

First published in the United States of America in 1991
by RIZZOLI INTERNATIONAL PUBLICATIONS, INC.
300 Park Avenue South, New York, New York 10010

Library of Congress Cataloging-in-Publication Data
Kahn, Louis I., 1901-1974.
    Louis I. Kahn : writings, lectures, interviews / edited by
  Alessandra Latour.
        p.   cm.
    Includes bibliographical references.
    ISBN 0-8478-1331-2 (HC). — ISBN 0-8478-1356-8 (PB)
    1. Kahn, Louis I., 1901-1974—Philosophy. 2. Architecture-
  -Language.   I. Latour, Alessandra.   II. Title.
NA737.K32A2   1991   90-50794
720′.92—dc20   CIP

All photographs of Louis I. Kahn appear courtesy of Esther Kahn.
Photographs on pages 49, 51, 52 by Gallob.
Photographs on pages 44 and 45 by Lawrence Williams.

Designed by Paul Chevannes
Printed in Singapore

Table of Contents

v

Louis I. Kahn in Venice, 1969.

7

Louis I. Kahn:
His Thought, His World

By Alessandra Latour

Words, for Louis I. Kahn, projected the same powerful imagery as his sketches, drawings, and the work itself. Words were not the fruit of mere skillful verbalization, of superficial expression, more or less articulated, more or less fluent and elaborated, but significant, precise, and carefully thought out terms that capture and portray a concept, an image, his conception of the world, his philosophy. For Kahn, the appropriate formulation of a discourse did not come easily, nor did the true elaboration of a project—the materialization of proper form—which meant the making of architecture that would express the real nature of things, represent the world he intended to build, secure the relationships he wanted to establish, create the institutions that would embody not just the circumstance of needs but the universality of inspirations in a city with an endless potential for growth.

For Kahn, elaboration of a concept, as well as bringing a project to fruition, required a lifetime process of learning punctuated by a series of "realizations" in which spontaneity and intuition merged with consciousness, with rationality. These realizations revealed a deep understanding, a profound knowledge of that mysterious, latent relationship between a sense of order and the transcendent dimension of religion or a dream. They revealed a conscience that allows complete expression, real freedom, and the fullness of one's being, overcoming the limitations of the ego, reaching the completion of the self: a careful and thoughtful distillation of the myriad images, ideas, manifestations around us, to attain an arduous but necessary harmony, almost unthinkable and unreacheable today. This speculation, this intense activity of tuning, this process of refinement, always permeated his words, speeches, writing; it was an investigation leading to a perfect agreement, a rare equilibrium, a real correspondence between "word," "image," "thought."

This collection of previously published writings, lectures, and interviews traces Kahn's thought process, extrapolating the diverse themes which became the leitmotiv of his philosophy—a speculative philosophy that disclosed his passion for research, his drive to question, his demand for constant verification, for dialogue, expressed with the same visual power found in his colors, lines, strokes, always sensuous and daring, visionary and realist, abstract and concrete. As his architecture sweeps us away through an atemporal dimension, albeit preserving a profound sense of both past and present, in the same way his thoughts project us toward unexplored grounds, allowing the mind to take flight, to wonder, while still bound to the universal values of human beings. We are confronted with the themes of presence, existence, order, commonality, measurable, unmeasurable design, form, realization, silence, light, beauty. They all come back to his constant search for a harmonious relationship between the constructed world, the artifact and nature, a search that also illuminates the lifelong aspiration of a great master to express poetry through architecture.

In the unfolding of this material, all his themes emerge in the order of their formulation, sometimes with insistence, sometimes with repetition, as something that should not be forgotten, a fervent reminder, a persistency about matters that should capture our attention, be the very core of our speculations. But the intention of this collection is not only to recapture Kahn's thought, it is also important to disclose his thinking process through time while providing the most complete documentation of his ideas. Only a few, short interviews have been eliminated, these being merely repetitive or partial in their formulation, or in a few cases those lacking permission to reprint. At the same time, many passages from "Wanting to be: The Philadelphia School" (1961) can be directly found in his other writings; therefore, it seemes more appropriate to present them in their original format.

Many people provided help in assembling this material. First, I would like to thank all the original publishers and the Louis I. Kahn Collection for allowing the reprinting of texts. I am particularly grateful to *Perspecta*, not only for its generosity on this particular occasion, but mainly for the key role it played in the excellent presentation of the work and thought of Kahn from the very beginning. Special thanks are also given to Dolores Gall and Julia Moore Converse for their full collaboration; to Daniel Friedman and Kostis Kouralis for their precious help in the collection of the texts; to Tom Stetz for his thoughtful advice; to David Morton, Lois Brown, and Vittoria Di Palma for their care in bringing this collection to publication; and a profound gratitude to Esther Kahn for the beautiful photographs, and always to Sue Ann Kahn for her valuable, affectionate, and constant support.

The Value and Aim in Sketching

There are no good or bad subjects, there are good or bad painters."—*Emile Gaudissard*
To the artist all in nature is beautiful. Those who are seized by the passion for truth
will learn to find beauty in the most ordinary objects. Only the untrained eye finds
ugliness in nature, through misunderstanding of the underlying philosophical truths;
for those subjects, previously considered inartistic, have been elevated to vie with any
other universally appreciated material. We should be less selective and more probing.
We must learn how a steamship is to be given its character as devotedly as how a
cactus plant can be given its particular character; or how a New York business building
is seen with an absolute detachment and devotion equal to that awakened by a cathedral.
Not simply the back alley streets of Europe with their quaintness, but also the busy
town with its architectural conglomerations; not only pompous estates but the mo-
notonous repetitions of the row house, should arrest our attention. By so thinking we will begin to understand the intrinsic character, and have respect for the
individuality underlying even the things that seemed to create no feeling within
us at first.

Drawing is a mode of representation. It makes no difference whether a watercolor
is tight, loose, or flabby; for if it discloses a purpose, it is of value, and the more we
understand the purpose the more valuable our watercolor will become.

A friend who visited the Rodin Museum asked me to explain what there was
about Rodin's sketches that could make seemingly sane people rave so much about
them. "Why, I think your sketches are much better. You ought to have them exhibited."
He was referring to some conscientious drawings I had made in life class at the

University. Of course I assured him that the reason for their obscurity was sheer neglect on my part, that I would have to break down some day, and show them to the world. I then went on to explain that drawing is employed by all the masters of the various forms of art in their own particular ways. The drawings this great sculptor made took form with his eye on the final results in stone. Although working with seemingly sloppy washes and careless lines, he was always thinking in terms of his chisel and hammer. They are great drawings because they embody the hidden potentialities of his medium. They are the true visions of a creator. A biographer of Rodin explained that his drawing betrayed the divine impatience of the artist who fears that a fleeting impression may escape him.

No object is entirely apart from its surroundings and therefore cannot be represented convincingly as a thing in itself; also the presence of our own individuality causes it to appear differently than it would to others. The simplest form, be it but a moulding, is only a part of a creative process. It is the interwoven relation of that moulding to the rest of the creation which makes it significant. It is this kind of relation that we should look for.

There is no value in trying to imitate exactly. Photographs will serve you best of all, if that is your aim. We should not imitate when our intention is to create—to improvise. When we are too much concerned about how So-and-so would have done it, or what Professor Blank will say about it, the drawing will lose in its general intention and value, and just become another sketch. We can never think clearly in terms of another's reactions; we must learn to see things for ourselves, in order to develop a language of self-expression. The capacity to see comes from persistently analyzing our reactions to what we look at, and their significance as far as we are concerned. The more one looks, the more one will come to see.

I try in all my sketching not to be entirely subservient to my subject, but I have respect for it, and regard it as something tangible—alive—from which to extract my feelings. I have learned to regard it as no physical impossibility to move mountains and trees, or change cupolas and towers to suit my taste. I try evolve a composition, and make every sketch count for as much value to me as may be gotten out of a design problem. To make a sketch of this sort requires, of course, the making of many impressions and notes "on the job." You must then get away from it all to work over and crystallize your thoughts in order to develop the picture in the form of a readable design. The impression of a cathedral, no matter how faithful you are to all the rules which govern the making of things appear tridimensional, will often only be an illustration of depth, height, and breadth; unless it has that element of the feeling for its design, and the lyrical rhythm and counterpoint of its mass, it becomes merely a stupid architectural perspective. In fact it is not necessary at all to follow the rules of perspective in making notes that will be of value to you. Did not the Chinese painters, who succeeded better than any others in representing space, ignore almost completely perspective as we practice it?

There exists in the thousands of sketches brought over from Europe entirely too much pose and artifice. It is a pity to allow our impressions to be dominated by the many cast iron styles of architectural representation. Why most of the drawings can only be expressions in terms of stylistic Ernest Born, or the shallow Chamberlain, is more than I can understand. If these are the only vocabularies with which one can record the masterpieces of Europe, I hold but little regard for those who blow their heads off about the feeling and grace of Rheims, and then show a flabby sketch of some buttresses as a proof of their understanding.

"The Value and Aim in Sketching," from *T-Square Club Journal*, vol. I, no. 6, May 1931, pp. 19-21; reprinted with permission of the Philadelphia Chapter of The American Institute of Architects.

Louis I. Kahn in his office, c. 1950 (Photo: John Ebstel).

Louis I. Kahn at the opening of the Richards Medical Towers show at The Museum of Modern Art, 1961.

13

"Standards" Versus Essential Space: Comments on Unit Plans for War Housing

It is well for architects to review their work critically and to draw conclusions which may benefit their own and others' future efforts. The evolution of the plans shown here and above is due to unsatisfactory experience with standard plans and the slight variations of such plans. After eight years of "organized housing" it seems time to analyze the actual value of plans developed for one-, two-, and three-bedroom units and their relation to actual use, now that many projects have been built and occupied.

To begin with, let us review such plans as the row house in Philadelphia, the row house in Baltimore, the shoe-box bungalow in Jersey or Long Island, and try to understand why it is that these houses which we have tried to improve still seem to be vastly preferred by the average person. Why do people prefer the ugliness of dickey-front houses, compressed in long rows, surrounded by a sea of concrete, to houses placed on the contours, related to sun and breeze, with garden living and community facilities? It is true, of course, that many localities offer no alternatives in the given price class, but it seems much more important to recognize these dwellings as composites of certain amenities accepted as essential, for otherwise they would not sell.

The most important advantage that we could find is the provision of essential space. Aside from that fact, these houses have been built as cheaply as the Government's houses. The operative builder offers no garden living space, the neighborhood is all house and street, and the row type used offers little flexibility when grade conditions are encountered. To maintain the various entrance levels to garage and to the front of the house, all trace of the natural beauty of the site is erased, imposing in addition drainage difficulties on adjoining ground. And yet he produces a house that satisfies a prime requisite of the house buyer or renter. His client gets a house with space in which to put his car, and a basement large enough for storage of a bicycle, a laundry, a workshop. To keep house is practically impossible if room is not provided for untidy work and storage. Architects may have succeeded in developing closely knit actual space for living, but this very space becomes bedlam when the bicycle and the baby carriage must be stored in the living room, the laundry washed in the kitchen and the chair repaired in the bedroom.

If we inspect our own Middletown plans, we realize that our apprehensions about the inadequacy of the storage space and the heater room were correct. The heater room was figured just large enough to take the units. The furnace is fired with some ease only after carefully planned movements are developed by the man of the house. Storage space, which should be at least 100 square feet, was made 30, to conform to the standards. Garbage and rubbish are kept in front of the house until removed. One of the greatest weaknesses of Government housing to date has been the lack of adequate minimums covering storage space, waste, and laundry. And yet, as we have seen, ignoring the vital requirements of essential space makes the house inadequate for all save the emergency market, while the lack of a thoughtful solution to the problems of waste and laundry can turn an otherwise satisfactory project into an eyesore.

The basement provided by the private builder, in addition to offering adequate space for rugs, trunks, kiddy car, baby carriage, garden tools, is also the heater room, coal storage area, and the laundry with its trays, washer, and other equipment. And yet the basement is no ideal solution. It means dragging the laundry upstairs and down, it is dank, poorly lighted, and increases the difficulties of drainage and connections to sewer lines. It was in an attempt to include the many advantages of the basement while eliminating its defects that the Coatesville and Washington plans were developed.

In essence, the scheme consists of nothing more than a transposition of the basement to the ground level, with one story of living space above. When developed into a typical four-family unit, some interesting features appear. There is open space between the utility blocks which serves very conveniently as a carport, a shelter for the entrance, or a covered play area. These openings also eliminate the distinction between "front" and "back," as there is free circulation through, rather than around, each building. No attempt was made to vary the size of the utility room with the number of bedrooms in a dwelling unit. The concrete post and beam construction shown on the model was developed to meet the building regulations of Washington, where buildings with more than two families have to be of brick construction.

It should be noted that the living room, kitchen, dining space, bathroom, heating stack, and stair form a unit, which is standardized for all dwelling types. With this unit, one, two, or three bedrooms are combined as required. The standard arrangement has two bedrooms while the necessary number of one- and three-bedroom dwellings may be obtained by interlocking the plans as shown. Where a pair of three-bedroom units are used together in one of the buildings, it is possible to develop a project storage room on the ground floor. This extra space, when distributed at points of vantage on the site, is very useful to the management for storage of screens, garden tools, etc., and may be used conveniently for gas and electric meters as well.

The living space on one level offers a very real possibility for economical planning which, to a great extent, offsets the added cost of extra space on the ground floor. Since, in the average two-story house the main living rooms are on the first floor, with larger windows required at this point, lintel problems develop which are avoided in the scheme illustrated. It is also difficult to provide adequate shelter at the entrance to the conventional house, a situation which resolves itself quite easily in this scheme.

In the Middletown plan it was logical to enter the kitchen side of the house. A plan with greater street frontage might have overcome the corridor entrance to the living room. The architects lost heart on this solution, because increased frontage for each dwelling would have raised costs too much.

Another advantage of the Washington and Coatesville plan is its adaptability to grade conditions. Because of the masonry construction of the ground floor, variations in grade from front to rear can be handled fairly easily, while drainage problems are simplified since some of the surface water can be passed through the carports.

Planners, in their attempts to control room orientation, have sometimes resorted to extravagant site development, or have changed the unit types on opposite sides of the street. The "ground-freed" house may be entered with equal ease from either side, permitting the architect to orient rooms and porches as he desires.

This scheme was developed for the Mutual Ownership Division of the FWA under Colonel Westbrook, an agency which was primarily interested in finding solutions for self-supporting projects. A close study had to be made of what people want rather than what the standards allow. The project for Coatesville, Pennsylvania, had to meet those demands. A study of our own previous attempts at housing and other work in the field, plus the encouragement to disregard past performances, led to the scheme just described, whose most important feature is recognition of the need for essential space, as distinguished from space required by the standards. Architects for this project were George Howe, Oscar Stonorov, and Louis I. Kahn. During the process of study, Mr. Howe and Mr. Kahn were appointed architects for a project of the Alley Dwelling Authority in Washington. For this project the Coatesville scheme was used, with changes to make it meet the stringent code requirements of the city.

It should hardly be necessary to state that the architects make no claims to complete authorship of the "ground-freed" house. The idea is an old one, and a very good one, and its application to housing offers distinct advantages, especially at the present time, when enthusiasm for site planning is tending to obscure the primary importance of the house. It is possible on any project to skimp on roads, planting and other elements, and to bring these up to par at some future date. The house, on the other hand, is completely inflexible once built. And if essential space is omitted at the beginning it can never be added. In view of these simple and inescapable facts, it is time to take another look at the standards and see what they mean in terms of family living.

" 'Standards' Versus Essential Space: Comments on Unit Plans for War Housing," by George Howe, Oscar Stonorov, and Louis I. Kahn in *Architectural Forum*, vol. 76, no. 5, May 1942, pp. 308–11; © 1942 BPI Communications, Inc., used with permission.

Louis I. Kahn in his office.

Monumentality

Gold is a beautiful material. It belongs to the sculptor.

Monumentality in architecture may be defined as a quality, a spiritual quality inherent in a structure which conveys the feeling of its eternity, that it cannot be added to or changed. We feel that quality in the Parthenon, the recognized architectural symbol of Greek civilization.

Some argue that we are living in an unbalanced state of relativity which cannot be expressed with a single intensity of purpose. It is for that reason, I feel, that many of our confrères do not believe we are psychologically constituted to convey a quality of monumentality to our buildings.

But have we yet given full architectural expression to such social monuments as the school, the community, or culture center? What stimulus, what movement, what social or political phenomenon shall we yet experience? What event or philosophy shall give rise to a will to commemorate its imprint on our civilization? What effect would such forces have on our architecture?

Science has given to the architect its explorations into new combinations of materials capable of great resistance to the forces of gravity and wind.

Recent experimenters and philosophers of painting, sculpture, and architecture have instilled new courage and spirit in the work of their fellow artists.

Monumentality is enigmatic. It cannot be intentionally created. Neither the finest material nor the most advanced technology need enter a work of monumental character for the same reason that the finest ink was not required to draw up the Magna Carta.

However, our architectural monuments indicate a striving for structural perfec-

18

tion which has contributed in great part to their impressiveness, clarity of form, and logical scale.

Stimulated and guided by knowledge we shall go far to develop the forms indigenous to our new materials and methods. It is, therefore, the concern of this paper to touch briefly on the broader horizons which science and skill have revealed to the architect and engineer, and sketch the faint outlines of possible structural concepts and expressions they suggest.

No architect can rebuild a cathedral of another epoch embodying the desires, the aspirations, the love and hate of the people whose heritage it became. Therefore the images we have before us of monumental structures of the past cannot live again with the same intensity and meaning. Their faithful duplication is unreconcilable. But we dare not discard the lessons these buildings teach for they have the common characteristics of greatness upon which the buildings of our future must, in one sense or another, rely.

In Greek architecture, engineering concerned itself fundamentally with materials in compression. Each stone or part forming the structural members was made to bear with accuracy on each other to avoid tensile action stone is incapable of enduring.

The great cathedral builders regarded the members of the structural skeleton with the same love of perfection and search for clarity of purpose. Out of periods of inexperience and fear, when they erected over-massive core-filled veneered walls, grew a courageous theory of a stone-over-stone vault skeleton producing a downward and outward thrust, which forces were conducted to a column or a wall provided with the added characteristic of the buttress which together took this combination of action. The buttress allowed lighter walls between the thrust points and these curtain walls were logically developed for the use of large glass windows. This structural concept, derived from earlier and cruder theories, gave birth to magnificent variations in the attempts to attain loftier heights and greater spans creating a spiritually emotional environment unsurpassed.

The influence of the Roman vault, the dome, the arch, has etched itself in deep furrows across the pages of architectural history. Through Romanesque, Gothic, Renaissance, and today, its basic forms and structural ideas have been felt. They will continue to reappear but with added powers made possible by our technology and engineering skill.

The engineer of the latter part of the nineteenth century developed from basic principles the formulas of the handbook. Demands of enormous building quantity and speed developed the handbook engineer who used its contents, more or less forgetting basic principles. Now we hear about continuity in structures, not a new word but recently an all important word in engineering which promises to relegate the handbook to the archives.

The I-beam is an engineering accomplishment deriving its shape from an analysis of the stresses involved in its use. It is designed so that the greater proportion of the area of cross section is concentrated as far as possible from the center of gravity. The shape adapted itself to ease of rolling and under test it was found that even the fillets, an aid in the rolling process, helped convey the stresses from one section to another in continuity.

Safety factors were adopted to cover possible inconsistencies in the composition of the material of manufacture. Large-scale machinery and equipment needed in its fabrication lead to standardization.

The combination of safety factors (ignorance factor as one engineer termed it) and standardization narrowed the practice of engineering to the section of members from handbooks recommending sections much heavier than calculations would require and further limited the field of engineering expression stifling the creation of the more graceful forms which the stress diagrams indicated. For example, the common practice of using an I-beam as a cantilever has no relation to the stress diagram which shows that the required depth of material from the supporting end outward may decrease appreciably.

Joint construction in common practice treats every joint as a hinge which makes connections to columns and other members complex and ugly.

To attain greater strength with economy, a finer expression in the structural solution of the principle of concentrating the area of cross section away from the center of gravity is the tubular form since the greater the moment of inertia the greater the strength.

A bar of a certain area of cross section rolled into a tube of the same area of cross section (consequently of a larger diameter) would possess a strength enormously greater than the bar.

The tubular member is not new, but its wide use has been retarded by technological limitations in the construction of joints. Up until very recently welding has been outlawed by the building codes. In some cases, where it was permitted, it was required to make loading tests for every joint.

Structure designs must discard the present moment coefficients and evolve new calculations based on the effect of continuity in structures. The structural efficiency of rigid connection, in which the sheer value and the resisting moment is at least equal to the values of the supporting member, is obtained by the welding of such connections. The column becomes part of the beam and takes on added duties not usually calculated for columns.

The engineer and architect must then go back to basic principles, must keep abreast with and consult the scientist for new knowledge, redevelop his judgment of the behavior of structures, and acquire a new sense of form derived from design rather than piece together parts of convenient fabrication.

Riveted I-beam plate and angle construction is complex and graceless. Welding has opened the doors to vast accomplishments in pure engineering which allows forms of greater strength and efficiency to be used. The choice of structural forms are limitless even for given problems, and therefore the aesthetic philosophy of the individual can be satisfied by his particular composition of plates, angles, and tubular forms accomplishing the same answer to the challenge of the forces of gravity and wind.

The ribs, vaults, domes, buttresses come back again only to enclose space in a more generous, far simpler way and in the hands of our present masters of building in a more emotionally stirring way. From stone, the part has become smaller and cannot be seen by the naked eye. It is now the molecular composition of the metal observed and tested by the scientist through spectroscopy or by photoelastic recordings. His finding may go to the architect and engineer in the more elemental form of the formula, but by that means it shall have become an instrumental part of the builder's palette to be used without prejudice or fear. That is the modern way.

Gothic architecture relying on basically simple construction formulas derived from experience and the material available, could only go so far. Beauvais cathedral, its builders trying to reach greater spans and height, collapsed.

The compressive stress of stone is measured in hundreds of pounds.

While not only the compressive, but also the bending and tensile stress of steel is measured in thousands of pounds.

Beauvais cathedral needed the steel we have. It needed the knowledge we have.

Glass would have revealed the sky and become a part of the enclosed space framed by an interplay of exposed tubular ribs, plates, and columns of a stainless metal formed true and faired into a continuous flow of lines expressive of their stress patterns. Each member would have been welded to the next to create a continuous structural unity worthy of being exposed because its engineering gives no resistance to the laws of beauty having its own aesthetic life. The metal would have now been aged into a friendly material protected from deterioration by its intrinsic composition.

This generation is looking forward to its duty and benefit to build for the masses with its problems of housing and health.

It is aware of our outmoded cities.

It accepts the airship as a vital need.

Factories have adopted horizontal assembly and shifting population has required the transformation of large tracts of virgin territory at least temporarily for complete human living.

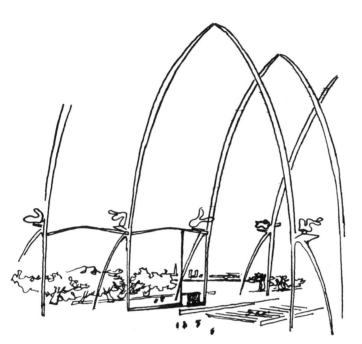

Section Thru Beauvais
after Auguste Choisy

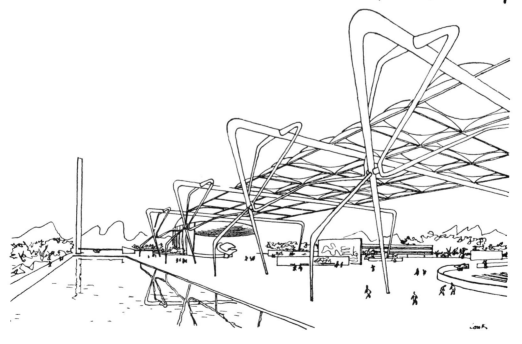

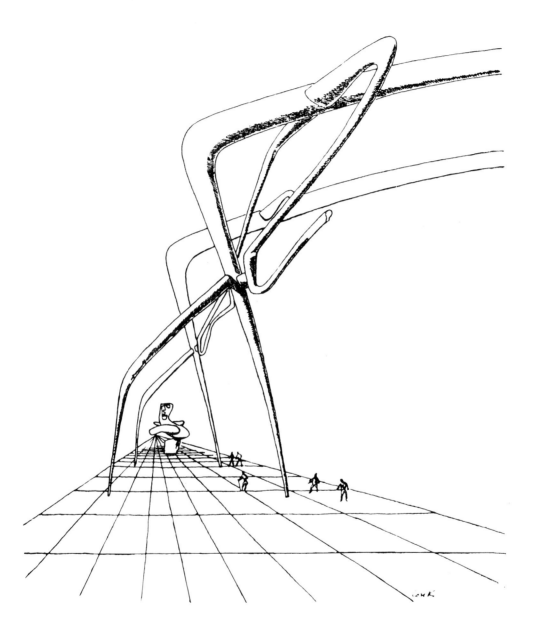

The building of a complete permanent town was attempted and almost built for the workers at Willow Run.

The nation has adopted the beginnings of social reform.

War production may become normal production on the same scale accepted as sound economics.

Still untried but pledged stand the noble principles of the Atlantic Charter.

In the days we look forward to must then the cathedral, the culture center, the legislative palace, world island—the seat of the congress of nations, the palace of labor and industry, the monuments to commemorate the achievements and aspirations of our time, be built to resemble Chartres, Crystal Palace, Palazzo Strozzi, or the Taj Mahal?

War engineering achievements in concrete, steel, and wood are showing the signs of maturity appropriate to guide the minds entrusted with the conception of buildings of such high purpose. The giant major skeleton of the structure can assert its right to be seen. It need no longer be clothed for eye appeal. Marble and woods feel at ease in its presence. New wall products of transparent, translucent, and opaque material with exciting textures and color are suspended or otherwise fastened to the more delicate forms of the minor members. Slabs of paintings articulate the circulation in the vast sheltered space. Sculpture graces its interior.

Outstanding masters of building design indicated the direction an architect may take to unravel and translate into simple terms the complexity of modern requirements. They have restated the meaning of a wall, a post, a beam, a roof, and a window, and their interrelation in space. They had to be restated when we recall the conglomerations that style copying tortured these elements into.

Efforts towards a comprehensive architecture will help to develop these elements and refine their meaning. A wall dividing interior space is not the same wall dividing the outside from the interior. Masonry shall always function as retaining and garden walls. It may be used for exterior walls for its decorative qualities, but be supplemented by interior slabs designed to meet more directly the challenge of the elements.

Structural ingenuity may eliminate the interior post, but as long as it must exist its place is reserved and its independence respected in the planning of space.

Structural problems center about the roof. The permanence and beauty of its surfaces is a major problem confronting science. The surfacing of the domes, vaults, and arches appearing as part of the exterior contours of the building may be an integral part of the structural design. Stainless metal, concrete or structural plastics, structural glass in light panes, or great reinforced glass castings may be the choice for domes and vaults, depending on the requirements, the climate, and the desired effect. The surfacing of flat roofs should be given equally serious consideration whether it is planned for use or not.

The citizens of a metropolitan area of a city and their representatives have formulated a program for a culture center endorsed by the national educational center. The citizens' committee collaborated with the architect and his staff of engineers. Costs were not discussed. Time was not "of the essence." Its progress was the concern of many.

From above we see the noble outlines of the building. Much taller buildings some distance from the site do not impress us with the same feeling of receptiveness. Its site is a prominent elevation in the outlying countryside framed by dark forests defining the interior of broad strokes in land architecture.

On the ground the first reaction comes from the gigantic sculptural forms of the skeleton frame. This backbone of the architect's central idea successfully challenges the forces which during its design challenged to destroy it. To solve the more minute complexities of the entire organism, its creator had drawn his conclusions and made his decisions from the influences of many people and things around him.

The plan does not begin nor end with the space he has enveloped, but from the adjoining delicate ground sculpture it stretches beyond to the rolling contours and vegetation of the surrounding land and continues farther out to the distant hills.

The immediate ground sculpture disciplines his mind in shaping it into stronger geometric planes and cubes to satisfy his desire for terraces and pools, steps and approaches. The landscape designer countered or accentuated these planes with again geometric and free forms interwoven with the lacy leaf patterns of the deciduous tree.

The plans reveal that the vast spans shelter smaller areas designed for specific use, which are divided from the whole by panels of glass, insulated slabs, and marble. These partitions are free of the structure and related only to the circulation pattern. The ground plan seems continuous. The great lobby is a part of the amphitheater which dips down to the stage. The light comes from above through an undulating series of prismatic glass domes.

Ahead, some distance from the entrance, is a great mural of brilliant color. As we approach it the forms clearly defined from a distance seem to divide into forms of their own, each with its own color power, clear and uncultured.

To one side is the community museum of sculpture, painting, and crafts. It exhibits the work of the younger men and women attending the vocational and art academies. Here they are accepted because their talents can be judged by those who have themselves been instructed in the basic principles underlying the use of a material. The emotional adaptations are left for the exhibitor himself to evaluate by contact, comparison, and experience.

Sculpture shows the tendency to define form and construction. Marble and stone is carved as of old. Castings in new alloys and plastics are favorite methods of obtaining permanency. Solids are interwoven with sheets and tubes of metal. The subject matter exhibited has no bounds. With the new materials and tools, chemical tints, and with manufacture at the artist's disposal, his work becomes alive with ideas. Metal sprays and texture guns, with fine adjustments have also become the instruments of the sculptor, painter, and craftsman. One of the younger men had cast within a large, irregular cube of transparent plastic other forms and objects of brilliant color. A sphere, planes at various angles, copper wire in free lines are seen through the plastic.

From these experiments in form the architect will eventually learn to choose appropriate embellishments for his structures. So far he has omitted them. His judgment leads him to free-standing forms in space.

Some of the younger artists are influenced by the works of an older sculptor who has developed a theory of scale in relation to space. He has argued that as the size of the structural work is increased the monolithic character of smaller work does not apply. He chose for large work a small consistent part or module of a definite shape, a cube, a prism, or a sphere which he used to construct block over block, with delicate adjustments to the effect of light and shadow, the overall form. His work seen from great distances retains a texturally vibrant quality produced by these numerous blocks and the action of the sun upon them.

Before we can feel the new spirit which must envelop the days to come we must prepare ourselves to use intelligently the knowledge derived from all sources. Nostalgic yearning for the ways of the past will find but few ineffectual supporters.

Steel, the lighter metals, concrete, glass, laminated woods, asbestos, rubber, and plastics, are emerging as the prime building materials of today. Riveting is being replaced by welding, reinforced concrete is emerging from infancy with prestressed reinforced concrete, vibration and controlled mixing, promising to aid in its ultimate refinement. Laminated wood is rapidly replacing lumber and is equally friendly to the eye, and plastics are so vast in their potentialities that already numerous journals and periodicals devoted solely to their many outlets are read with interest and hope. The untested characteristics of these materials are being analyzed, old formulas are being discarded. New alloys of steel, shatterproof and thermal glass and synthetics of innumerable types, together with the material already mentioned, make up the new palette of the designer.

To what extent progress in building will be retarded by ownership patterns, dogmas, style consciousness, precedent, untested building materials, arbitrary standards, outmoded laws and regulations, untrained workmen and artless craftsmen, is speculation. But the findings of science and their application have taken large steps recently in the development of war materials which point to upset normally controlled progress and raise our hopes to the optimistic level.

Standardization, prefabrication, controlled experiments and tests, and specialization are not monsters to be avoided by the delicate sensitiveness of the artist. They are merely the modern means of controlling vast potentialities of materials for living, by chemistry, physics, engineering, production, and assembly, which lead to the necessary knowledge the artist must have to expel fear in their use, broaden his creative instinct, give him new courage, and thereby lead him to the adventures of unexplored places. His work will then be part of his age and will afford delight and service for his contemporaries.

I do not wish to imply that monumentality can be attained scientifically or that the work of the architect reaches its greatest service to humanity by his peculiar genius to guide a concept towards a monumentality. I merely defend, because I admire, the architect who possesses the will to grow with the many angles of our development. For such a man finds himself far ahead of his fellow workers.

"Monumentality" from *New Architecture and City Planning, A Symposium*, ed. Paul Zucker (New York: Philosophical Library, 1944) pp. 77–88.

Louis I. Kahn in Moscow, 1965.

Louis I. Kahn in Moscow, 1965.

Toward a Plan for Midtown Philadelphia

Expressways are like **RIVERS**

These **RIVERS** *frame the area to be served*

RIVERS *have* **HARBORS**

HARBORS *are the municipal parking towers*

from the **HARBORS** *branch a system of* **CANALS** *that serve the interior*

the **CANALS** *are the go streets*

from the **CANALS** *branch cul-de-sac* **DOCKS**

the **DOCKS** *serve as entrance halls to the buildings.*

Architecture is also the street. There is no order to the movement on streets. Streets look alike, reflecting little of the activities they serve. Carcassonne without walls, cities without entrances, indiscriminate movement without places to stop. The design of the street is design for movement.

Fifty years ago before the automobile and the skyscraper, this map looked the same. The open space system is substantially the street system which occupies about 30% of the site. Except for the Vine Street Expressway the streets have retained their dimensions. Yard spaces have disappeared with the growing density and coverage of buildings. Recently with the greater increase in cars, parking lots have become the new open spaces. In general parking lots and garages take over other uses now on the secondary streets between the main shopping streets. Movement through the city is difficult. A parking ban is now being tried which has increased the flow of traffic and accentuated the value of off-street parking. Those streets cleared of parking still have the conflicting *staccato* movement of buses or trolleys and the *go* intentions of the car moving in the same lanes.

It is intended by the drawings which follow to *redefine* the *use of streets* and separate one type of movement from another so that cars, buses, trolleys, trucks, and pedestrians will move and stop more freely, and not get in each other's way. This system utilizes the old street, setting aside widening and other costly improvements as untimely before a more effective use of present street area is tested. However, the widening of Lombard Street as an expressway planned by the Philadelphia City Planning Commission is important. It would accomplish the demolition of decidedly bad slums and help frame the area known as CENTER CITY.

By designating specific streets for the staccato movement of buses and trolleys, specific streets for go traffic, and others as terminal streets for stopping, the efficiency of street movement would be increased considerably. Cars may enter the areas—and not be ruled out as many of today's planners propose. Zoning would grow naturally out of the type of movement on a street. Architecture would tend to be related to the type of movement.

This system of movement is not designed for speed but for order and convenience. The present mixture of staccato, through, stop and go traffic makes all the streets equally ineffectual. The orderly discrimination of traffic of varying intentions should tend to facilitate flow and thereby encourage rather than discourage entrance of private cars into the center of town.

It is further intended by this system to stimulate more imaginative development of our shopping areas along the lines of the new suburban shopping centers which already provide a pattern of movement sympathetic to the pedestrian and the motor. In town, this distinction of types of movement could also give rise to new building and merchandising ideas. Chestnut Street as a pedestrian way with a single trolley line becomes virtually a 60-foot promenade. Trees could be planted or shelters built for shade, and the free zig-zag lines of the movement of people from one side of the promenade to the other would tend to free the design of shops from their present linear limitations.

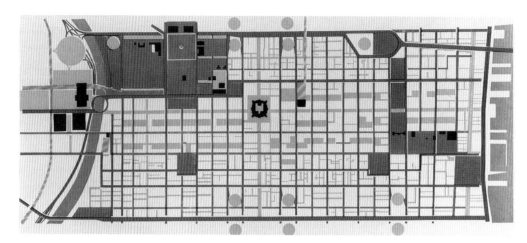

Proposed Movement Plan

THROUGH STREETS—rivers or expressways (red) as a part of their design are provided with harbors in the form of free or low-cost Municipal Garages for all day use of cars and within reasonable walking distance of offices and shops.

GO STREETS—or canals (brown) afford access to the center city, free of trolleys, local buses, and parked vehicles and with a reduced number of intersections.

STOP STREETS—or dock streets (yellow), blocked from uninterested through traffic, for staccato movement of trolleys, local buses, parking and service.

Existing Movement Plan

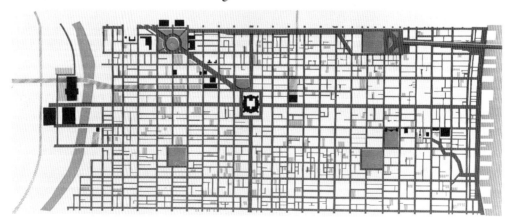

DOCKS—(yellow) space for deliveries and loading, for parking, service stations, and short-time commercial parking garages. Existing minor streets, increased where needed, are zoned for these purposes and blocked to through traffic. Many parking garages now existing are located in suggested dock areas.

PEDESTRIAN WAYS—(green) are primarily shopping streets unharassed by cars and trucks, allowing the movement of trolleys or local buses for the convenience of shoppers and office workers.

Building Plan For Midtown Philadelphia

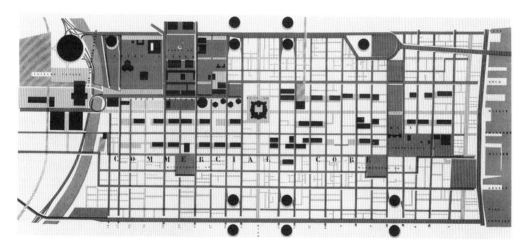

Expressways

"Go" Streets—through motor traffic; no
parking no trolley cars or local buses

Municipal Parking buildings

"Stop" Streets—parking and service; trolleys
and local buses no other through traffic

Docks—parking and service; parking
buildings

Commercial Parking Garages

Pedestrian Ways—trolley cars and local buses no private motor traffic

The harbor gateways are proposed as parking towers built at the same time as the expressway on Lombard Street and at the suggested points to be acquired by the Parking Authority on Vine Street. Each tower would house about 1500 cars. The garage buildings in the dock areas between Market and Chester, Chestnut and Walnut, are proposed as built by private enterprise aided in acquisition and standards by the Parking Authority.

The COMMERCIAL CORE is accentuated in this study for the purpose of suggesting that the contemplated development of the Chinese Wall—Pennsylvania Boulevard area (known as Penn Center) should not be isolated from the Core. The strength of the new development lies in tying it together with existing shopping and commercial patterns.

It is suggested that the address of Penn Center should be extended to include the area from 18th Street to the river, thereby tying in the Pennsylvania Station at 30th Street with its suburban station at 17th. Present Penn Center plans call for development from City Hall to 18th Street only. The bus station proposed at 18th Street by the City Planning Commission would serve both ends of the extended Penn Center. The NEW CITY HALL including the courts and technical buildings is located in the Triangle Area as part of our enlarged CIVIC AND CULTURAL CENTER at Logan Square. This move anticipates stimulation of developments westward and reclamation of the Schuylkill River for recreation. This relatively inexpensive area would allow for the continued development of the expanding functions of our city government and would eventually reveal itself as the new Philadelphia Landmark—an impressive entrance to the center city at its rail and motor gateway.

Over part of the railroad yards of the 30th Street Station, a TRANSPORTATION GATEWAY is proposed, tying together two levels of passenger tracks, the high level freight line, a trucking level, and a helicopter air connection as a transportation interchange and a freight center. This would consolidate some of the services of the Pennsylvania Railroad now spread over a large area, and serve the needs of the Post Office and the new Bulletin building.

Detail of Existing and Proposed Harbors

Detail of existing blocks in the center city shows present trend in the appearance of parking lots and garages on minor streets between main shopping streets, present movement mixture, and frequent intersections.

Proposed changes separate the mixture of movement, creating streets for staccato movement only and for go movement only. Terminal areas for docking, free of through

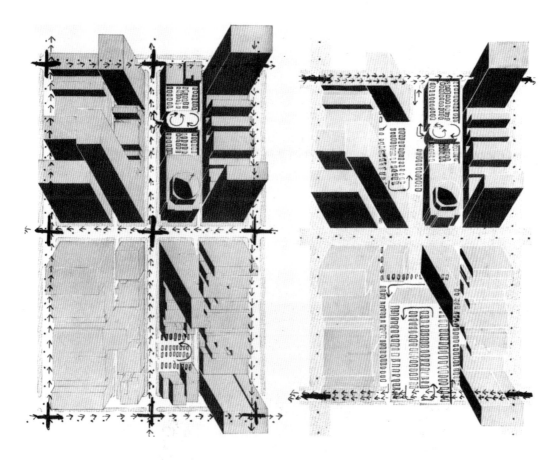

movement, provide delivery, loading, and parking for buildings now fronting on the main shopping streets, enlarging on the present location of parking on the minor streets. Shopping streets without go traffic become freer for people to walk and shop. Only the trolley remains to tie together the linear shopping area stretching for about three miles.

House and Harbor

The row house studies shown here were made for the Philadelphia City Planning Commission to suggest, on an equal economic basis, improvements over the present row house system used by the operative builders in the northeast Philadelphia area.

33

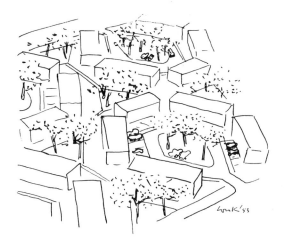

The principle of harbor entrances applied to the street system offered decided advantages of adaptability to terrain and drainage, preservation of trees, safety, and off-street parking, and resulted in a grouping of buildings with more distant outlook and privacy. The garage and front door entrance on the harbor opens up the entire rear of the house as the garden and outdoor living area.

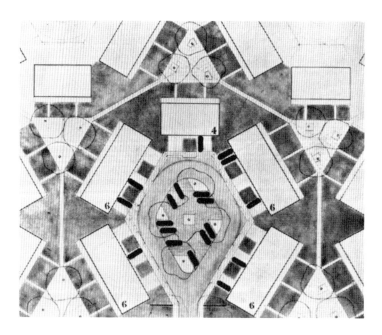

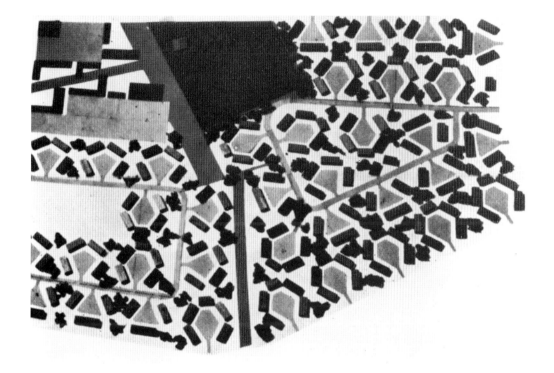

Row house construction on the gridiron street system with rear drive completely obliterates the original site characteristics of trees, streams, and contours. The front faces a through street with parking, the rear alley connects with the cross streets and is the garage entrance of the house. Practically the only green area is the terraced lawn in front of the house. The various cul-de-sac or harbor types shown in the site plan adjust to closer interlocking of land and to the varying conditions of contours. The interlocking discipline was devised again to satisfy densities comparable to the economics of the present row house.

Existing Movement Pattern

This type of drawing made fifty years ago would show dots in all the streets—no arrow, no crosses. The symbol of staccato movement would well have applied to the delivery wagon, carriage, and horse-drawn trolley. Now on the same streets trolleys, buses, trucks and cars with varying speeds, purposes, and destinations travel

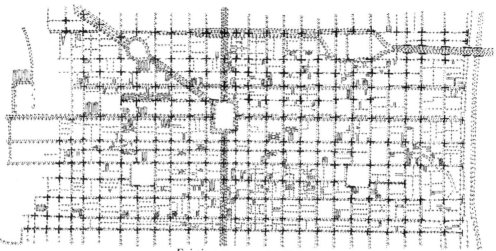

Existing movement pattern.

together. Uninterested traffic destined to places outside the center may choose streets at will. Motion is further restrained by loading, deliveries, and parking. Frequent intersections frustrate movement.

Vine Street, widened to expressway dimensions, has the same number of intersections as before. The original plans for the expressway, which were not realized by the Philadelphia City Planning Commission, called for a depressed cartway with entrances by ramp to cross streets.

Parking lots and garages are developing to some extent where they are most needed. Demolition of unprofitable or unfit buildings usually result in a parking lot wherever it happens. These places to stop now exist in the stream of movement. The slowest vehicles set the pace of movement.

Proposed Movement Pattern

The added movement symbol is the wound-up street or municipal garage at the strategic gateway interchanges off the Vine and Lombard expressways. These, with the expressways of the Delaware and Schuylkill, frame midtown Philadelphia. Though the number of intersections have been decreased, the gridiron pattern of the streets are intact. Staccato movement is on its system of streets separated from all go traffic. The main interior streets of Broad and Market intersecting at City Hall have been converted into linear docks. Skyscrapers, banks, and department stores on these streets are thereby provided with an automobile entrance and a place for people to park. The trend indicated on the existing movement map of parking lots and garages on minor streets between main shopping streets is extended, and these places are designed as terminals. Buses and trolleys are retained on the main shopping streets for public transportation and to keep the linear business area tied together. This plan will provide docking space for trucks on all streets except the go streets.

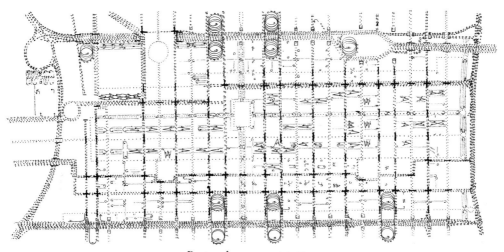

Proposed movement pattern.

•••• *staccato* → *go* ↻ *parking* > *garage* + *intersection*

The tower entrances and interchanges, wound-up parking terminals, suggest a new stimulus to unity in urban architecture, one which would find expression from the order of movement. The location and design of these entrances are an integral part of the design of the expressway financed and constructed as a unit. It is not an isolated real estate venture which could lead to compromise and the distortion of the system. At night we know these towers by their illumination in color. These yellow, red, green, blue, and white towers tell us the sector we are entering, and along the approach, light is used to see by and give us direction in ideas of lighting in rhythm with our speed. From these entrances a system of canals or interior streets feed the various activities of center city life.

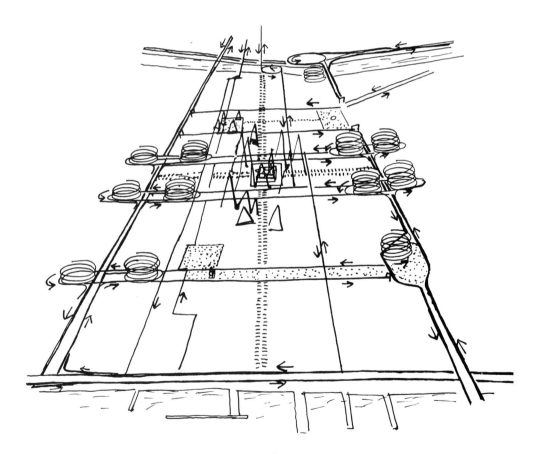

Shopping

Shopping streets would have no go traffic. People meet in shopping places. Promenades would induce new and revive old and even ancient merchandising ideas. Now the shopping areas are islands in a sea of traffic. They could be an interweaving of people, glass, escalators, trees, gardens, and exhibits. We would walk through our Christmas decorations not only peer at them through windows.

The wares, holiday symbols intermingled with the trees, patios, music and fashion shows remind one of the seasons. Gardens finger through the shops and the exhibits which show how things are made. The scale of the architecture is in sympathy with the "path of feet and the eye"—*George Howe.*

Shopping is walking. Walking is also resting—in shade, at the sidewalk café, looking at the sculptor's exhibit in the garden. Shopping promenades lead to a larger area—the site of the theaters, dance hall, bowling alleys, concert hall, places for food and refreshment, and places with such fun devices as the pin ball machine, juke box, and shooting galleries. Diverse entertainment now found on cheap streets—classed as "honky tonk"—are actually healthy energies—part of our blue jean era, needing the more friendly environment of the planned fun center.

Market Street as a dock.

Chestnut Street as a pedestrian way.

39

Millcreek Redevelopment Project

Mill Creek Redevelopment Project for the Philadelphia City Planning Commission

An arrangement of ten 15-story low-rent square apartment towers to house 600 families on a 10½ acre plot. Off-street parking is combined with service entrances. Circular green areas evolved after a study of paths in the conventional manner. The pathways resulting from this system seem to flow more gracefully into one another and lead with considerable directness to desired points. Over the entire area, trees are planted for shade and rest. Each level of a tower is divided into four apartments. Each level is a lot. Ninety-one deep balconies stretching the full length on the east and west sides give a generous outdoor play and plant space for each apartment. The concrete structure is designed to free the apartment spaces of columns and shaped to brace the building, support the balconies, and enclose the central core.

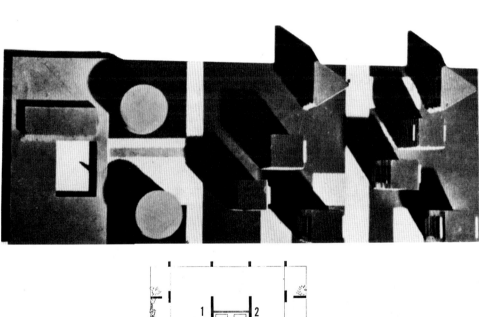

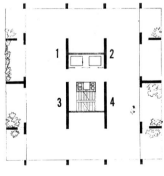

LOUIS I. KAHN 1953

Redevelopment Project New Haven

The Apartment Redevelopment Project for New Haven provides off-street parking in line with the present streets, with the bulk of parking under the shopping building to the right. The apartment towers are similar to those proposed for Mill Creek. The circular tower is, in fact, a square building with encircling balconies.

Penn Center

The Penn Center is an unusually large parcel of land in the middle of town opened for development after the demolition of the old Broad Street Station and of the elevated tracks referred to as the "Chinese Wall." The property is owned by the Pennsylvania Railroad, which company has been cooperating with the City Planning Commission in the overall plan for the area. A recently appointed board consisting of George Howe, Edmund Bacon of the Planning Commission, and Robert Dowling, city developer, are the design consultants for the Railroad. The later suggestions illustrated here have been submitted to the design board and are proposals growing out of a continued interest in this vital area over a period of several years.

The plan of Penn Center as proposed by the Pennsylvania Railroad now extends from City Hall to 18th Street. It is recommended by the plan to develop the block from City Hall to 15th Street as a slab office tower running north and south, from 15th to 16th as two off-set parallel slab towers running east and west, from 16th to 17th to be developed in the same way as the block from 15th to 16th Street. A five-story building covering the block from 17th to 18th Street is to be a bus terminal and communication center. This plan has changed slightly from time to time and still is undergoing modification, but it is substantially the plan known as the Dowling Plan.

The plan of Penn Center as illustrated is based on the following ideas.

That Penn Center be extended west from City Hall to the 30th Street Station across the Schuylkill River along the new Pennsylvania Boulevard to tie the Suburban Station area to the new developments at 30th Street Station. The extension of the address of Penn Center in this manner is intended to stimulate the real estate activities along the south side of Market Street, now not considered a part of the area.

That a park be created from 18th to 20th Street from Market Street to Pennsylvania Boulevard as an open space tying Logan Square to the north with Rittenhouse Square to the south along the axis of 19th Street. This would connect the in-town residential center of Rittenhouse Square and stimulate further developments of the civic and cultural center around Logan Square.

That the present receptiveness of the open space created by the demolishing of the "Chinese Wall" area be retained. The two proposals, showing in one case two towers and in the other case four towers from 15th to 17th Street, tend to meet the objectives of open space. In both cases, there is equivalent office space to that provided by the Pennsylvania Railroad plan.

The round glass building 270 feet in diameter proposed in the block from 17th to 18th Street provides a bus station on the concourse level below grade connected to traffic by ramps from the new park. The first floor of the building is an entrance to a

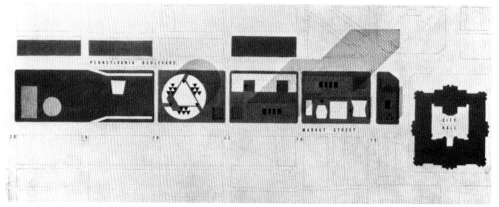

Esplanade Plan.

Alternate Esplanade Plan.

44

hotel which is planned around the perimeter of the building, and an entrance to a department store which occupies the central core of the building. The combination of the hotel with the department store offers an economy of air conditioning and an economy in the cost construction. The low building near City Hall allows for an unobstructed view of one of the most symbolic buildings of Philadelphia. Eighty-foot-square gardens on the concourse level below the street open to the sky and connect with the platform on which buildings stand.

Separated shop enclosures under a single low shelter are designed for the free movement of people from Market Street through to Pennsylvania Boulevard.

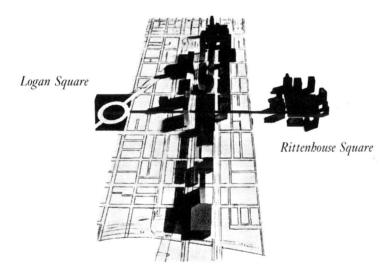

Logan Square

Rittenhouse Square

Alternate Esplanade Plan
Photo by Lawrence Williams

In Gothic times, architects built in solid stones. Now we can build with hollow stones. The spaces defined by the members of a structure are as important as the members. These spaces range in scale from the voids of an insulation panel, voids for air, lighting and heat to circulate, to spaces big enough to walk through or live in.

The desire to express voids positively in the design of structure is evidenced by the growing interest and work in the development of space frames. The forms being experimented with come from a closer knowledge of nature and the outgrowth of the constant search for order. Design habits leading to the concealment of structure have no place in this implied order. Such habits retard the development of an art. I believe that in architecture, as in all art, the artist instinctively keeps the marks which reveal how a thing was done. The feeling that our present day architecture needs embellishment stems in part from our tendency to fair joints out of sight, to conceal how parts are put together. Structures should be devised which can harbor the mechanical needs of rooms and spaces. Ceilings with structure furred in tend to erase scale. If we were to train ourselves to draw as we build, from the bottom up, when we do, stopping our pencil to make a mark at the joints of pouring or erecting, ornament would grow out of our love for the expression of method. It would follow that the pasting over the construction of lighting and acoustical material, the burying of tortured unwanted ducts, conduits, and pipelines, would become intolerable. The desire to express how it is done would filter through the entire society of building, to architect, engineer, builder, and craftsman.

Proposed City Hall Building

The requirements of generous public areas, meeting rooms, and exhibit spaces which could be located in an area not requiring natural light, suggested a building of large floor area. Each of the three hexagonal areas in plan is 20,000 square feet, and where the three are used on one level a gross area of 60,000 is made available. The ceiling of the exhibition entrances to the departments of Health, Recreation, Zoning and Public Works are 21 and 33 feet high. The general work spaces of the larger departments have a 21-foot ceiling with smaller offices on mezzanine levels. This structure rising the equivalent of 18 stories in height would contain about 500,000 square feet of net space, excluding the public areas. The floor plans at this stage of study are undivided loft spaces as shown on the plans. The model shows only the basic geometry of structure with the mezzanine floors omitted. The pattern of possible vertical open shafts through the structure is regular, and several additional shafts would appear upon further study of the plumbing and other mechanical needs. At present, only the vertical circulation of elevators and stair shafts with spaces for ducts and conduits is indicated.

The space frame tower was developed to satisfy a desire to express one of the endless potentialities of three dimensional construction and to make such choices as would integrate structure with the programmed space needed for working and for the harboring of the mechanical requirements. It is an exploration of the resultant forms of extending a triangular space frame system in a vertical direction. The floor plans are not directly over each other, shifting in a triangular relationship with each other as a result of the geometry of the structure. The entire building is trussed by the cross

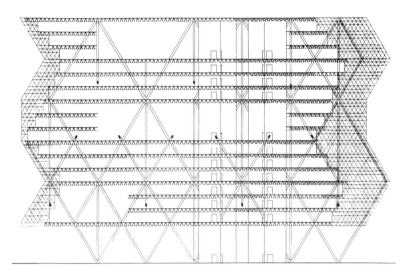

Louis I. Kahn, Architect
Anne G. Tyng, Associated Architect

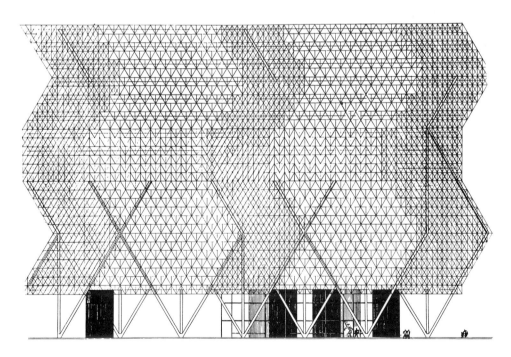

47

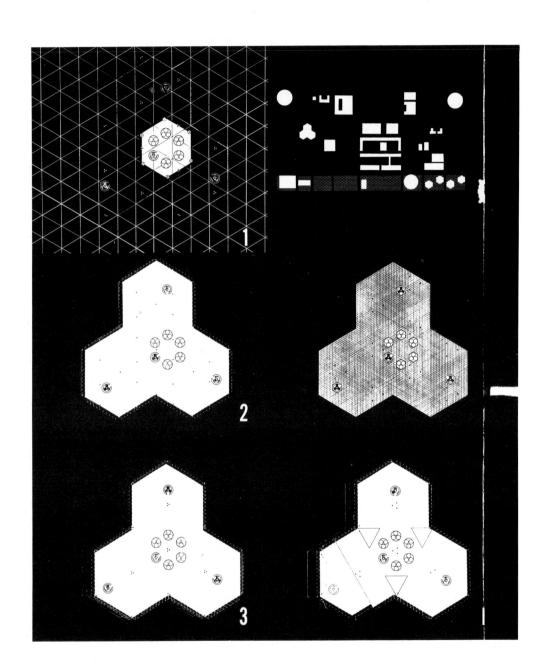

49

framing and intersecting of the column system.

The precast, prestressed concrete struts forming the triangulated frame come to a point every 36 feet. These major levels shift to meet the angles of the struts. In the full building height of 216 feet there are six major levels. Each of these levels may be divided into three floors of 12 feet floor to floor. The two mezzanine levels between major levels stiffen the frame. Uninterrupted struts reaching the full height would be braced at a point about 20 feet above the floor. The floor construction is three feet deep, composed of precast lightweight concrete tetrahedrons, the walls of which are just thick enough to cover the reinforcing.

In the octotedron spaces of the floor structure are exposed the conditioned air ducts and wiring conduits. The floor slab over the tetrahedrons is poured on insulation panels which absorb the sound. The ceiling pattern itself tends to break up sound. The air ducts are round pipes spaced three feet apart and follow the structural module and are installed at the pouring of the ceiling structure. Their openings point upward to the ceiling, with the air filtering down after striking the slab. This continuous mechanical system provides a complete flexibility of space division. Such a system is now being used for the Art Gallery Building at Yale University.

First Study of The City Hall Building

The building is conceived as an alternating space frame system of trussed spaces 27 feet in height and free spaces of equal height. The trussed space rests on membrane-connected triangulated frames clustered around the vertical circulation, leaving the remaining space free of supports. The trussed space would contain departmental offices and other work spaces. The central, column-free space on the plan below would be

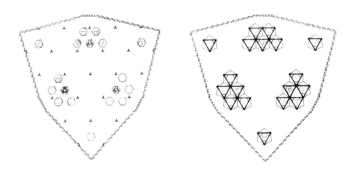

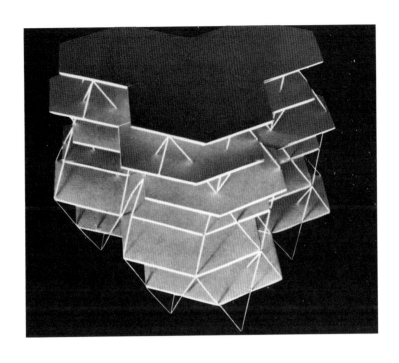

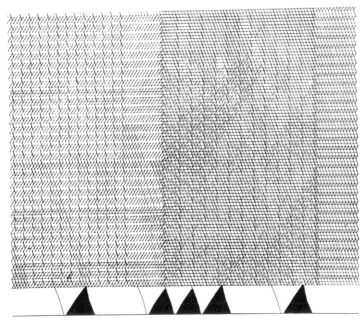

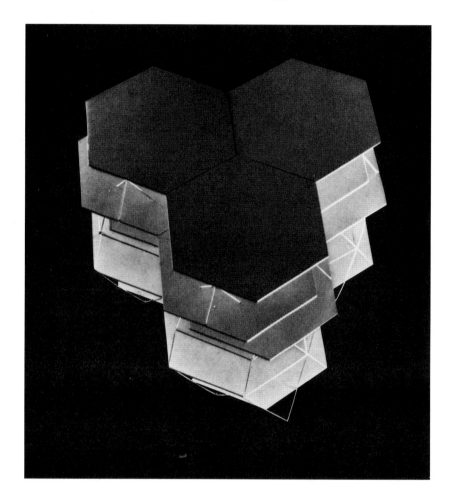

the entrance rotunda for exhibits, auditorium spaces, or meeting halls. The 27-foot-high space on either floor can be made into two stories.

"Toward a Plan for Midtown Philadelphia," reprinted from *Perspecta 2: The Yale Architectural Journal*, 1953, pp. 10–27.

On the Responsibility
of the Architect

Excerpts from the studio discussion originated at Yale with the participation of Pietro Belluschi, Philip Johnson, Louis Kahn, Vincent Scully, Paul Weiss

Considering a definition, Architecture is a life emerging from inseparable aspects of mind and heart. It has to do with the full complexity of making Architecture work in the fullest psychological sense. It works because it is motivated. It fills the desires and the needs. And so should the Tower work, as a psychological satisfaction. It should not work if it can't be used from the inside, if it's done without love and integrity. The Tower was done with love and I should say it is architecture. It belongs to Mr. Wright personally. It belongs not to the sociological aspect of architecture so much as to the physics book of architecture. Architecture should start a new chain of reactions. It shouldn't just exist for itself; it should throw out sparks to others. That is really the judgment of a piece of art, that power. If the Tower has this power to throw out sparks, to make you want to build one of these things, then I believe it functions. If it doesn't necessarily function as an experimental laboratory, then Wright should be fired by the Johnson Co. The form itself does excite us. If you can define one building as sculpture as separated from architecture. I think there is something wrong with both definitions. As sculpture it must be judged from the standpoint of its being sculpture as a piece of architecture, and if it isn't a piece of sculpture, then it must be a poor piece of architecture. It has to satisfy the tenets of sculpture in both cases. It's got to be a piece of sculpture. It is a built-up type of sculpture made of small pieces rather than of a single monolith.

As you know I am constantly in the formative stage, being influenced by very diverse things. But I think the only test of a real architect is his being an artist. I think there is a distinction between the professionals and the architect—there are only a few architects and plenty of professionals. I do not believe starting with form, necessarily, is the way to produce architecture, but I think it's a highly strong and natural way to begin. I think we all start with intuitive doodles which eventually express ourselves. I know that somehow I get a design suddenly. If the concept is strong, the design almost falls in place. Our great trouble is to try to fare into nonexistence many leftovers of ragged thinking which leaves us with very small pieces to be fixed and that is the design. I believe the concept should be equal to that of planting a seed, in which the concept, that is, the result you are going to get should be quite clear. As you progress and develop, the form will be modified, and you should welcome this, because the concept will be so strong that you cannot destroy it. How you accomplish all this comes with the knowledge of how a thing is done, knowing the process you must go through. The whole thing is a building process. It's very different, in my opinion, from conceiving the end product and then finding a means of doing it. There is a regular training that is necessary to do this because with this training comes assurity. I believe you must know about the mechanical equipment and also about your affinity for structural members.

The schools fail, because there isn't that element about them which brings out the artist, which somehow makes the competitive feeling of art. They can't instill the will to work in you, to discover yourself, as little as it can be discovered. If a man is really an artist, he looks not with too studious an eye at what others have done; the will is to produce something coming from the inside of you. He must have an instrument of work; therefore, he uses whatever he understands as a means, but he does not copy.

I agree they [originals] probably should be copied, but I still feel that the man who is going to be significant in his own right is not going to use that method. He is too impatient. He is not as deliberate as that. There are things bubbling in him that are completely different from any such process of copying. So I feel the artist looks at work fleetingly with a certain amount of humility, with a feeling of wishing that he had done it, but he does not copy.

"On the Responsibility of the Architect," reprinted from *Perspecta 2: The Yale Architectural Journal*, 1953, pp. 47–50.

Architecture and the University

Proceedings of a conference held at Princeton University, December 11–12, 1953

I studied at the University of Pennsylvania and, although I can still feel the spiritual aspects of that training, I have spent all my time since graduation unlearning what I learned. . . .

Design as a Circumstance of Order

I believe that we are speaking about order when we are speaking about design. I think design is circumstantial. I think order is what we discover the aspects of, so as to get a plan—a plan of a city or building, or even of a poster. If you develop a sense of order—enrich it through design by the exercises of design—you can also recognize those qualities of people who are very consistent, qualities which are beautified in their work. I think we are constantly confusing design and order. Order includes all the designs of construction—mechanical and spiritual; and design is merely the process of fitting them into conditions and coming up with a certain experience which strengthens and even enriches the order.

May I suggest that the student can be judged as to his conceptual tendency pretty early and before he gets to school? If he writes a literary composition, you can certainly tell whether he's an exceptional person. I think the watching of those characteristics before the graduate level is reached would be a practical way of distinguishing the conceptual mind from the practicing, methodic mind.

Buildings are not Monoliths

I've made notes and I think they are confusing, but they are based on what I feel are inadequacies in the school where I teach. I'd say one fault is that buildings are considered as monoliths. If we take the usual attitude that the ducts and the electric lighting and the air conditioning and the insulation and acoustics will take care of themselves, you will find that form will not grow out of the understanding of these elements and you will just be repeating what others have done. Therefore, we have these things exposed on the drawings. Also we ask the student to make what we call structural elevations. Next we ask the student to make a drawing of how he would enclose the building. I believe the building is not a monolith and that every means must be found to understand the building. One of them is of course engineering, and we take it out of the auditory field and put it in the visual field. Demonstrations coupled with auditory means would do wonders. We find also that some things cannot be drawn. It is impossible. In the explanation of space, which I am taking a great interest in, we are building with hollow stones, not solid stones. We just don't paste certain facilities on our buildings and cover them up. We know also that we call in outside people because we, ourselves, feel the inadequacy of our training and our knowledge— and we are trying to put all the responsibility of discovering what may be the character of the buildings today on someone else, and not on the profession, so to speak. I know the nature of space is something we really don't know much about. We arrive at shapes too quickly because we take the end products of the creativeness of other people and read into them certain appropriateness; whereas, we should arrive at these forms ourselves through some internal inspection of the spaces to be read. I believe that we should study the masters of today from the standpoint of how they can make beginnings for us, but not from the standpoint of the buildings themselves. We should study what means they go through in order to arrive at their conclusions—and their conclusions are theirs. If you can find the people who take the attitude that we should start all over again, you will find there are many potentials which have definitely not been explored—engineering potentials, particularly. We must bring everything down to stamp size, so that we can see it and feel it; not as so many details. Then we might be able to play the piano of composition which equals, in a sense, the architecture of building.

Architecture and the University, (Princeton: The School of Architecture, Princeton University, 1954), pp. 29–30, 46, 67–68; reproduced with the permission of The Louis I. Kahn Collection, University of Pennsylvania and Pennsylvania Historical and Museum Commission.

Louis I. Kahn in Moscow, 1965.

1954

How to Develop New Methods
of Construction

Excerpts from a talk at a conference on architectural illumination, School of Design, North Carolina State College

We should try more to devise structures which can harbor the mechanical needs of rooms and spaces and require no covering. Ceilings with the structure furred in tend to erase the scale. The feeling that our present-day architecture needs embellishment stems in part from our tendency to fair joints out of existence—in other words, to conceal how parts are put together. If we were to train ourselves to draw as we build, from the bottom up, stopping our pencils at the joints of pouring or erecting, ornament would evolve out of our love for the perfection of construction and we would develop new methods of construction. It would follow that the pasting on of lighting and acoustical material, the burying of tortured unwanted ducts, conduits, and pipelines would become intolerable. How it was done, how it works, should filter through the entire process of building, to architect, engineer, builder, and craftsman in the trades.

"How to Develop New Methods of Construction," *Architectural Forum*, November 1954, p. 157; © 1954 BPI Communications, Inc., used with permission.

Order Is

Order is
Design *is form-making in order*
Form emerges out of a system of construction
Growth is a construction
In **order** *is creative force*
In **design** *is the means—where   with what on when   with how much*
The nature of space reflects what it wants to be
     Is the auditorium a Stradavarius
       or is it an ear
     Is the auditorium a creative instrument
         keyed to Bach or Bartok
        played by the conductor
      or is it a convention hall
In the nature of space is the spirit and the will to exist a certain way
    Design *must closely follow that will*
    Therefore a stripe painted horse is not a zebra.
    Before a railroad station is a building
    it wants to be a street
    it grows out of the needs of street
      out of the order of movement
    A meeting of contours englazed.
Thru the nature—why

*Thru the **order**—what*
*Thru **design**—how*
A Form emerges from the structural elements inherent in the form.
>> *A dome is not conceived when questions arise how to*
>> *build it.*
>>> *Nervi grows an arch*
>>> *Fuller grows a dome*
Mozart's compositions are designs
>>> *They are exercises of **order**—intuitive*
>>> ***Design** encourages more designs*
>>> *Designs derive their imagery from order*
>>> *Imagery is the memory—the Form*
>>> *Style is an adopted order*
*The same **order** created the elephant and created man*
>>> *They are different designs*
>>> *Begun from different aspirations*
>>> *Shaped from different circumstances*

Order does not imply Beauty
>>> *The same order created the dwarf and Adonis*
Design is not making Beauty
>> *Beauty emerges from selection*
>>>> *affinities*
>>>> *integration*
>>>> *love*
Art is a form making life in order—psychic
Order is intangible
>>> *It is a level of creative consciousness*
>>> *forever becoming higher in level*
>>> *The higher the order the more diversity in design*
Order supports integration
From what the space wants to be the unfamiliar may be revealed to the
  architect.
From order he will derive creative force and power of self criticism
to give form to this unfamiliar.
Beauty will evolve

"Order Is," reprinted from *Perspecta 3: The Yale Architectural Journal*, 1955, p. 59.

Two Houses

The Kitchen wants to be the Living Room.
The Bed Room wants to be a little house by itself.
The car is the room on wheels.
In searching for the nature of the spaces of house
might they not be separated a distance from each other
theoretically before they are brought together.
A predetermined total form might inhibit what the
various spaces want to be. Architectural interpretations
accepted without reflection could obscure the
search for signs of a true nature and a higher order.
The order of construction should suggest an even
greater variety or design in the interpretations
of what space aspires to become and more versatility
in expression of the ever present problems of
levels, services, the sun, the wind and the rain.

Each house is a cluster of square areas 26 feet on a side. They grow out of the same order. The designs are different.

ADLER: Stone piers 3'6" square in the four corners of each square area. Each square is a whole structure. Criss-cross timber roof rests on the inner edges of the piers. Each square roof area is supported independently, drained independently and seen as an entity from the ground and from above. Piers gathered to form space for closets, bath rooms, fire places, vertical shafts, for ducts and a well for a stairway. The system of criss-cross joists inherently makes possible the construction for well and also the cantilever to complete the roof or the floor. To satisfy the order the design purposely created the piers heavier than necessary for support.

DEVORE: Six 18" square brick piers to the square. Roof joists are pairs of 2 × 12's inclined to each other at 60°. Spaces between piers enclosed by brick cavity wall and by glass. Brick of cavity walls laid in non supporting manner to distinguish from the brick supporting piers. Hollow lead "little houses" are inserted in the unprotected spaces left on the piers. One of these is open at the top in each square roof area acting as a roof drain and has a tongue for spouting.

60

The intention in these two houses is an order of construction which provides the avenues to harbor today's complex mechanical requirements including complete air conditioning.

In the Adler House the ducts are visible. In the De Vore house, round black ducts are tucked in the "V" areas of the roof system and are not visible. Both systems express their purpose, though the circumstances lead to the use of different materials and different devices. Design is not a product, it is a means.

"Two Houses," reprinted from *Perspecta 3: The Yale Architectural Journal*, 1955, pp. 60–61.

A Synagogue: Adath Jeshurun of Philadelphia

The assembly building rests on a circular plaza cut into the slope of a five-acre estate.

The retaining wall following the rise in the land casts a half-moon shadow on the plaza.

The car dock is inclined with the land and designed for slow movement.

Parking is separted from movement by posts as tall as a man about 20 feet apart, which also serves to light the cobbled paving of the dock.

The circular sidewalk follows the six percent slope of the dock at and above the plaza level and continues on to dip below the plaza level for the circulation needs toward east.

The rest of the site will be developed as places for relaxation and the enjoyment of nature's designs.

Beth Knesset or House of Assembly is on two levels each for a different purpose. On the lower or plaza level is the auditorium and its needs for social and cultural purposes. The higher level is the Synagogue.

Beth Sefer or House of Books (school) adjoins the lower level of the Knesseth. The classrooms communicate with a long interior open court for study and contemplation.

Three major column clusters of nine columns each in the form of an open triangle 26 inches on the side support a tetrahedral space slab. These three areas of support unfold loosely to form entrance porticoes and porches on the north and south and unfold and again unfold to form Beth Midrash or Study Chapel on the east behind the Bimah.

Each column cluster harbors a stairway as though captured in a great hollow trunk. The columns thus spread grips the floor and roof structure like outspread fingers.

It is what the space wants to be. A place to assemble under a tree.

"A Synagogue: Adath Jeshurun of Philadelphia," reprinted from *Perspecta 3: The Yale Architectural Journal*, 1955, pp. 62–63.

This Business of Architecture

A lecture at Tulane University, New Orleans

In my talk today, there is one thing I want to tell you right off. In one sense, what I mean by saying that architecture need not necessarily be beautiful, I mean that the approach in solving a problem doesn't start with beauty, with the consideration of what you think is beautiful. It starts with many more things which, if it results in beauty, good. If it is ugly but has the elements of architecture in it, it has hopes of becoming beautiful, too; by its exercise, by selection, it could become beautiful. But to start with the notion; this is beautiful, therefore I accept it; this is not beauty, and I don't accept it; then I shall design all Mies's buildings for him. You see, in that sense of beauty, I think you've got nothing.

Mainly, I think, I should like to talk about design. But instead of design for design's sake, it is how to approach the problem of design, or, rather, what sets up the framework; what sets up the atmosphere within which design is possible? And the word "order" appears at that point. Order, I say, in that exercise precedes design. Actually, order does not precede any part of the mental process in any way. It is only as a matter of convenience to us; as some means for separation, by saying that first we try to get the nature of our problem from the nature of spaces that we actually want to enclose or even leave open. And from this very nature of the space, we devise one which we sense it wants to be. Or we leave the tenets of order which we can use in the process of design. Design being the means. Design being that part of the exercise of creation which takes in circumstantial conditions—the amount of money, type of client you have, whether you are designing in Philadelphia or New Orleans. The art gallery or the auditorium, still design-wise, is a different problem. But from the standpoint of order, what an auditorium should be is the same problem in New Orleans as it is in Philadelphia. Order, you see, stands as a kind of philosophical abstraction of the nature of the space which is an auditorium. In other words, you can't hold on to order. It isn't a matter of problems like that. Order is a philosophical abstraction. It is that quality, it is the seed element of your design; it's a part which when planted gives you your design. That isn't to say with house seed, you should always get a petunia, which means you should always get an auditorium. But whether you use brick or cinder block, or whether it is a big auditorium or a small auditorium, are all design problems; they have nothing to do with order, except they're drawn from order and to convey that even to yourself is most difficult. Every time I speak about order I always feel very unsure. I don't know really what words to use to make it explainable, because people expect something very tangible. But it isn't. You might say a very simple explanation of order may be that to build a brick wall requires the order of the header and stretcher system of laying a brick wall; but whether you use Flemish bond or English bond is a matter of design. That is an extremely simple example.

Yale Art Gallery

The form work was made from floor to floor, and this line was accented in the design; because what we tried to do in the expression of the building was to show in every way how it was built. This form work was made of small floor boards, and the little holes that you see there indicate the through-ties in the form work. These were left in as holes in the concrete so that in every way, how it was made is apparent. We accentuated the struggle of building; of building from floor to floor, because that joint is a critical thing in the construction. When you take the forms off, something always happens in a very ugly soupy way. Whereas, if you actually know that, and you place in there something which is very positive; you put this in it (pointing to the form joint) so you can really see it, then it sets up its own pattern. And I believe that these joints are the beginning of ornament. It's true certainly of the old buildings. It's when you change your form of construction. It's true of anything I know, that the ornamentation is really the joint problem. . . .

At Yale, now, we are giving a problem which is a civic center. Please forget the word civic and please forget the word center. That's important. If you think of civic, what do you think of? You think of the city hall, you think of the firehouse, the post office, you think of the other things that go into a civic center. Actually, the present tendency is not for us to meet in the city hall to discuss problems. You are not really a participating part of any meeting house, which was at one time held in what we call "city hall." The post office is a service. The courts are an outcome of our service in connection with self-protection.

One of the strongest elements which we have not thoroughly explored is the power of communication. We don't realize how much power it actually has. Religion is a form of communication. As a matter of fact, a meeting house at one time was a form of communication, and we don't use that any more. Heaping of wares on a table, that is to say on a table of a shopping center, is a form of communication. Sensitiveness to that, and the impulse of gregarianism, therein lies somewhere an expression of what we call a civic center today. But we don't know what it is. And if you accept the term "civic center" quite in its form as we know it and its usual connotation, I think we do not add anything to the creation of a civic center. If we are talking about a table, we are saying, what is a table? If we are talking about a chair, what is a chair? Although we know very well. But nevertheless, we should do that. If we say, civic center, we should say, what is a civic center? In the same way, when we say an auditorium, if we accept it on the old basis, or rather on the basis as we know it, it just becomes a matter of perfecting sight lines, perfecting acoustics, accepting even in a general way the usual terms that appear. Whereas, it may not be at all the kind of thing you want to accept if you actually go into the problem very deeply.

Apartment Towers at Mill Creek

This represents a housing project which we are doing in the Mill Creek area. There we established those towers which represent four living units on each level. What is the order of design in this case? We said that it is of no great advantage to live in an apartment house, but an apartment house is necessary. Certainly, once you compare living in a house with living in an apartment house, the nature of the living is probably somewhat different. But certainly there are still humans there. We said that an apartment house should be equal as far as possible to a house. And when it became quite evident economically that an apartment house was necessary, we said that we would put the house up in the air; but we never said that the rooms would be put into an apartment building. In doing so we said, what if these people want to live in a place next to the ground because they want a little plot of ground. That's one thing they want. They can't have the advantage of living on the ground floor because it would be impossible. Therefore, we said that every step up would be considered a level rather than a floor; and it is actually a contour which we have created for ourselves at that level, so that on any contour level or any level, instead of a floor, we had a yard. These yards become generous balconies which were twenty feet by seven. You might say that's too generous, but it isn't when you consider that this is a public

64

housing project where balconies are the first thing you throw out of the picture because the government will say, "we will not use public funds in that way; it would be highly criticized." The very nature of the problem dictated that we must have that which resembles a house as much as possible, up in the air, and that we are not going to call the floor a floor but a level, and that each house must have cross ventilation. We therefore, design-wise set up a system of construction which made the columns a support for the balcony as well as the support of the building, and then when the government comes around and says you can't have balconies, we say you can't have a building because they support the building.

I would have liked to carry the balcony all the way to the very end, but I could not justify the columns. Design-wise it was possible to do this and still justify it. But it's fairly large, and it is wide enough to swing a cat in; a very nice indoor sport of all children.

The interior columns were also reduced because a column on the interior inhibits the whole freedom of the design and makes it very difficult to meet the square foot requirements. So therefore, we took all the columns out of the interior; we put them all on the outside. The interior core, which represented the housing for the elevator, scissor stairs, and other things you needed in the core, became the other column. So therefore, the interior room of vertical circulation became the column of this tower, and the exterior was the column for the wind bracing of this tower, plus the support of themselves. That was the design means used to carry out the premise that we needed balconies to begin with, because we, in looking at the nature of the problem, demanded that these houses needed to have a yard. The nature of the problem demanded a yard.

The idea that brought about that kind of thinking also brought about the possibility of consolidating the yards of the houses. Usually, the attitude being a Queen Anne front and a Mary Ann back to your house. The Queen Anne front and the Mary Ann back is not present in this house because these are also crowded little houses in which the yards are consolidated into one area, which makes the area rather larger than smaller.

Now, this site happens to be the acropolis of this particular area. It's a very high left-over piece of ground and inexpensive. It was just left there with very few people living there. And that is what started the possibility of this apartment project. Although these towers are not very far apart, they are much farther apart than in any other housing project.

These towers are also juxtaposed in such a way that they don't face each other. And because they are towers and not long slabs, they tend to make visible the rest of the area around. You don't feel as though these towers are a barrier to what's beyond. The arrangement of such towers in a large scheme gives a castlelike arrangement in which there are endless views. There is no end to what you can see as you walk around these towers.

From "This Business of Architecture," reprinted from *The Student Publication of the School of Architecture of Tulane University*, 1955, unnumbered pages.

Louis I. Kahn with Norman Rice and Holmes Perkins at a faculty jury review at the University of Pennsylvania, 1968 (Photo: Eileen C. Ahrenholz).

66

1956

An Approach to Architectural Education

The center of Philadelphia is being given new life by the developments around Independence Mall and Penn Center. The completion of the Vine Street Expressway, the planning and the eventual completion of the Lombard Street and Delaware Avenue Expressways, will frame the area with new traffic rivers eliminating the necessity for thru traffic and freeing all the street-ways for a new order of movement.

This order of movement with its system of municipal garages integrated with the entrances from the expressways will mark the gateways to the center. These gateways together with commercial garages on the interior and the assignment of most streets for parking should satisfy the motorists objective of a place to stop for shopping, recreation, and business. Public transportation and pedestrian ways would belong to a separate system of movement on other streets. Zoning for land use will grow naturally out of the street zoning for movement. Architecture will tend to relate to the street character.

The Triangle Redevelopment Area of which Penn Center is a part and the area along the river south of it to Walnut and east to 20th may be considered as the site for the greater recreation, culture, and civic center of the city.

The redevelopment of this area, the mall, and other areas in relation to the new movement and garage system, is the subject of many possible studies in Architecture and environment.

Tower Buildings are likely to become gigantic space structures consolidating many uses in one complex, in order to economize in the services of communication—sanitation, heating, and air conditioning. This consolidation will tend also to free the ground for the re-establishment of plant life and the parking of vehicles.

Tower design is a timely problem for students in Architecture preparing for an approach to the study of these future buildings. Though circumstances may change, the location and nature of the centers of redevelopment, an approach to design through a comprehension of order, reflecting the nature and spirit of what a space or a street wants to be, could lead to an architecture of cities.

The office tower is built essentially for investment. The fixed cost and the calculated financial return is the program handed the architect. His problem therefore is to build on a specific lot so much space for so much money. The efficiency of the plan is measured by the amount of usable space both near and away from natural light in proportion to the amount of space given over to services and corridors.

Little time elapses from the real estate transaction to the finished drawings.

The financial scheme must be put into effect immediately.

More or less the tower (or slab) results from an assembly of competitive materials and techniques unsympathetic to integration and to development into an expressive and inspiring architecture. Any experienced builder or promoter feels he knows enough to bring together such responsible engineers, technicians, and material men to result in an intelligent assembly of a physically functioning office building without the aid of an "expensive" architect. Consequently the average promoter, though he must employ an architect, does not regard him as a master coordinator-builder but rather as a designer of exteriors and selector of tasteful finish materials. His fee is whittled down accordingly and it is not uncommon for the architect to accept part of his fee in promotion stock.

The "treatment" of the facade is recognized by all interested and responsible as belonging solely to the architect. Sometimes the promoter interferes and insists on a horizontal motive against the wishes of the architect who may feel a vertical tendency. The facade is regarded as an enclosure playing no part in the structural conception of the building. This is intellectualized into a standardization of function—as a skin. The architect has much fun and uses much money making sketches of all possible "treatments."

But the face is no casual matter of structure in a building hundreds of feet high.

As the face to the sun, to the wind, and the rain, it can well be conceived as the beginning of the structure able to break up or receive the rays of the sun or become a buttress against the force of wind and thus becoming an integral part of the conception contributing in the development of a higher order of construction.

The many storied trabeated construction with columns of essentially the same dimensions as the building rises and elevator spaces in high proportion to the usable space seem to negate the competitive objectives of more space for less money and cannot be accepted by the questioning mind of the architect as solved.

The conception of a straight tower or slab of equal dimension from base to roof though possible to construct does not express the crushing-down forces and upsetting side forces acting on it.

The mind sees a building of a construction growing from a base crossing its members as it rises against the forces of wind.

Gravity and wind and the logic of space in proportion to its service suggest a tower pyramidal in form.

"An Approach to Architectural Education," reprinted, with changes, from *The Pennsylvania Triangle*, vol. 42, no. 3, January 1956, pp. 28–32.

Space   Form   Use

A library building should offer a system of spaces adaptable to needs in time; the spaces and their consequent form as a building should originate from broad interpretations of use rather than the satisfaction of a program for a specific system of operation. A space order for a library which encompasses the many possible relationships of books, people and services could possess a universal quality of adjusting to changing human needs, translatable into an architecture. A library design around the incipient influences of standardized book storage and reading devices could lead to a form with two distinct space characteristics—one for people, one for books. Books and the reader do not relate in a static way. Books or the means of reading may themselves take another form, making the stack system, for instance, obsolete. In the stages of design for building here shown, thoughts were centered around the desire to find a space construction system in which the carrels were inherent in the support which harbored them. Reading within a cloistered space with natural light in nearness to the building surfaces seemed good. The library at Durham built in the first century of the Gothic era is described by a chronicler:

> The North syde of the Cloister... was all fynely glased from the hight to within a little of the grownd and in every wyndowe iii Pewes or carrells, wherein... the Monks dyd resort. And in every carrell was a deske... And over against the carrells against the church wall did stande great almeries (or cupboards) of waynscott all full of books.—*Sturgis*

Then from the smallest characteristic space harbored in the construction itself,

69

the larger and still larger spaces would unfold. This pattern of spaces, if inherent in a construction system, would closely approximate what the architect thought the space "wanted to be," and how they could be made. Wall-bearing masonry construction with its niches and vaults has the appealing structural order to provide naturally such spaces. Concrete and steel, the obvious economical form making system of our time, are natural to big openings, not harbored little spaces. But the needs of sun control challenge the large openings, and the exterior walls must be more sensitive to orientation. A search for a high order of construction which could embody the appropriate sun protection and the little harbors of reading would, if found, sing out joyously as architecture. To combine sun control and support in the same structural material could be conspicuously wasteful of structural power. However, a continuous hollow column of concrete or steel, around the entire exterior would act as a vertical space frame capable of supporting a long-span, prestressed slab. This could satisfy the problems of orientation and be another approach in the search for the construction of characteristic spaces.

The design:

The pyramidal form places the larger areas required closer to the ground, and with its cross plan, admits more light deeper into the building. Spaces for books and for reading are not distinguished from each other. High spaces exist for undivided areas and low spaces for small rooms and divided areas. Carrel spaces are not developed within the fabric of the structure, but rather carved out for a system of space dividing wood furniture hugging the windows. The column and bay system remains consistent as the building form steps back, giving a clear story light to the high interior spaces and the intermediate levels looking out over these high spaces. The structure is composed of concrete columns supporting a two-way system of square bays made of precast, lightweight, domed coffers that provide spaces for lighting and air conditioning. These coffers, formed of sound absorbing material, become the deck and side forms for cast in place concrete beams and floors. The domed coffers reflect light from centered fixtures. Air conditioning ducts are housed between coffers and under the beam system. Columns are reduced in size as loads diminish but all perimeter columns are designed to take one additional story. Future expansion is thus possible in small units of space. These can be added when and where needed without destroying the original conception of the structure in mass and detail. Sun control on the south elevation is by means of stationary horizontal shades projected from the building at an angle and made of lead-coated metal in deep open mesh of geometric pattern. There are three rows of shades per floor. Shades over adjacent window bays are staggered vertically and overlap at mullions. Sun control on the west elevation is by means of vertical V-shaped stationary lead-coated, open-mesh metal fins in two layers with spacing staggered on inner and outer faces. Views from the interior are to the southwest and northwest between fins.

"Space Form Use: A Library," reprinted from *The Pennsylvania Triangle*, vol. 43, no. 2, December 1956, pp. 43–44.

Louis I. Kahn in Venice, 1969.

Louis I. Kahn in Venice, 1969.

Order in Architecture

Order of Spaces Integrated with Order of Construction

The Trenton Bath House is derived from a concept of space order in which the hollow columns supporting the pyramidal roofs distinguish the spaces that serve from those being served. The 30-by-30-foot spaces under the roofs remain undivided and the eight-by-eight-foot hollow columns provide the needs of smaller spaces.

The enclosing walls of the major spaces are placed beyond the confines and flush with outer walls of the columns to allow the sun to enter.

The enclosing walls of the basket room are brought well under the roof to protect the area from rain. Each roof as it rises ends in an oculus. The one over the basket roof is glazed.

This Bath House had simple space requirements. The Community Building now being planned on the same site as the Bath House is a further development of this concept of space order. Spaces of a variety of dimension and character supported by their own space needs lend themselves to the development of meaningful form by space distinctions in a more complex hierarchy of spaces.

Order of Movement and Renewal of the City

A street wants to be a building.

The new spaces that want to be will emerge from the designs drawn from an order of movement.

An order of movement that distinguishes staccato from go movement and includes the concept of stopping.

The zoning of streets for characteristic movement must precede the zoning of the land they serve.

Expressways are rivers that need harbors.

Streets are canals that need docks.

The architecture of stopping is equal in importance to the great walls that surrounded the medieval cities.

Carcassonne was designed from an order of defense. A modern city will renew itself from its order concept of movement which is a defense against its destruction by the automobile.

Center City is a place to go to—not to go through.

Great vehicular harbors or municipal entrance towers will surround the innermost center of the city. They will be the gateways, the landmarks, the first images that greet the visitor. Their place in this order and their strategic locations will demand of the designers meaningful form as a composite building of many uses. Its street story may be a market, the outer ring towards the light may be used as a hotel or for offices, and the inner core for storage. The main body of the tower gateways between the outer perimeter and the inner core will be the wound-up street of vehicular arrival and stopping.

The spaces and buildings within the gateways must embody and strive for the fulfillment of gregarian tendencies. Only the consolidation of all centers—cultural academic, commercial, athletic, health, and civic—into one Forum will inspire renewal of a city.

Decentralization disperses and destroys the city. So-called shopping centers away from the Center are merely buying. Shopping cannot exist away from the city's core.

An arena placed outside the city for reasons of parking is isolated from its other living companions. Its existence outside is limited, unenlivened by the other places where people gather. In the Center its space will stimulate ideas for its use and strengthen other places of meeting and commerce by its presence.

The center need not be large. It now is more complex than the village green. Consolidation and its lofty spires are contained within the scale of walking. The moving sidewalk extends the area of that scale.

The Center is the cathedral of the city.

LOUIS I. KAHN 1957

Order of Movement and the Plaza

City streets and plots are structures containing services of ever increasing complexity and importance. The building platform or plaza attempts to derive meaningful form out of the realization that a street "wants to be" a building equally organized as to space and structure as any other piece of architecture.

The plaza base 700 by 700 feet square is composed of three levels.

On the street level the diagonally opposite corners of the plaza are designed for ramp entrances around 80′ diameter openings for ventilation and light. These ramps lead to the parking and service spaces below. The opposite corners of the plaza are for the docking of taxis and buses off the street. On all four sides of the plaza are three pedestrian courts 80 by 80 feet square penetrated by 40-foot-diameter air shafts.

Stairs lead from these courts to the higher level plaza, and escalators wedged between these stairs give pedestrian access to and from the parking below.

A shopping concourse between the parking levels and the upper plaza is entered from these 12 court entrances surrounding the square. The arrival of a motorist at the lower level is greeted with natural light and fresh air from the circular openings overhead. The escalators leading to the granite paved courts at street level are framed by a great variety of shops and entrances through the concourse. The many shopping areas and the conveniences for those working in the tower and for the public gives shopping continuity and adds to the gaiety around this strategically located building.

The circular ventilators lined with granite would be inscribed as time goes on.

The shadow of these circular forms would be as effective as the shade of a tree and benches would be placed near and around them.

Order of Structure of a Building That Rises

The tower is an experimental exercise in triangulation of structural members rising upward to form themselves into a vertical truss against the forces of wind. Forces of gravity are secondary in a tower rising high. This structure is in contrast with the accepted, many-storied trabeated construction corrected for wind.

The facades of a tower are usually regarded as an enclosure playing no part in the structural conception of the building. As they face to the sun, to the wind and the rain it can well be conceived as the beginning of the structure able to break up or receive rays of the sun or become a buttress against the force of wind, thus becoming an integral part of the conception contributing in the development of a higher order of construction. In this tower the members of the structure in their undulation upward and around present various conditions to the sun and the wind.

The concrete struts forming the triangulated frame come to a point every 66 feet with nine of these intersections occurring in the total height of 616 feet. The column capitals at these intersections, 11 feet deep, are spaces for service needs. The smallest elements of triangulated structure are three-foot-deep tetrahedrons of the floor slabs which harbor the horizontal distribution of light and air. The 3,000,000 square feet of space has ceiling heights varying from eight to 55 feet for offices, public spaces, and assembly. To shade the building from the sun and to hold its panels of glass, a permanent scaffolding of aluminum is planned to cover the entire exterior. From a distance windows, per se, would not be apparent. A lacey network of metal reflecting the color of the light and its complementary color of shadow would be seen by the passerby.

"Order in Architecture," reprinted from *Perspecta 4: The Yale Architectural Journal*, 1957, pp. 58–65.

Spaces Order and Architecture

An address given at the Royal Architectural Institute of Canada Golden Jubilee Assembly,
revised and edited by Kahn

Architecture is the thoughtful making of spaces.

Reflect on the great event in architecture when the walls parted and columns became.

It was an event so delightful and so thought wonderful that from it almost all our life in architecture stems.

The arch, the vault, and the dome mark equally evocative times when they knew what to do from how to do it and how to do it from what to do.

Today these form and space phenomena are as good as they were yesterday and will always be good because they proved to be true to order and in time revealed their inherent beauty.

In the architecture of stone the single stone became greater than the quarry. Stone and architectural order were one.

A column when it is used should be still regarded as a great event in the making of space. Too often it appears as but a post or prop.

What a column is in steel or concrete is not yet felt as a part of us.

It must be different from stone.

Stone we know and feel its beauty.

Material we now use in architecture we know only for its superior strength but not for its meaningful form. Concrete and steel must become greater than the engineer.

The expected wonders in concrete and steel confront us. We know from the spirit of architecture that their characteristics must be in harmony with the spaces that want to be and evoke what spaces can be.

Forms and spaces today have not found their position in order though the ways of making things are new and resourceful.

The continual renewal of architecture comes from changing concepts of space.

A man with a book goes to the light.

A library begins that way.

He will not go fifty feet away to an electric light.

The carrel is the niche which could be the beginning of the space order and its structure.

In a library the column always begins in light.

Unnamed, the space made by the column structure evokes its use as a carrel.

A man who reads in seminar will look for the light but the light is somewhat secondary.

The reading room is impersonal. It is the meeting in silence of the readers and their books.

The large space, the small spaces, the unnamed spaces, and the spaces that serve. The way they are formed with respect to light is the problem of all buildings. This one starts with a man who wants to read a book.

dedication

ritual

    is the chapel

a chapel of a university

ritual is inspired

dedication is personal

Inspired by a great teacher the fortunate young man winks to the chapel as he passes. He feels dedication and performs his own ritual. He was there though he never opened its door.

The rally centers there and inspires its own ritual.

A man is honored there.

dedication is its essence.

When I first came to Pisa I went straight in the direction of the Piazza. Nearing it and seeing a distant glimpse of the Tower filled me so that I stopped short to enter a shop where I bought an ill-fitting English jacket. Not daring to enter the Piazza I diverted to other streets toward it but never allowing myself to arrive. The next day I went straight for the Tower touched its marble and that of the Duomo and Baptistry. The next day I boldly entered the buildings.

So it is with a university chapel.

Possibly a space protected by an ambulatory entered from an open arcade in a dimensioned garden.

Space for those who never go there, those who must be near and don't enter and those who go in.

house   a house   home

In a certain space it is good to sleep.

In another it is good to dine or be with others.

The serving spaces and the free spaces combine and are placed to the garden or to the street to suggest their use.

House implies a place good also for another. It is that quality which is closer to architecture.

It reflects a way of life.

It does not make small spaces for small people.

Spaces transcend function.

A house is more specific.

The Renewal of City.

> The new spaces that want to be will emerge from the designs drawn from as order of movement. An order of movement that distinguishes staccato from go movement and includes the concept of stopping.

> The zoning of streets for characteristic movement must precede the zoning of the land they serve.

> A street wants to be a building.

> Expressways are rivers that need harbors. Streets are canals that need docks.

> The architecture of stopping is equal in importance to the great walls that surrounded the medieval cities.

> Carcassonne was designed from an order of defense. A modern city will renew itself from its order concept of movement which is a defense against its destruction by the automobile.

> Center City is a place to go to—not to go thru.

> Great vehicular harbors or municipal towers will surround the innermost center of the city. They will be the gateways, the landmarks, the first images that will greet the visitor. Their place in order and their strategic locations will demand of the designer more meaningful form as a composite building of many uses. Its street story will be a market, the outer ring towards the light may be used as a hotel or for offices and the inner core for storage. The main body of the tower gateways between the outer perimeter and the inner core will be the wound up street of vehicular arrival and stopping.

> The spaces and buildings within the gateways must embody and strive for the fulfillment of gregarian tendencies. Only the consolidation of all centers—cultural, academic, commercial, athletic, health, and civic—into one Forum will inspire renewal of a city.

> Decentralization disperses and destroys the city. So-called shopping centers

away from the Center are merely buying centers. Shopping cannot exist away from the city's core.

An arena placed outside the city for the same reason of parking is isolated from its other living companions. Its existence outside is limited, unenlivened by the other places where people gather. In the Center its spaces will stimulate ideas for its use and strengthen other places of meeting and commerce by its presence.

The center need not be large. It now is more complex than the village green. Consolidation and its lofty spires is contained within the scale of walking. The moving sidewalk extends the area of that scale.

The Center is the cathedral of the city.

The column or wall defines its length and breadth; the beam or vault its height.

Nothing must intrude to blur the statement of how a space is made.

The forms characterizing the great eras of architecture present themselves and tempt us to adapt them to concrete and steel. The solid stones become thinner and eye deceiving devices are found to hide the unwanted but inevitable services. Columns and beams homogenized with the partitions and ceiling tile concealing hangers, conduits, pipes, and ducts deform the image of how a space is made or served and therefore presents no reflection of order and meaningful form.

We are still imitating the architecture of solid stones.

Building elements of solids and voids are inherent in steel and concrete. These voids are in time with the service needs of spaces. This characteristic combined with space needs suggest new forms. One quality of a space is measured by its temperature by its light and by its ring.

The intrusion of mechanical space needs can push forward and obscure form in structure.

Integration is the way of nature. We can learn from nature.

How a space is served with light air and quiet must be embodied in the space order concept which provides for the harboring of these services.

.The nature of space is further characterized by the minor spaces that serve it. Storage rooms, service rooms, and cubicles must not be partitioned areas of a single-space structure, they must be given their own structure.

79

The space order concept must extend beyond the harboring of the mechanical services and include the "servant spaces" adjoining the spaces served.

This will give meaningful form to the hierarchy of spaces.

Long ago they built with solid stones.
Today we must build with "hollow stones."

"Spaces Order and Architecture," reprinted with permission from *The Royal Architectural Institute of Canada Journal*, vol. 34, no. 10, October 1957, pp. 375–7.

Louis I. Kahn with Carlo Scarpa and Carlos Vallhonrat, 1969.

New Frontiers in Architecture: CIAM in Otterlo 1959

Talk at the conclusion of the Otterlo Congress

I have had the good fortune to observe the plans and work of the men here, and have seen that almost everyone started with the solution of the problem, given the conditions upon which design was made. But I think I may say freely that very few started with a kind of sense of realization of the problem and then inserted design as its natural extension—a circumstantial thing, because I really do believe that design is a circumstantial thing. I believe that a man must realize something before he has the stimulation within himself to design something. I believe that there are many in our profession who rely entirely upon the actual design and very little on the way of thought as to what a thing wants to be, before they try to develop the design—the solution of the problem.

Design is very comparable to a musical composition, for a composer has a sense of music before he composes. I would say that if a dish fell in Mozart's kitchen he would know the difference between the noise of it and the music of it. Another man would run with the noise of it and make a career out of it, because it is different. But Mozart would choose the difference and say, "Yes, dissonance awards to music," and he would have discovered something else in the realm of music. He would compose from this realization—that the falling dish had a meaning in music—where another person would take the noise only and think that he could make a career of it.

I might talk a little about realizations, because realizations are to me a finer part of us than, say, thought. Knowledge is a servant of thought and thought is a satellite of feeling.

If one was to ask, "What is feeling?" I think you could say that it is the residue of our mental evolution, and that in this residue was an ingredient which is thought. And this ingredient somehow was a spirit in itself, and one time it said to feeling, "Look, I have served you well, I have helped you to become man, and now I want to go out for myself. I want to be a satellite, I want you to consider me as something independent of you. I will come back to you, I must." Thought goes independently and deals with other thoughts of other men, and from it comes a postulate. But still a postulate must say to feeling, "How am I doing?" It must!

Now realization, I think, is thought and feeling together. Because feeling itself is completely unable to act, and thought also is unable to act, but thought and feeling combined create a kind of realization. This realization can be said to be a sense of order; a sense of the nature of sense.

Often when one says order, one means orderliness, and that is not what I mean at all. I do not mean orderliness because orderliness has to do with design but has nothing to do with order. Orderliness is nothing tangible about order, it is simply a state of comprehension about existence, and about a sense of a sense of existence. From it you can get a sense of the existence will of something. The existence will, let us say, of a form, of a need, which one feels. The existence will of this need can be sensed through a realization. From the realization you get much richness of design— design comes easily. This is the reason why I mention Mozart again. Mozart could lose his composition and rewrite it verbatim after he had lost it, because he did not deal with his design per se. It had a very definite order-sense about it which made the design something that could be easily varied but still be the same.

Now I said that what a thing wants to be is the most important act of an object. It is for the architect to derive from the very nature of things—from his realizations— what a thing wants to be.

In the center of a very large city, maybe I cannot use Amsterdam as an example as it is a city of a different nature, but certainly in Paris, Rome, New York, in Philadelphia or in any other large city, the street in the middle of the town wants to be a building; it does not want to be just a street, and that is realization. If you think of it only as a street, then it never can occur to you that the construction of it is anything but a left-over thing in which you use the meanest ways of making it, because you will not see it.

But if you think of it as being that which it really wants to be—and that is a building—you will not have to dig it up every time a pipe goes bad. You will have a place for these things. You will have a place for walking under, you will have a place for other things, and it will occur to you what this building is which is called a street, and then you will realize that you are actually walking on or riding on the roof of this building. That is a very important thing to realize about a street in the middle of a town, because it is really a contour, it is really a level, and it really is a building.

The same is true of an auditorium. An auditorium wants to be a thing—it wants to be an instrument. It cannot be any old instrument, because acoustically it is true that a large auditorium has a different tempo, a different sound from a small auditorium. No matter how much you try, you cannot make a really large auditorium unless you use artificial means to create a tonality which is other than the actual tonality of the volume which you are encompassing. I don't agree with solutions which say, "I shall build a form and then I will correct it acoustically." This, I would say, is sheer design. I accuse design for such approaches because designers invariably start with square wheels and eventually have to use round ones. But they discard the square wheels to be different. Also they start with short-necked giraffes. The giraffe cries out to have a long neck. But no, the designer says, "I do not want it." So he makes the giraffe with a small neck. Eventually, of course, it turns out, "for practical reasons, damn it," that a giraffe had to have a long neck, and so it is. But a man who watches his realizations does not care what a giraffe looks like. As a matter of fact if you think of it, a giraffe is a pretty ridiculous animal; from the standpoint of design it does not make any sense. But in the same way, a porcupine comes to the Order of Things and says, "I want to be a porcupine," and the Order says, "My God, what an idea. Whoever dreamed up this ugly thing." "Oh!" he says, "but I still want to be a porcupine." And Order says, "Well I have really not much to do with this." And this is true. Nature is not concerned with form, only man is concerned with form. It makes it according to circumstances. If it meets the order of things in the nature of things, it will make any form that answers to the very nature of things. That is why we have what we call such peculiar-looking animals. Because there is a certain existence will in this kind of thing which produces itself into this kind of animal and nature is not concerned about form—but we are. So, therefore, the existence will of something, an auditorium, a street, a school, will be the thing which makes the form. Think of a school for a minute. A school. What is the existence will of a school?

If you get a program from a school board, the first thing it will say, in our country, is that it must have a nine foot fence around it—wire fence—and that it must have stainless-steel doors and the corridors must be no less than nine feet wide, and that all its classrooms must be well ventilated and have good light and all be a certain size. They will give you many things which will help the practitioner make a pretty good profit out of his commission by following the rule of rules. But this is not an architect at work. An architect thinks of a school possibly as being a realm of spaces within which it is well to learn. I think schools, for instance, have now gotten away from the original spark or the existence will or seed of "school."

Think of a man under a tree, talking to a few people about a realization he had—

a teacher. He did not know he was a teacher, and those who listened to him did not consider themselves pupils or students. They were just there, and they liked the experience of being in the presence of one who had a realization—a sense of order. This is the way it began. But around such a man there was a need that also grew. You felt that his existence also had a need content. Around him were people who realized that they would like to send their children to this man, too—that it was nice to know, to realize—the things he realized. So, therefore, a need was automatically felt for this thing, for this phenomenon, for this seed, for this beginning, which is called "teacher" and "student."

Every city is made up of institutions. If you were to consider the making of a city you would have to consider the organization of the institutions. But you have got to review those institutions and really know what those institutions are. The institution of learning must have in its mind—must have in its sense—the realm of spaces which are good for learning, and not a program which says that you must have so many of this, or so many of that, but a realm of spaces which you feel is sympathetic to learning. So, therefore, you may go into a space which may be a Pantheon-like space. You would name it absolutely nothing—it would just be a good place to arrive in which you say "school"—from which may come other spaces: small or large, some with light above, some with light below, some big spaces made for many people, some small spaces for a few people, some small spaces for many people, and some big spaces for only a few people, some seminal spaces, spaces to meet in some other ways, never naming any more of them either "classroom" or "auditorium" or "seminal" or anything, just realizing that there is a sense to the realm of spaces where it is good to learn. That is all you have to know. The program is nothing. The program is a hindrance. You must answer the program.

The economic thing is not the budgetary thing. The economic thing is to build what I have just described. The budgetary thing is the program which is based on another program, which is based on yet another program, all of which are stupid, and you simply have nothing but a struggle to produce that which should cost much more than what the budget allows, and you can never never express the real thing. Now if you create the realm of spaces you are also feeling the institution—you are making the institution alive—that which you call part of the city.

You were talking about urbanism. Well, I would like to add this one point, that urbanism is a study of institution of housing, the institution of movement, the institution of schools, the institution of anything you like. You see, they are all institutions really because around them somehow there must be an idea—a need must have been established.

Now, if this is what a school is—a realm of spaces where it is good to learn—

84

then it is the occupation of the architect to change the programme, to make the programme alive to the very existence will which started the school.

The spirit of the start is the most marvellous moment at any time for anything. Because in the start lies the seed for all things that must follow. A thing is unable to start unless it can contain all that ever can come from it. That is the characteristic of a beginning, otherwise it is no beginning—it is a false beginning.

Now therefore, that moment under a tree was the beginning of the institution of "school" which has gone completely haywire because it has been handled by too many men who assumed a feeling for it, but who have long lost the meaning of it, and the architect must constantly be there to revive the existence will sense of this thing.

Now you take in our country, a city hall. You go by it but it is really a place you don't participate in any more. There is no assembly held there. It is a place where the mayor does not want to be. It is a place where you pay fees and taxes, but everything it does not represent, represents it. Participation—the original existence will, that which made city hall a city hall, a village green, a place for getting together (and participation was the most important part of it) does not exist any more.

Suppose you wanted to meet here, upholding certain cultural, social, or other interests of our democracy, you now have no place to meet. The city hall which was the place to meet is now something else. It must be again a realm of space where people should meet—where fountains play. When Picasso comes to Philadelphia, he should not have to go to the Sheraton Hotel, which he has to do now, you see. There is simply no place you can take him. Here in Europe you are very fortunate in having much more of a sense of this than we have in our country. I merely bring this out because it comes as a ready kind of example.

Now take the institution "house." A house has to answer, I think, three important things: it has to, answer "house," symbolically house, it has to answer "a house" which is the problem. A house is a circumstantial house. It indicates how much money you have. It means who your client is. It means where it is or how many rooms it has. It means a lot of things. But the architect lies in his ability to make house, not a house. That is what architecture really is. "A house" can be the professional, but the architect lies in "house" itself—symbolically "house." He has to find somehow a realm, of spaces where it is good to live. Sometimes he must find it with very little space, but essentially that is his job and he must do it so, he does not name the rooms, bedrooms and living rooms and kitchens, he has got to do it in such a way that it is obvious because of the way they are served, that these things are there and that they are there rightfully and they want to be there. It is a realm of spaces really, which you call "house." Then there is one thing that the architect can do nothing about, and that is "home." A "home" has to do with the people in it, and it is not his business, except that he must prepare this realm to make it suitable for "home." But these three characteristics—or rather I would say aspects—of house, must be there.

Now one can go wrong. I will give you an example which I think is significant. If I were to describe a chapel for a university, a university as one where there is nothing partisan, nothing denominational. M.I.T. Chapel, for instance, is a chapel which is done with immediate calling on the ingredients of a chapel: stained glass, ornamental work, and all the paraphernalia which you must need to make a chapel. Actually they are a very minor consideration in a chapel. I would say that it comes from a kind of personal ritual. If I were a student of architecture and I got a good criticism from my professors—a criticism which gave me a sense of dedication to my work, a good criticism—then I would be happy, really happy, and I would go by the chapel and wink at it. I wouldn't have to go in, it wouldn't be necessary, nor would I wink at the gymnasium—I would wink at the chapel.

So, what is a chapel really? A chapel, to me, is a space that one can be in, but it must have excess of space around it, so that you don't have to go in. That means, it must have an ambulatory, so that you don't have to go into the chapel; and the ambulatory must have an arcade outside, so that you don't have to go into the ambulatory; and the object outside is a garden, so that you don't have to go into the arcade; and the garden has a wall, so that you can be outside of it or inside of it. The essential thing, you see, is that the chapel is a personal ritual, and that it is not a set ritual, and it is from this that you get the form. The form is derived from this, and not from changing, modifying, making modern that which was already set for you as a chapel.

Now, existence will then, of trying to grasp the realm of spaces or defining the character of space which is good for a space, is, I tell you from the little that I have had a chance to develop it, the most delightful, most fulfilling experience of all. How to do it is infinitely less important than what to do, for it gives you the means to do it. You can hire anybody to do it. Even those who are untrained in how to do it will find by whatever means they can how to do it, if they would only know what to do. Of course you will make many mistakes if you don't know how to do it and I think that the horrible ones may effect even what you do. But essentially this is the role of the architect, and if you think of planning, it is certainly this.

Now, in the planning aspect of it—since we are talking about urbanism—I have made a few observations. When I think of a street, I don't think of a street per se, and I don't dismiss it. I stop when I think of a street and I say, "A street? What is a street? Must I assume that a street is a street?" No. A street is either a stream or it's a river or it's a dock. It is something which is different in characteristic depending on the order of movement which I can sense.

In our streets today there is a new order of movement. The order of movement is not a horse and carriage movement, but our streets are still horse and carriage streets. The only difference is that we don't have hitching posts in the streets, we have gasoline pumps. But the streets are quite the same. Nowadays if you go through the streets of Paris, you don't have the same sense of going through the streets that you had before. You are constantly watching for your life, and not watching the environment of the street.

The meaning of street: There is a type of character, of movement, of go (as Smithson has pointed out), which is a definitely deliberate thing and a kind of place (which is a much better word than I could ever think of) for this street. It is a sort of an arrival, sort of a place where—well, it's a place—that is the right word for it. And it's still the same street, only now you're redefining it. You are giving it a new life by redefining it. Then you place those services next to these things, so that you don't have them haphazardly develop—like a garage here or there—which tends to destroy the imagery of a city.

The original imageries of cities based on defense, were all based on the order of defense. All the walls, and all the details were made, not by the architect but by the order of defense. It was circumstantially that particular design because it was on a mountainside, or because it had a certain kind of stone, or it had a river close by. Those were circumstances that made one city look different from another. But the order of defense made very stark decision as to what, when, or where, to defend yourself. It was inconceivable to have a city which did not account for this aspect.

It is also inconceivable today for a city not to have an order of movement; to define every element of movement for what it does, so that one can make form around it. It is a form-making thing. I believe that zoning should start with streets, not with buildings. If you zone streets, as Smithson did in his project—give it its use in other words—then you are giving automatically the use of environments and buildings.

In other words, the common activity you can have in a street depends on the movement, and it depends on the design of this movement. In the design of this movement are also buildings. It isn't only just a street.

Then there are the buildings which make you stop. The buildings which you call garages, but which I call gateways. I call them places which really are monumental structures, which simply are wound-up streets. It is the street come to conclusion. These are the sculpture—the image of a city that you come to now. You can have them very close. You can have them farther away. But you are entering a series of defined forms which are derived out of the order of movement, which is a very positive beginning for a city.

Now I saw one project, and I don't mean to point this out as being an example of any kind, but I noticed one project where buildings were placed next to an old town very regularly around the periphery. They were grouped at the entrance points so that one could see them. I did not like this. I would like to place a gate at the entrance. But I would not like to use people, upon people, upon people, upon people, as a symbol for an entrance to a town. No. These should be placed somewhere else. Because an apartment building only wants to be a house, but it can't be a house, so it must be a house upon a house, upon a house, upon a house, upon a house, upon a house. When you build a house, upon a house, upon a house, it must still satisfy house. Therefore, as a gateway, it seems to be the wrong element to enter that part of the city. What you should have is a gate, and it belongs to the order of movement, and does not belong to apartment buildings which are not part of the order of movement. An apartment building is a thing you arrive at—but it is not part of the movement. Therefore, if you have this conception of movement first then the entire design would change. The design would not be the way you have made it—not made movements out of people and toilets going up, and up, and up. It wouldn't be so.

Speaking about spaces, I said that architecture was the thoughtful making of spaces. I think that could be said in many ways. I have often thought about whether it was a full definition, and it really is not. However, for the moment, if we think of spaces, what are architectural spaces?

I think an architectural space is one in which it is evident how it is made; you will see the columns, you must see the beams, or you must see the walls, the doors, or the domes in the very space which is called a space.

If you try to think of points from which we can reach points of departure in architecture, we can very easily state that a space in architecture is one in which it is evident how it is made, and that the introduction of a column or any device for making a roof is already thought of from the standpoint of light, and no space is really an architectural space unless it has natural light. Artificial light does not light a space in architecture, because it must have the feeling in it of the time of day and season of the year—the nuances of this is incomparable with the single moment of an electric bulb. It is ridiculous to think that an electric bulb can do what the sun can do or the seasons can do. And this is what gives you a real sense of space architecturally—it's natural light. Then, at night, it becomes a totally different space. And almost a realization of this tells you that you should not have your electric lights where the sun comes in, because it is so ridiculous to try to imitate it. Why not make it entirely different? Have your chandeliers doing all sorts of gay things about being night.

I have seen theories about putting lights where the daylight comes in but how ridiculous it is really to follow this when you think in terms of spaces being served

88

by the sun—by the light of the day—it's so marvellous.

The making of spaces is the making of light at the same time. When the light is destroyed, the rhythm is destroyed, and the music is destroyed, and music is terribly important to architecture.

There is a side thing I should mention before I forget it. I think that music is more akin to architecture than either sculpture or painting. If you think of music, it is very, very close to architecture, and I think personally, that every architect should learn to write music. It is wonderful to realize that when a man writes music he is not enthralled by the beauty of what he sees as a kind of writing—he is enthralled by what he hears. The musician hears what he writes—he doesn't see it. The architect comes over and looks at his drawings and says: "Oh, isn't it wonderful! I think I'll make a blow-up of it and put it in my living room!" To the musician his writing means something beyond itself—it means sound, it means organization of sound. An architect must be able to read the life that comes into his works through his plans. His realm of spaces is analogous to a sheet of music. His columns and his beams and his walls should be almost assumed. You must say that in this interior space I must have light. Because I have made a space therefore I must have light. I must assume that it must be some kind of order. I am looking for something. I am looking for the space-making of this in my plan. I think a sheet of music and an architectural plan are the same thing.

Every space must have its own definition for what it does, and from that will grow the exterior, the interior, the feeling of spaces, the feeling of arrival. All these things indicate themselves once we think of them as being a realm of spaces—a hierarchy of spaces—and not just simply a feeling. It is just not enough to say: "I feel this should be larger here and bulge out here," and so forth. This you can also do—it is absolutely all right to do it—but it must have an internal kind of structure which permits you to do it, just as the musician has his formal structure and discipline which permits him to play on almost any instrument. It depends on his genius. In the same way, and I think some of you are familiar with my personal way of saying that spaces must be distinguished. The serving areas of a space and the spaces which are served are two different things. It is very likely that a plan starts this way, and the architect says: "Oh, don't touch this!" The client says: "I need an office, I need a toilet, I need a closet, I need a few things in here," and the architect says: "Oh, don't do this, this is a wonderful thing on a podium and you cannot touch it," and the client says: "But I need it!" And the architect says: "Put it down in the cellar. You can't have it around here. This is really very important and everything depends on it." Actually this is where the architect goes wrong. This is a very limited man at work, because what he could probably come out with may actually be better, and he will get the spaces he needs, and will have contained elements which can serve those spaces.

The architect must find a way in which the serving areas of a space can be there, and still not destroy his spaces. He must find a new column, he must find a new way of making those things work, and still not lose his building on a podium. But you cannot think of it as being one problem, and the other things as being another problem.

Actually, these are wonderful revelations because modern space is really not different from Renaissance space. In many ways it is not. We still want domes, we still want walls, we still want arches, arcades, and loggias of all kinds. We want all these things and, with that belief, need them. But they are not the same in character because a space today demands different things. If I build a dome it does not have to talk back to me. It must be quiet. A Renaissance dome can talk back to me, and it's all right, but not a modern one. So therefore, something in the fabric of making this thing is already the ingredient of making it not speak back to you.

Another characteristic of this dome is that it must have temperature control. I must want it warm when it is cold out, and cool when it is warm out. This is a very definite demand of modern society. If we don't have it radically so, it certainly will gradually become so by the pressures and fury of business, or whatever it is that will make you do it.

There is another thing—light must also be there. If you see all these things only after you have made a great form—suppose you got the right engineer, let's say Candela or Nervi to do the building for you—and then you said, "Now, how shall we light it?" Then you're wrong. Or if you then said, "How shall we breathe in this place?" you are also wrong. In the very fabric of making it must already be the servants that serve the very things I've talked about—its timbre, its light, and its temperature control; the fabric of the construction must already be the container of these servants.

I spoke before about "beginnings." I should like to go back to that now and talk more about it. I should like to talk of the Renaissance, and of Giotto in particular.

Giotto was a wonderful painter. But why was he wonderful? Because he painted the skies black in the daytime, and painted dogs that couldn't run and birds that couldn't fly, and people who were larger than buildings—because he was a painter. He was not an architect, he was not a sculptor.

The prerogatives of the painter allow him—the very fact that he can draw in this way allows him—to do that very thing. The extent of his fantasy is within his realm, definitely within his realm.

But Giotto also satisfied the need by being true to the allegory, let us say, of St. Francis in this case. So he found that St. Francis kept the right company in the painting. People understood it. The combination of both the beautiful sense of the rights of the painter that Giotto very thoroughly understood—felt—combined the life of St. Francis with the mystical atmosphere which was necessary to bring it to a religious sense, of nobility, of sacrifice, of things which are religious.

Chagall, a lesser painter, also felt the same kind of freedom. Modern painters have the same freedom. I do think, however, that modern painters have not as yet established a form.

Giotto did establish a form because others followed him immediately. The artists immediately sensed that they had a life to begin with from what Giotto had set up as the prerogatives of the painter. But modern painters have not indicated a form. Now I mean not necessarily form as it finally is, I mean really preform.

Preform is archaic form. In the preform actually exists more life, more of the story that can come after, than anyone who walks from it and nibbles at it can ever attain. In the preform—in the beginning, in the first form—lies more power than in anything that follows. And I believe that there is much to be gained by this thought if it comes through your minds, not only through mine, in what it can mean to you, because I am really worried about the beautiful things that exist around us today.

I can worry about the Seagram Tower. She is a beautiful bronze lady but she is all corsetted inside. She wears corsets from the first to the fifteenth story, but you can't see the corsets. She is a beautiful bronze lady, but she is not true. She is not that shape on the inside.

Now the preform may be a protoform. It may not be a beautiful thing in the eyes of the beholder, but to the artist it is a beautiful thing. It is the form before beauty, as we know it, sets in.

Think of sculpture for a minute! The Greeks in their archaic sculpture (and of course in the sculpture that later followed, too, but not so much as in the archaic, sculpture) symbolized aspects of man by indicating images of man. The torso was really an ever-serving servant—it did not have lung trouble—it was an ever-serving thing. The arms were ever capable. The eyes could not see, but could see forever.

It was this aspect which you catch very definitely. The helmet of the archaic warrior was more heraldic than it was useful. He could not go to battle with this thing—he would be knocked on the head in no time. He couldn't walk with it. But that wasn't the point. The sculptor realized he was indicating, symbolizing, something constantly. That was the important aspect—that sculpture knew that it was not indicating man at all.

Later, sculpture thought that it would perfect—"Look how ugly the lady's arms are, and look how disproportionate this torso is!" They misinterpreted the spirit—which is the beginning, from which sculpture actually began—which was the symbolizing of aspects of realizations in man. Using man because he was very concerned about it.

Now, how to do it in architecture? Well, I tried to explain, by saying what a space was, what a thing wants to be. There are new problems, tremendous new problems today, which have not been touched by the architect because he is thinking about exterior forms. He is thinking of all kinds of extraneous things before he arrives at a kind of realization of what a space really wants to be.

If you could only have the opportunity, where you can express more than just a single space or two or three, or a simple composition, like the campus of a university, some such thing as this which is a symphony really.

What is a campus of a university? Let's talk about it a little. It is really a realm of spaces which may be connected by ways of walking, and the walking is a protected kind of walking (it seems logical that it is protected). You consider it as high spaces together with low spaces, and various spaces where people can sort of find the place where they can do what they want to do.

In the few university buildings I have done, I came to several realizations with regard to space in that sense. I simply said, in a university building which was a laboratory for medical people, that the air you breathe should never come in contact with the air you throw away. That's all. Then I said that a scientist is like an artist—he is like an architect: he does not like to work as they do at M.I.T., in corridors with names on them. He likes to work in a kind of studio. A place which he can call his own, or with his confrères, working on a problem. He feels it very well if his space is a deadend of some kind, or a traffic way, or a place you would build a tunnel, or a place you take the elevator, or where the duct shafts are, and that you have limited the space, so that he cannot ever succeed in experimenting because his space is always being taken away from him by utilities which are in the way.

In the Medical Research Building at Pennsylvania, I developed characteristics within the studio itself where you can get darkness and light, not by pulling shades, but by simply characterizing the building so that there are natural places where darkness exists, and natural places where light exists.

Now in the art gallery at Yale University—and I'll criticize my own gallery freely—I only came to a very slight conclusion there about order. The realization there was something which was not fully understood by me; had it been, the design would probably have been different. Though, I must say that it has certain aspects which are very good still. If I were to build a gallery now, I would really be more concerned about building spaces which are not used freely by the director as he wants. Rather I would give him spaces that were there and had certain inherent characteristics. Then the visitor, because of the nature of the space, would perceive a certain object in quite a different way. The director would be fitted out with such a variety of ways of getting light, from above, from below, from little slits, or from whatever he wanted, so that he felt that here was really a realm of spaces where one could show things in various aspects.

I would say that dark spaces are also very essential. But to be true to the argument that an architectural space must have natural light, I would say that it must be dark, but that there must be an opening big enough, so that light can come in and tell you how dark it really is—that's how important it is to have natural light in an architectural space.

In discussing Giotto and the prerogatives of a painter I mentioned realm. I should like to elaborate on what I mean by a realm. The realm of architecture is a realm within which all other things are. In the realm of architecture there is sculpture, there is painting, there is physics, there is nursing—everything is in it. But the emphasis is on architecture. Architecture is the king of this realm. It is the reason for its existence altogether. And I think you know this realm best when you can touch the walls of its limits—when you know you've reached the point where, when you go across the wall, you are in a different realm. When you are able to touch the limits of it—not the limitations, but the limits, knowing how far you can go—I think at that point you really understand the realm.

When I went to school, we had a reference library divided into various architectural periods: Egyptian, Greek, Roman, Gothic, and so on, and this was my realm of architecture. If I had a cemetery to design, nothing could be better than a walk up to the Egyptian area where I could find what I needed. That was just the kind of life I led, and it was most delightful; I looked through the books and saw wonderful examples I could follow. Now when I got through with school, I walked around the realm and I came to a little village, and this village was very unfamiliar. There was nothing here that I had seen before. But through this unfamiliarity—from this unfamiliar thing—I realized what architecture was. Not right then, because I was then dealing with answers, but Le Corbusier raised the question for me, and the question is infinitely more powerful than the answer. So through the question—the power of it—the real thing was brought out.

As one person remarked, "A good question is greater than the most brilliant answer," and that is true. A good question is one that touches realization; it touches order, whereas an answer is very fragmentary in comparison to it. I never really got to architecture by simply taking convenient things; it was through the unfamiliar that I had learned and realized what architecture really was.

I think that striving to not be afraid when you are confronted with the unfamiliar is a wonderful thing. It is something we can recognize in your CIAM meetings. I find, however, that you occupy so much time in explaining the circumstantial aspects of your problem; you spend so much time in talking about contours, and about design,

93

and about all these things, all of which are terrifically important but are not really the essence of it. Because if you are making an auditorium, you are dealing with people who are to hear. The main thing about the auditorium is that you must hear and that it must have a certain tonality in order to hear properly. Therefore, your first concern is: what do you realize about an auditorium? If you must make it out of ice cubes, that is the next thing because you are building it in Iceland. But that is incidental, that is circumstantial: the design is circumstantial. What material you use is circumstantial; it is a design problem; it is a practical absolute problem. The design is the making of your composition, so that you can play the music. That is all very important. It is the imagery. It is the first thing you see. It is the tangible thing.

The realization of what is an auditorium is absolutely beyond the problem of whether it is in the Sudan, or in Rio de Janeiro. Therefore, your getting to the essence of what you are trying to do in creating what it wants to be, should be the first concern—should be the first act—of an architect explaining his project to another architect, and not all the circumstantial things, the amount of money you had, and the difficulties of regulations and so forth. I think that it is the circumstantial things which show with what brilliance you have attacked the problems of design with which you were confronted. But those are design problems; they are not problems in my opinion of the real essence of architecture today. The present is not a time of style whatsoever, it is a time of groping—a time of discovery. It is a time, you might say, of realization. Our problems are all new, our special demands are new, and it is a time, therefore, more concerned with trying to create better institutions from those we already have established. Our institutions are very much down. They are not good institutions now, because the spaces which must serve them are antiquated. We must find the realm of spaces which can now serve these institutions well. To think about what a school should be, and what those other things should be, is terribly important. To establish the right kind of budget, the right kind of approach to what really should be provided for these things, should be the concern and the preoccupation of CIAM in the expression of your problems.

The group that was talking just the other day came to a point where there was a kind of—a sort of feeling of—tension about this very issue. It was about the issue of the approach to the problem—of realizations about things. The climate of discussion should be such that people can go back home with a feeling that they owe nothing to anybody; because actually a man who discovers things that belong to the nature of things does not own these things. The designs belong to him but the realizations do not. If you copy Le Corbusier's designs you are somewhat of a thief. But if you take that which is in essence architectural from him, you take it very freely, because it does not belong to him either. It belongs to the realm of architecture. The fact that he

94

discovered it is a very fortunate thing for us, but it does not belong to him. In the same way, music does not belong to Mozart, but his compositions do.

I would like to conclude here, but first I mean to show my appreciation to Aldo who simply talked about a door. I think it is a wonderful thing to review the aspects of architecture from that sense. The mere fact that one can get to be totally preoccupied with this sort of thing is wonderful, because from it can grow many wonderful things; it could lead a man to realizations which go far beyond the problems of a door or a gateway.

I think it is not just the preoccupation with the little things, about whether you will put toilets here or there, or whether you have so much opening in the wall, it is a much broader thing, it is a climate within which these things can develop well, which means it must have a framework.

A city has a framework which is based on movement. The movement must also include a place to stop, where the pedestrian begins, which means there is a square; there is a place where he can stop. But it is not the same square as the European square is now. It is not the same in duplicate, because it is somehow a different thing. We are really walking on wheels, and as such it becomes quite different because you can now bypass a city; you can simply say: "I'll go somewhere else."

I think that cities will become greater as time goes on, but there won't be as many of them, as I think that a city cannot produce enough of the power, which you call city, in small places. I believe also that shopping centers in our country are not shopping centers—they are buying centers, that is all they are—and they can never develop into shopping centers, that is too wonderful a thing. They are devices for buying, that's all. They are as stupid as anything when the cars are away. They look like some of the abandoned American West. You see nothing and more nothing in most of them. Well, now I think I would like questions.

Discussion:

QUESTION: You mentioned the Seagram Building in your talk. Would you elaborate on it further?

KAHN: The Seagram Building is, I think, one of the really beautiful buildings of the world today. It stands there, a tall and marvellous looking building but it does not tell the true story of the architecture; it is a facile thing. It is stillborn on a sort of podium. As it stands now, the only thing left for some architects to do, who are jealous of it, is to make it out of silver, so that it will not cost 88 dollars per square foot, but 200 dollars per square foot.

However, the building is not honest, because the wind forces are not being expressed. Hidden in the building are great forces which offset the wind. The building, though, does not express the fact that these forces are in play. The force of gravity is nothing, you can easily calculate that. But the wind stresses are not so easily calculated, and there is a great form-making thing about them.

If this building expressed the force of wind, I am sure that when an ordinary man passed by he would look at it, more than he does now, even if it were done brutally. He would stop to think of it, of how it was done, and how it works, whereas he gives the present building far less thought. What we have here is another example of the short-necked giraffe approach. It is forcing a thing into a preconceived notion as to what it might look like. With the other approach you simply allow it to look like what it wants to be; as nature does with the porcupine—you let it tell you something about it; about the forces of truth from which you can derive a way of life. So it is important that these forms do come out.

Another thing is that I feel strongly that a building should not be considered as having no ending. I believe that an ending, as a sawed-off thing, is an indication of our society; a kind of frustrated way of looking at things. But if you believe in architecture sufficiently, you must put an ending to a thing, so that it is evident that you are not going to build some more. Nobody is going to build above it anyway. You know you must end it, and it is a good thing to indicate it if you can feel what it should be.

QUESTION: Architects seem forever to be wrangling about originality and the use of other men's ideas. What are your opinions on this?

KAHN: I don't think that you should be limited by the fact that someone has sort of opened the door for you, not at all. But it must be an opened door which isn't going to lead to your saying, "Now how can I make it different, so I can open another door?"

There is such a thing as the phenomenon of the man who somehow can do the unfamiliar thing and that it be right. The unfamiliar thing, however, cannot exist without already feeling that you need it. You should feel the need of it, as I said about Giotto. Giotto actually brought people to a state of need for his paintings. And I think a work of art must have that quality of need. I would say that a work of art is like an axe. An axe is created by a man, not by society. But society leads him to produce the axe because there is a certain need for it. At first the axe was not perfect. It probably fell off the handle and you had trouble with lifting it. But society demanded that it be developed—it needed it.

Art is definitely something of that nature. Art is the making of meaningful form. It is very much a part of our life, and is actually the concrete product of religion—feeling at its greatest moment is religion. Not ritualistic religion. I mean religion from which we derive such feelings as nobility—that religion.

QUESTION: When you spoke of a gateway, with reference to our project for instance, a gateway is something that is open or closed, and my feeling is that I did not even want a gateway, that I just wanted it open and that the trees and garden are there as a kind of symbol of the gateway.

KAHN: When you say you did not want it, one must question this for a moment, because it is not what you want, it is what you sense is the order of things which tells you what to design. It is then you can say that you want this or that as a way of satisfying this realization which you must of course believe in. It cannot be something that is imposed on you—you believe in it. In other words, the realization you have about movement, which says, it must be open, so that you can come in easily, is what you believe in. I do not disagree with this being open, but in my opinion, you cannot come too suddenly to an entrance in our movement, in our time. In a horse and carriage movement you can, for it is very incidental, slow-moving thing. It is very easy to contemplate an entrance through horse and carriage movement, but with a car it is a different kind of entrance, it is a much more deliberate, quick-moving, and demanding kind of entrance. You must see the entrance, and you must be prepared for it before-hand. Now, I don't say that your project is so big that it requires this kind of thought. I am only using it as an example, as I said, with all apology. I just did not think that a house was a proper gateway symbol. I did not mean a gateway with gates, I meant a gateway only as a kind of symbol. The distinction is that you realize that a gateway is necessary, and it is not the casual kind of thing you know about. When you are in a car you actually can lose your own entrance.

QUESTION: What do you feel about group work and partnership in architecture?

KAHN: Well, I think, that an act of architecture—not a professional performance in building a building, which is a different thing—cannot be done by more than one person. Whereas performing a building, doing a service and making it work, can be done by any number of people, by an organization as well. But that which has to do with making a space what it wants to be, that must be very jealously guarded by the man who does it. He cannot share this. It would be like asking two painters to paint one portrait. It is just impossible.

97

I think certain realizations can come through teamwork. The cross stimulization of one person working with another, and resulting in realizations, is very possible. But again, I think, that if an artist is an artist he has to guard very, very religiously his personal work. He cannot share his work with another. Those who are willing to share and work together should only be willing to do so for a certain period of time.

I have always had my apprehensions about partnerships because of the very fact that eventually one person or the other will try to claim ownership to that part which he cannot divulge from the other. If the partnership is really a significant thing, then it is very hard to do. I think that the more the artist, the more it is one person.

I am one who does not believe that we should have a collaborator, sculptor, or painter, in a team with the architect doing a building. I believe that an architect is entrusted with the making of spaces—the thoughtful making of spaces—and if he defines these spaces by the very way in which they are made, then in the fabric of the making, already exist all the places where painting and sculpture can exist—if it wants to exist. The sculptor or the painter can come in at that moment, if you like.

I am not saying that collaboration is impossible. I am just saying that I believe that the architect never allows himself to create spaces so defined that the painter is inscribed by the knowledge of where he should paint. The painter may very well come to the architect and say "Look I want to collaborate with you," and he knows very much what the architect is trying to do, and in this way can help him enormously. In most cases, however, the architect's work has not been concerned with the architecture. In order to make the painter understand what the architect is driving at, architects should produce architecture.

In connection with this let me talk a little about ornament. I feel that the beginning of ornament comes with the joint. The way things are made, the way they are put together, the way one thing comes to the other, is the place where ornament begins. It is the glory of the joint which is the beginning of ornament. The more a man knows the joint, the more he wants to show it. The more he wants to show the joint, the more he wants to show the distance. And if he wants to have it show the distance, he wants to exaggerate and caricature things which ordinarily are small. The beginning or ornament lies also in the challenge against the elements. The problems are there.

Now, one can also apply ornament. There is no reason why one can't apply it. But one must apply it with humor, and know he is applying it. But one must satisfy the other things too. It isn't merely a question of saying: "I need ornament, because these things are too bulky and I'm going to put something on so that it has more life in it." This is meaningless, as we all know.

I don't really believe it is even bad to exaggerate a beam's action—to give it more the power of the effort. But I do believe that if exaggeration is employed in a little way, it loses itself. In other words a short span cannot afford to be exaggerated—it becomes ridiculous. However, the larger the span the more the column says to the beam, "I like you," and puts its arms out and becomes definitely something which can be developed, and the expression of the joint between the column and the beam will be the ornament.

Reprinted from Oscar Newman, *New Frontiers in Architecture: CIAM in Otterlo 1959* (New York: Universe Books Inc., 1961), pp. 205–16.

Louis I. Kahn with Carlo Scarpa, 1969.

World Design Conference

Excerpt from the debate on "Our Country: The Total Image" at the World Design Conference, Tokyo

"Realization means harmony of a system in which a definite subjective condition reaches a condition of sensible order. Architecture is the ideational affirmation of space; the fact that most buildings, despite their internal differences, look alike, is because they lack Realization. Realization is not a mere ideology, but a philosophy with an emotional background."

"World Design Conference," reprinted with permission from *Industrial Design*, vol. 7, no. 7, 1960, p. 49.

On Philosophical Horizons

Excerpt from a panel discussion with the participation of Lawrence B. Anderson, John M. Johansen, Louis I. Kahn, and Dr. Morton White

I want to talk a bit about realization. I like to think that the transcendence of thought in the individual is philosophy, and the transcendence of feeling of an individual is love or religion. Realization is the combining of these transcendencies. It is not the individual thought; it is not the individual feeling. It is a kind of fact of both.

Realization stems from this. Realization may be said to be a harmony of systems that lead you to a feeling of form rather than design.

Form doesn't have shape or dimension. It simply has a kind of existence will.

Design is the means by which you bring into being that which form seems to indicate. In form you might say the spoon has to have a container and an arm. You bring it into existence by designing it as deep, or shallow, or long, or short, or made of gold, silver, or wood.

In speaking of the city I like to feel that it is a realization; that there is a distinction between city and institution. Institution is a working organization of the city. A city, specifically like Philadelphia or Rome, is a symbol of that which is an undeniable focus of getting together; the feeling that man as being cannot be denied; that may take ugly forms, ugly shapes, but you can't deny it.

I wish to speak about realization in this sense and in relation to institution.

I believe the institutions of our city are rotten to the core. If we get a program from a school board which says: Don't forget the nine-foot fence around your school, a lobby so many square feet, corridors nine feet wide, all classrooms alike—you have a red light budget that goes with it. I think nothing can come out of it in the way of what the architect is able to do.

If you were to define architecture in a few words you would say architecture is the thoughtful making of spaces. It is the duty of the architect to find what is this thoughtful realm of space, what is school—and not just take the program of the institution but try to develop something which the institution itself can realize is valid.

That is a challenge.

What is a school? It was a man sitting under a tree talking to a student who didn't know he was a student, simply talking about what occurred to him as a realization. Later of course the need for such a thing came about. Certainly the mother and child, hearing about this man, wanted him to live forever. Others took on the role of teacher. Pretty soon rules were built around the teacher and pretty soon the group developed into our present institutions which have absolutely no resemblance to the existence will which generated from the man under a tree talking to a few people.

I believe it is the duty of the architect to take every institution in the city and think of it as his work, that his work is to redefine the progress brought by these institutions; not to accept programs but to think it terms of spaces—in the case of the school he may even present a large entrance space which you can't name and from there he may go to a development of spaces, spaces small, large, with light coming from above to the side, but spaces that seem to indicate a good place where learning is possible.

Every space, including the corridor itself, should not be just stuffed with lockers because it happens to be a good way of solving a problem. Quite a difference between the economic problem and the budgetary problem.

In the same way, if you were given the problem of designing a chapel for a university, certainly you would not bring out all your palette of stained glass and mosaics or devices which you know a chapel must have, but simply think of it as a place which for the moment you won't define because it is too sacred. Then you put the ambulatory around, and then you put an arcade around the ambulatory so you don't have to go into the ambulatory, and a garden around the arcade so you don't have to go into the arcade, and then a fence around the garden so that you don't have to go into the garden.

Ritual is inspired, not set. I think it begins with the sense of a man who gets a criticism from a fine teacher and this instills in him a sense of dedication and he goes by the chapel and winks at it—he doesn't have to go in. He doesn't wink at the gymnasium, he winks at the chapel.

So it is not taking out your familiar tools in the development of space. It is the realization of the kind of space.

I think the city would grow great and I think the city is the true cathedral of our living. Man learns about man. He learns even how to walk graciously from man. He discovers walking by looking at another man.

Our institutions and their programs must be attacked. Architects must give great empty spaces for the institutions—those spaces must be both things of life and ways of life.

If you look at the Baths of Caracalla—the ceiling swells a hundred and fifty feet high. It was a marvelous realization on the part of the Romans to build such a space. It goes beyond function.

"On Philosophical Horizons," *AIA Journal*, vol. XXXIII, no. 6, June 1960, pp. 99–100; reproduced with the permission of The American Institute of Architects, 1735 New York Avenue, NW, Washington, DC 20006.

On Form and Design

Speech at the 46th meeting of the Association of Collegiate Schools of Architecture held at the University of California at Berkeley, Berkeley, California, April 22–23, 1960

As you know, I am a teacher which means really I am teaching myself and whatever rubs off, the student gets. When questions are brought before you by students I feel that the answers to these questions cannot be given offhand. I have always felt rather humble in the presence of a student.

During the time when I was thinking about form and design and making distinctions between the two I thought that the unmeasurable aspects of our existence are the ones that are the most important. Such things as thought, feeling, realization are all unmeasurable. It seems that this is also the concern of scientists.

I am concerned with realization because I believe from realization do we really design. Realization stems from the transcendence of our own feeling into the feeling of ourselves as others, and it actually represents the fact of feeling itself. The transcendence of thought is philosophy. We live by our own feelings and our own thoughts but when we come to realizations we transcend our own feelings and our own thoughts. Realization, I feel, stems from the fact of thought and the fact of feeling.

Now I say all this because I believe one can understand a form much better if one understands realization. You might say that realization is the sense of harmony of systems and belong to that which wants to exist and it is a sense of the order of things.

Design, when we come to it, is what we call on to put into being that which we realize.

During a seminar which was held at one of the universities, we gave ourselves the problem of trying to discover the nature of schools, not a school, not a program of a school, but simply school itself. The recognition of the singularity that you are different from another person gave rise to the idea that a man speaking to two people is not the same man talking to ten or the same man talking to a thousand.

One could speak to a thousand when speaking of a formula. When you are discussing knowledge, when you are discussing thought and feeling, we know we are a different person speaking to two or four or eight, and that you are very much attuned to your own singularity and to the singularity of others. From this you come to the realization that school is not a series of rules as you would get from a school board, but rather a realm of spaces wherein it is good to learn.

The architect when confronted with a problem of building a school has to start all over again and derive his source of design from where school began. Form is really inner image, something which does not have shape or dimension, but something which has the reflection of the order of things which makes the realm of spaces for the activity of school particular and not like other spaces.

When you reflect on the spaces of a city hall it is a space where you pay fees and taxes, the courts are there, but the participation is not there any more. The various organizations that feel responsible toward our way of life politically do not have any place in a city hall. It has lost its sense of participation.

I have often thought that our city halls are a quarry. It contains the spaces which do not represent participation. I believe it should be a city place where a dignitary, let us say a man like Picasso, could stay. He shouldn't be taken to the Sheraton Hotel. Why shouldn't he stay at the city place. Let us say it is a kind of chateau and the mayor has a key to it.

I see then a city place, a realm of spaces which can be used by the various organizations that uphold the interests of our democratic way of life. Men interested in housing, men interested in health, in art, in all the aspects of human activity. Many of these organizations hold their meetings in borrowed places. Their work is terrifically responsible but they have no home whatsoever.

When we are given a city hall to design we are told that it is nothing more than an office building. Is it just an office building? I think definitely not. There is an existence will about a city hall which is much beyond that of business space. It wants really to house the interests of the citizens. Those Citizens who are interested in the affairs of the city should be given the key to a space where they can meet.

This doesn't occur to us when we are given a program by the city authorities to design a new city hall. We simply fill the prescription like a druggist, never altering the program, never realizing that a city hall is a different kind of thing entirely. That it is a realm of spaces where these organizations can be given their proper place to meet and to uphold the interest of our democratic way of life.

Now we get a program from the school board which reads like this: the school must have a nine foot fence around it, of corrugated galvanized iron; it must have a lobby entered by stainless-steel doors because they are easy to maintain; the lobby is measured by so many square feet per person and the corridor must be no less than nine feet wide and preferably contain the lockers and the rooms must all be of the same size, well-ventilated and with good light, and enough to hold thirty people in each class.

Just see how far it is from the original phenomenon of a man who simply could not help but convey what was in his mind to a few people, from which school actually started.

Is school that kind of a place? No. It is really a realm of spaces where it is good to learn. If an architect visualizing these spaces feels the need for pantheon space to enter which is one hundred feet square, which cannot mean lobby, but simply a room, good to enter, so one feels the power of a place to learn—he should propose such a thing.

And then these spaces, which are high and low and lighted from above and the side, may be small spaces for a number of people, may be large spaces for just a few people, but in any case one cannot help but visualize even a corridor as spaces where it is good to learn.

Why must we begrudge the ten minutes that it takes to go from class to class? Is not coming out of class also learning? Of course it is. But in the wake of lockers all around you and great ventilating fans and everything else that spells just function, just use and just solutions of problems, I am afraid that the architect cannot convey in this way spaces for learning.

Architecture must be in the making of spaces so well attuned to the needs of the spaces and the needs of the spaces must be separated from the spaces themselves. They must have their own construction so they do not interfere in any way with the clarity and with the beauty that is called a place of learning.

I believe if we made spaces which more fully express the activity in many that the institutions themselves would sense the importance of changing their programs. I believe they will make enormously more allowances to the architects if the architects' examples were more reflective of the power of architecture itself.

Architecture is the thoughtful making of spaces. But these spaces must be clearly defined in their making. I believe we cannot have little things placed in a space created by a large span. The effort of the span belongs to the space. Often times we make larger spans and we crowd into them little rooms, little anterooms and closets, toilets, whereas these small spaces I think should have in their way a span so the spaces themselves become clearly made and its architectural quality seen.

Form to me is this inner image. It has no shape. It has no dimension. It somehow reflects that which belongs to itself. It is a harmony of systems which belong to a thing. It is a sense of the order of things. Design is that which puts it into being.

When a dish fell in Mozart's kitchen he knew the difference between the noise of it and the music of it. Where another man would probably run from the noise, he made a career out of it. Mozart knew the dissonance which it suggested to him belonged to music but not to him, but the way he used dissonance in music did belong to him.

The design of an architect belongs purely to him but that which he adds to architecture does not belong to him. It is the part which you might say is the realization of his work. He draws from realization which immediately belongs to the realm of architecture itself.

If we look at the work of Le Corbusier, look at the work of Aalto, of Mies, I think it is well to consider just what is there about Mies, what is there about Le Corbusier, what is there about Aalto that belongs to architecture itself? That which is inevitable or eternal as it is, that naturally belongs to architecture.

When you see imitation of men like Mies, imitation of Le Corbusier and Aalto, you know that men who imitate them do not really understand architecture because they are unable to draw from their particular designs that which represents the architectural qualities behind them. They are only able to see a way of doing it. To me it is much more significant to know what to do than how to do it as far as architectural consciousness is concerned.

To me architecture is the making of spaces, the thoughtful making of spaces and the concern is just what kind of spaces now represents the enclosure or the enclosing character of activities of man.

In the case of a house it is, I think, of great architectural importance to know house rather than a house. You can do nothing about home because it is the people that make a home but house, I believe, should be foremost in the architect's mind. Is he accomplishing house or is he just accomplishing a house? And certainly all the circumstantial character lies in a house, that which represents a kind of way of life or a realm of spaces where it is good to live is in house itself.

I believe that when you see an architectural drawing of a building that it is more akin to music than it is to, let us say, painting and sculpture. We often talk about painting and sculpture being highly associated to architecture. I believe that music is infinitely more akin to architecture than either of these. A musician sees it as something he hears. I believe a sheet of plan of an architecture should read like a realm of spaces and light. One should be able to read the light that comes into those spaces. It is a music of spaces in light. I believe spaces are not architectural spaces unless they have natural light because all the answers of the time of the day and the season of the year should enter these spaces and play on those spaces.

With artificial light it is but a single moment in light. Natural light is infinite in its giving to the spaces.

A column or a vault chosen in the making of a space is a kind of religion in the making of these spaces. A column is a releaser of light. In addition to giving light, it gives us the point from which we can reach gravity. It is different entirely from a wall because a wall does not release light unless you puncture it, whereas a column says that it stands between the one and the other, is a great source of light or a place you can go through. It tells you this. And a vault also tells you the same. It is a way of bringing light into the space and one should be able to see on a plan that it is a light-giving thing. One should feel the light coming into the spaces.

This is not true of our plans. We see partitions coming across the construction, not following the lines of construction because it is so easy to make these constructions that we forget that a column is definitely a position in the making of space. We talk about interpenetration of partitions—let us say the placing of the partitions near columns and all of that, all of which tends to make the plans less readable, less powerful in their emergence of space.

106

I like to think that form has no shape or dimension. It is something in the way of realization; that this realm of spaces belongs to this activity; another realm of spaces belongs to another activity.

Our buildings have a tendency to look completely insensitive to an activity. They tend to look alike. Office buildings look like apartment buildings, maybe with a few balconies that differentiate one from the other; actually they appear alike, the same kind of building.

Actually an apartment to be an apartment building should be a house over a house over a house and a house must have a yard, even if the yard is upstairs. Somehow the consciousness that you are still doing a house when you are doing an apartment building must be there and must be evident as differentiated from office space, which certainly doesn't have the same kind of will as that of an apartment building.

An auditorium wants to be a building. Sure it can't be a fiddle but it really wants to be very sensitive to sound and it is different from a convention hall. But we tend to make them quite the same.

I am doing a Unitarian Church in Washington. The form image that I had was from listening to the Unitarians. I felt the auditorium was a question and the school of the Unitarian Church was that which raised the question. I felt that the school should be the walls of the question. In my first designs I too literally made this image. I made a square. The exterior of the square where the rooms represented the school, the interior of which was an auditorium. I found great resistance to this because it was very rigid. The amount of school space was always much greater than what was necessary. And I found that in the design that I could do very much better by accepting the incompleteness of the form by saying that the amount of the space necessary to surround the auditorium had to be less than a square done in a categorical way could give.

I found that there were rooms that came to the auditorium but did not complete the walls, and then I completed the walls in a way which said I cannot get enough school space to complete this but what the premise is must remain. I still felt the school must surround the auditorium.

I felt the expression of the Unitarian idea is that they both come together rather than be separated. You may disagree with my holding so very closely the form realization and design which I applied to give it expression, but that you may attribute to my own limitation, but I did try to separate them. I wanted to try to express an activity of man which was different from another activity of man.

I had been asked to be the architect for an Academy of Biology in San Diego. I had no program whatsoever. They went to see the buildings that I am doing at the

University of Pennsylvania. They said how many square feet do you have there? I said one hundred and nine thousand square feet. They said that's about what they need. It has to be a laboratory, we are interested in one thing—we believe that cancer does not belong to medicine. We believe it belongs to population, not to medicine. We believe we can have people come in who can use their minds, who have powers of realization. What do you think the building should be like?

I said the first thing you want to do is build a chateau so you can come to this place and talk about these realizations. There would be fine, generous spaces which need not be all named for their purposes, just the wonderful spaces to come to. It would certainly have places of meeting. There would be places of dining, maybe you might have places where people could stay overnight, gymnasium, swimming pool, arcades, seminar rooms, and so on.

One would say: Where are the laboratories? We are talking about laboratories too. Essentially it is a laboratory building but you must not forget that the place of meeting is almost of major importance. The laboratory buildings were conceived as little courtlike buildings which were designed more by the scientists than the architect and presented a kind of gardenlike spot. You saw more walls than building. But they represented what the scientist himself feels represents the kind of space he needs to do his work without answering to a general scheme of laboratory.

Then down the road when laboratory function is understood, when the men knew what they were going to do and knew the men they were going to employ to go after directional research, there you had a factorylike mechanism, deliberately made as a mechanism, not pretty, not time lost but something strong which truthfully works as a deliberate directional research laboratory.

These were the three kinds of spaces I thought were good for such an activity as they outlined it without any program. But in this case the architect in a way did write the program and they felt very sympathetic to it.

Thank you very much.

"On Form and Design," reprinted with permission from *The Journal of Architectural Education*, vol. XV, no. 3, Fall 1960, pp. 62–65.

Marin City Redevelopment

Critique

It's difficult to comment after the completely sound dissertations by Reay and De Mars, and the wise comments of Albert Mayer. However, I have things in mind. First, I know you cannot change the design of yesterday and you cannot predict the design of tomorrow. We know what designs look like now that we thought only five years ago would be valid five years later. You can only design today. I mean precisely this day. I do think there is a distinction, however, between form and design. You can design a form in many, many ways, but the form itself is a set thing, essentially, which is indestructible as a form. I think of a house and a home. A house is probably not the greatest act of the architect but symbolically *house*, which represents a place where it is good to live, is probably a greater attainment than building a specific house. A home you can do nothing about, because it has to do with the people in it, but you can certainly anticipate this by the charm and warmth and direction its design gives. Design is a personal act: the making of a form is rather different. I think the making of a form represents the greater achievement of the architect because from it many designs can be made. However, though the architect may have invented a form, the force of order is so great in it that it already belongs to everybody as soon as it is created; so the architect is left with the design that he produces as a result of his realization which led to form. These are the things that came to my mind when I was looking at this project. Just what is its form concept? And what is the design interpretation of this form concept?

There should be, I think, very strong points which are indestructible in a plan for a village (as De Mars called it, and I think it's a very happy name for such a development). I don't particularly sense them here, except in a physical way, but I see them in a sociological way—in the way there would be no distinction made between one type of dwelling and another. In an apartment building one must satisfy the same premises as in a house; it is actually a place to live in and therefore it is quite equal in its position in a village to a house. But I sense that here an apartment house is built quite differently. In the house there's a certain respect for shading, overhang, roof structure—a kind of indigenous quality casually distinguishable as Californian— whereas the apartment house is no different from a house. I would say it's a house, upon a house, upon a house—and that each house must have a yard and that therefore the yard must be as apparent in the apartment building as it is for the house.

If the premises are carried out strongly I believe that a way of life can be represented in full, and this may become the basis for a form from which designs can be made. If these form realizations can be stated so that designs may result, even made by other architects who follow the realization of form, I think the project may turn out to be something of an excellent example in the direction of the development of these villages. There is a distinction between working design-wise, and building in variety with a *realization*. If I may define realization, it is a kind of harmony of system. I think that there is a tremendous harmony of system that has been established by the architects of this program, and this is its most commendable part. In the variety which they say must be—and I think it must be—and with the belief that one type of dwelling is not subjugated to another, and with the emphasis given to that which is already high by making it higher, there are aesthetic realizations as well as psychological realizations. I believe that in many places the design itself could have been worked over a little bit more. The casual fences, stairways, the kidney-shaped ponds, the trees in pots, and all these little devices are, from my point of view, for the birds. They are purposeful in creating charm, but I doubt whether you can do it by such means. As handled by the usual aborigine who goes in there to build they would be mangled to pieces: few people can do that sort of thing.

I believe you've treated too lightly the question of the pond, which is considered an essential part of the functioning community. In a village, the avenues of going and coming, the points where one takes a bus, the difference in grade between one level and another must be treated in a more ordered way. The sculpture of the ground itself, forming a logical framework for the development of houses, should not be quite so casually considered. I think it should be thought of as mandatory overall design, without worrying whether you are encroaching on the prerogative of the architect who follows. I would like to see more rigid statements of the points which must be given form from the beginning, as a point of departure from which design can come. It should be more than a casual and uncontrolled statement regarding overhangs, and so forth. These need not be made the same way by all people. The pond, since it is mandatory, should be quite formalized instead of so casual. I was hoping that such things as schools, institutions, the center part of town, would be given a little less of the feeling of the houses, which are much more subject to variation than those things which you say in a school.

Talking about institutions for a minute. I believe it is one of the most important duties of an architect to look into spaces which make up institutions. I believe they are too casually considered in filling out the program as put down by the school board or the city authorities. I believe that school started under a tree with a man who didn't know he was a teacher talking of his realizations or concepts to people who didn't know they were students. And because it really touched the need in man so greatly, out of it grew an institution called *school*. Think of the many different forms it had in Greek, Roman, or other periods that followed. But today you get a program from the school board that sounds like this: there should be a 9-foot fence around the property and there should be a lobby, measured by so many square feet per person: there should be stainless steel because it's so easily maintained; there should be corridors so wide because that's the minimum and then you have rooms that are all well ventilated and lighted. But is this actually a realm of spaces where it is good to learn? I doubt it. In California there is a much freer attitude, there are more possibilities, you can consider the outdoors and indoors more casually; but that isn't what I mean. I don't mean design. I mean raising the level to what you may call a realm of spaces where it's good to learn, where you may come into a space which you don't name at all, only because it is a good place to come into as a place to learn.

In the same way, what is a city center place? It is a casual kind of thing—I don't believe that it is. I think it should have human spaces which have as much of a sense of nobility as you can give them. If you look at the Baths of Caracalla—I'm not comparing them with the project that you're involved in—we know that we can bathe just as well as under an 8-foot ceiling as we can under a 150-foot ceiling, but I believe there's something about a 150-foot ceiling that makes a man a different kind of man. I would like to see firmed up those things which represent the institution as against, let's say, the more intimate concerns of houses. I believe that realizations in this sense are infinitely more design-fertile than *starting* with design, than the purposeful making of charm and that kind of thing. I think the project has such excellence that it doesn't need a lengthy comment; I'd like to see it successful, and I see certain aspects of it that may turn out to be unsuccessful because there is less a statement of the form, that which is not changeable, than a great variety of individual design compositions. A figure is a form, a composition is a design; and it is the figure aspect that it would be nice to feel in the plan, so that it would be easily recognized by anyone who passes it, who could say: I see the logic of this, I see the sense in it. From this, growth can come much more readily than by a casual riding with the contours of the land in a sort of circumstantial way.

"Marin City Redevelopment," reprinted with permission from *Progressive Architecture*, vol. XLI, November 1960, pp. 149–153.

1961

Form and Design

A young architect came to ask a question. "I dream of spaces full of wonder. Spaces that rise and envelop flowingly without beginning, without end, of a jointless material white and gold." "When I place the first line on paper to capture the dream, the dream becomes less."

This is a good question. I once learned that a good question is greater than the most brilliant answer.

This is a question of the unmeasurable and the measurable. Nature, physical nature, is measurable.

Feeling and dream has no measure, has no language, and everyone's dream is singular.

Everything that is made, however, obeys the laws of nature. The man is always greater than his works because he can never fully express his aspirations. For to express oneself in music or architecture is by the measurable means of composition or design. The first line on paper is already a measure of what cannot be expressed fully. The first line on paper is less.

"Then," said the young architect, "what should be the discipline, what should be the ritual that brings one closer to the psyche. For in this aura of no material and no language, I feel man truly is."

Turn to Feeling and away from Thought. In Feeling is the Psyche. Thought is Feeling and presence of Order. Order, the maker of all existence, has No Existence Will. I choose the word Order instead of knowledge because personal knowledge is too little to express Thought abstractly. This Will is in the Psyche.

All that we desire to create has its beginning in feeling alone. This is true for the scientist. It is true for the artist. But I warned that to remain in Feeling away from Thought means to make nothing.

Said the young architect: "To live and make nothing is intolerable. The dream has in it already the *will to be* and the desire to express this *will*. Thought is inseparable from Feeling. In what way then can Thought enter creation so that this psychic will can be more closely expressed? This is my next question."

When personal feeling transcends into Religion (not a religion but the essence religion) and Thought leads to Philosophy, the mind opens to realizations. Realization of what may be the *existence will* of, let us say, particular architectural spaces. Realization is the merging of Thought and Feeling at the closest rapport of the mind with the Psyche, the source of *what a thing wants to be*.

It is the beginning of Form. Form encompasses a harmony of systems, a sense of Order and that which characterizes one existence from another. Form has no shape or dimension. For example, in the differentiation of a spoon from spoon, spoon characterizes a form having two inseparable parts, the handle and the bowl. A spoon implies a specific design made of silver or wood, big or little, shallow or deep. Form is "what." Design is "how." Form is impersonal. Design belongs to the designer. Design is a circumstantial act, how much money there is available, the site, the client, the extent of knowledge. Form has nothing to do with circumstantial conditions. In architecture, it characterizes a harmony of spaces good for a certain activity of man.

Reflect then on what characterizes abstractly House, a house, home. House is the abstract characteristic of spaces good to live in. House is the form, in the mind of wonder it should be there without shape or dimension. *A* house is a conditional interpretation of these spaces. This is design. In my opinion the greatness of the architect depends on his powers of realization of that which is House, rather than his design of *a* house which is a circumstantial act. Home is the house and the occupants. Home becomes different with each occupant.

The client for whom a house is designed states the areas he needs. The architect creates spaces out of those required areas. It may also be said that this house created for the particular family must have the character of being good for another. The design in this way reflects its trueness to Form.

I think of school as an environment of spaces where it is good to learn. Schools began with a man under a tree who did not know he was a teacher discussing his realization with a few who did not know they were students. The students reflected on what was exchanged and how good it was to be in the presence of this man. They aspired that their sons also listen to such a man. Soon spaces were erected and the first schools became. The establishment of school was inevitable because it was part of the desires of man. Our vast systems of education, now vested in Institutions, stem from these little schools but the spirit of their beginning is now forgotten. The rooms required by our institutions of learning are stereotypical and uninspiring. The Institute's required uniform classrooms, the locker-lined corridors and other so-called functional areas and devices, are certainly arranged in neat packages by the architect who follows closely the areas and budgetary limits as required by the school authorities. The schools are good to look at but are shallow in architecture because they do not reflect the spirit of the man under the tree. The entire system of schools that followed from the beginning would not have been possible if the beginning were not in harmony with the nature of man. It can also be said that the existence will of school was there even before the circumstances of the man under a tree.

That is why it is good for the mind to go back to the beginning because the beginning of any established activity of man is its most wonderful moment. For in it lies all its spirit and resourcefulness, from which we must constantly draw our inspirations of present needs. We can make our institutions great by giving them our sense of this inspiration in the architecture we offer them.

Reflect then on the meaning of school, *a* school, institution. The institution is the authority from whom we get their requirements of areas. A School or a specific design is what the institution expects of us. But School, the spirit school, the essence of the existence will, is what the architect should convey in his design. And I say he must, even if the design does not correspond to the budget. Thus the architect is distinguished from the mere designer. In school as a realm of spaces where it is good to learn, the lobby measured by the institute as so many square feet per student would become a generous Pantheon-like space where it is good to enter. The corridors would be transferred into classrooms belonging to the students themselves by making them much wider and provided with alcoves overlooking the gardens. They would become the places where boy meets girl, where the student discusses the work of the professor with his fellow student. By allowing classroom time to these spaces instead of passage time from class to class, it would become a meeting connection and not merely a corridor, which means a place of possibilities in self-learning. It becomes the classroom belonging to the students. The classrooms should evoke their use by their space variety and not follow the usual soldierlike dimensional similarity, because one of the most wonderful spirits of this man under the tree is his recognition of the singularity of every man. A teacher or a student is not the same when he is with a few in an intimate room with a fireplace as in a large high room with many others. And must the cafeteria be in the basement, even though its use in time is little? Is not the relaxing moment of the meal also a part of learning?

As I write alone in my office, I feel differently about the very same things that

I talked about only a few days ago to many at Yale. Space has power and gives mode.

This, with the singularity of every person, suggests a variety of spaces with a variety of the ways of natural light and orientation to compass and garden. Such spaces lend themselves to ideas in the curriculum, to better connections between teacher and student, and to vitality in the development of the institution.

The realization of what particularizes the domain of spaces good for school would lead an institution of learning to challenge the architect to awareness of what School *wants to be* which is the same as saying what is the form, School.

In the same spirit I should like to talk about a Unitarian Church.

The very first day I talked before the congregation using a blackboard. From what I heard the minister speak about with men around I realized that the form aspect, the form realization of Unitarian activity was bound around that which is Question. Question eternal of why anything. I had to come to the realization of what existence will and what order of spaces were expressive of the Question.

I drew a diagram on the blackboard which I believe served as the Form drawing of the church and, of course, was not meant to be a suggested design.

I made a square center in which I placed a question mark. Let us say I meant it to be the sanctuary. This I encircled with an ambulatory for those who did not want to go into the sanctuary. Around the ambulatory I drew a corridor which belonged to an outer circle enclosing a space, *the school*. It was clear that School which gives rise to Question became the wall which surrounds Question. This was the form expression of the church, not the design.

This puts me in mind of the meaning of Chapel in a university.

Is it the mosaics, stained glass, water effects, and other known devices? Is it not the place of inspired ritual which could be expressed by a student who winked at chapel as he passed it after being given a sense of dedication to this work by a great teacher. He did not need to go in.

It may be expressed by a place which for the moment is left undescribed and has an ambulatory for the one who does not want to enter it. The ambulatory is surrounded by an arcade for the one who prefers not to go into the ambulatory. The arcade sits in the garden for the one who prefers not to enter the arcade. The garden has a wall and the student can be outside winking at it. The ritual is inspired and not set and is the basis of the form Chapel.

Back to the Unitarian Church. My first design solution which followed was a completely symmetrical square. The building provided for the schoolrooms around the periphery, the corners were punctuated by larger rooms. The space in the center of the square harbored the sanctuary and the ambulatory. This design closely resembled the diagram on the blackboard and everyone liked it until the particular interests of every committee member began to eat away at the rigid geometry. But the original premise still held of the school around the sanctuary.

It is the role of design to adjust to the circumstantial. At one stage of discussion with the members of the church committee a few insisted that the sanctuary be separated entirely from the school. I said fine, let's put it that way and I then put the auditorium in one place and connected it up with a very neat little connector to the school. Soon everyone realized that the coffee hour after the ceremony brought several related rooms next to the sanctuary, which when alone were too awkwardly self-satisfying and caused the duplication of these rooms in the separated school block. Also, the schoolrooms by separation lost their power to evoke their use for religious and intellectual purposes and, like a stream, they all came back around the sanctuary.

The final design does not correspond to the first design though the form held.

I want to talk about the difference between form and design, about realization, about the measurable and the unmeasurable aspects of our work and about the limits of our work.

Giotto was a great painter because he painted the skies black for the daytime and he painted birds that couldn't fly and dogs that couldn't run and he made men bigger than doorways because he was a painter. A painter has this prerogative. He doesn't have to answer to the problems of gravity, nor to the images as we know them in real life. As a painter he expresses a reaction to nature and he teaches us through his eyes and his reactions to the nature of man. A sculptor is one who modifies space with the objects expressive again of his reactions to nature. He does not create space. He modifies space. An architect creates space.

Architecture has limits.

When we touch the invisible walls of its limits then we know more about what is contained in them. A painter can paint square wheels on a cannon to express the futility of war. A sculptor can carve the same square wheels. But an architect must use round wheels. Though painting and sculpture play a beautiful role in the realm of architecture as architecture plays a beautiful role in the realms of painting and sculpture, one does not have the same discipline as the other.

One may say that architecture is the thoughtful making of spaces. It is, note, the filling of areas prescribed by the client. It is the creating of spaces that evoke a feeling of appropriate use.

To the musician a sheet of music is seeing from what he hears. A plan of a building should read like a harmony of spaces in light.

Even a space intended to be dark should have just enough light from some mysterious opening to tell us how dark it really is. Each space must be defined by its structure and the character of its natural light. Of course I am not speaking about minor areas which serve the major spaces. An architectural space must reveal the evidence of its making by the space itself. It cannot be a space when carved out of a greater structure meant for a greater space because the choice of a structure is synonymous with the light and that which gives image to that space. Artificial light is a single tiny static moment in light and is the light of night and never can equal the nuances of mood created by the time of day and the wonder of the seasons.

A great building, in my opinion, must begin with the unmeasurable, must go through measurable means when it is being designed and in the end must be unmeasurable. The design, the making of things, is a measurable act. In fact at that point, you are like physical nature itself because in physical nature everything is measurable, even that which is yet unmeasured, like the most distant stars which we can assume will be eventually measured.

But what is unmeasurable is the psychic spirit. The psyche is expressed by feeling and also thought and I believe will always be unmeasurable. I sense that the psychic Existence Will calls on nature to make what it wants to be. I think a rose wants to be a rose. Existence Will, *man*, becomes existence, through nature's law and evolution. The results are always less than the spirit of existence.

In the same way a building has to start in the unmeasurable aura and go through the measurable to be accomplished. It is the only way you can build, the only way you can get it into being is through the measurable. You must follow the laws but in the end when the building becomes part of living it evokes unmeasurable qualities. The design involving quantities of brick, method of construction, engineering is over, and the spirit of its existence takes over.

Take the beautiful tower made of bronze that was erected in New York. It is a bronze lady, incomparable in beauty, but you know she has corsets for fifteen stories because the wind bracing is not seen. That which makes it an object against the wind which can be beautifully expressed, just like nature expresses the difference between the moss and the reed. The base of this building should be wider than the top, and the columns which are on top dancing like fairies, and the columns below growing like mad, don't have the same dimensions because they are not the same thing. This story if told from realization of form would make a tower more expressive of the forces. Even if it begins in its first attempts in design to be ugly it would be led to beauty by the statement of form.

I am doing a building in Africa, which is very close to the equator. The glare is killing, everybody looks black against the sunlight. Light is a needed thing, but still an enemy. The relentless sun above, the siesta comes over you like thunder.

I saw many huts that the natives made.

There were no architects there.

I came back with multiple impressions of how clever was the man who solved the problems of sun, rain, and wind.

I came to the realization that every window should have a free wall to face. This wall receiving the light of day would have a bold opening to the sky. The glare is modified by the lighted wall and the view is not shut off. In this way the contrast made by separated patterns of glare which skylight grills close to the window make is avoided. Another realization came from the effectiveness of the use of breeze for insulation by the making of a loose sun roof independently supported and separated from the rain roof by a head room of six feet. These designs of the window and wall and of the sun and rain roofs would tell the man on the street the way of life in Angola.

I am designing a unique research laboratory in San Diego, California.

This is how the program started.

The director, a famous man, heard me speak in Pittsburgh. He came to Philadelphia to see the building I had designed for the University of Pennsylvania. We went out together on a rainy day. He said, "How nice, a beautiful building. I didn't know a building that went up in the air could be nice. How many square feet do you have in this building?" I said, "One hundred and nine thousand square feet." He said, "That's about what we need."

That was the beginning of the program of areas. But there was something else he said which became the Key to the entire space environment. Namely that Medical Research does not belong entirely to medicine or the physical sciences. It belongs to Population. He meant that anyone with a mind in the humanities, in science, or in art could contribute to the mental environment of research leading to discoveries in science. Without the restriction of a dictatorial program it became a rewarding experience to participate in the projection of an evolving program of spaces without precedence. This is only possible because the director is a man of unique sense of environment as an inspiring thing, and he could sense the existence will and its realization in form which the spaces I provided had.

The simple beginning requirement of the laboratories and their services expanded to cloistered gardens and Studies over arcades and to spaces for meeting and relaxation interwoven with unnamed spaces for the glory of the fuller environment.

The laboratories may be characterized as the architecture of air cleanliness and area adjustability. The architecture of the oak table and the rug is that of the Studies.

The Medical Research Building at the University of Pennsylvania is conceived in recognition of the realizations that science laboratories are studios and that the air to breathe should be away from the air to throw away.

The normal plan of laboratories which places the work areas off one side of a public corridor and the other side provided with the stairs, elevators, animal quarters, ducts, and other services. This corridor is the vehicle of the exhaust of dangerous air and also the supply of the air you breathe, all next to each other. The only distinction between one man's spaces of work from the other is the difference of the numbers on the doors.

I designed three studio towers for the University where a man may work in his bailiwick and each studio has its own escape *stairway sub tower* and *exhaust sub tower* for isotope air, germ-infected air, and noxious gas.

A central building to which the three major towers cluster takes the place of the area for services which are on the other side of the normal corridor plan. This central building has nostrils for intake of fresh air away from *exhaust sub towers* of vitiated air.

This design, an outcome of the consideration of the unique use of its spaces and how they are served, characterizes what it is for.

One day I visited the site during the erection of the prefabricated frame of the building. The crane's 200-foot boom picked up 25-ton members and swung them into place like matchsticks moved by the hand. I resented the garishly painted crane, this monster which humiliated my building to be out of scale. I watched the crane go through its many movements all the time calculating how many more days this "thing" was to dominate the site and building before a flattering photograph of the building could be made.

Now I am glad of this experience because it made me aware of the meaning of the crane in design, for it is merely the extension of the arm like a hammer. Now I began to think of members 100 tons in weight lifted by bigger cranes. The great members would be only the parts of a composite column with joints like sculpture in gold and porcelain and harboring rooms on various levels paved in marble.

These would be the stations of the great span and the entire enclosure would be sheathed with glass held in glass mullions with strands of stainless steel interwoven like threads assisting the glass and the mullions against the forces of wind.

Now the crane was a friend and the stimulus in the realization of a new form.

The institutions of cities can be made greater by the power of their architectural spaces. The meeting house in the village green has given way to the city hall which is no more the meeting place. But I sense an existence will for the arcaded city place where the fountains play, where again boy meets girl, where the city could entertain and put up our distinguished visitors, where the many societies which uphold our democratic ideals can meet in clusters of auditoria in the city place.

The motor car has completely upset the form of the city. I feel that the time has come to make the distinction between the Viaduct architecture of the car and the architecture of man's activities. The tendencies of designers to combine the two architectures in a simple design has confused the direction of planning and technology.

The Viaduct architecture enters the city from outlying areas. At this point it must become more carefully made and even at great expense more strategically placed with respect to the center.

The Viaduct architecture includes the street which in the center of the city wants to be a building, a building with rooms below for city piping services to avoid interruption to traffic when services need repair.

The Viaduct architecture would encompass an entirely new concept of street movement which distinguished the stop-and-go staccato movement of the bus from the "go" movement of the car. The area framing expressways are like rivers. These rivers need harbors. The interim streets are like canals which need docks. The harbors are the gigantic gateways expressing the *architecture of stopping*. The terminals of the Viaduct architecture, they are garages in the core, hotels, and department stores around the periphery and shopping centers on the street floor.

This strategic positioning around the city center would present a logical image of protection against the destruction of the city by the motor car. In a sense the problem of the car and city is war, and the planning for the new growth of cities is not a complacent act but an act of emergency.

The distinction between the two architectures, the architecture of the Viaduct and the architecture of the acts of man's activities, could bring about a logic of growth and a sound positioning of enterprise.

An architect from India gave an excellent talk at the University about the fine new work of Le Corbusier and about his own work. It impressed me, however, that these beautiful works he showed were still out of context and had no position. After his lecture I was asked to remark. Somehow I was moved to go to the blackboard where I drew in the center of the board a towering water tower, wide on top and narrow below. Like the rays of a star, I drew aqueducts radiating from the tower. This implied the coming of the trees and fertile land and a beginning of living. The buildings not yet there which would cluster around the aqueduct would have meaningful position and character.

The city would have form.

From all I have said I do not mean to imply a system of thought and work leading to realization from Form to Design.

Designs could just as well lead to realizations in Form.

This interplay is the constant excitement of Architecture.

"Form and Design," from Vincent Scully, Jr., *Louis I. Kahn* (New York: George Braziller Inc., 1962), pp. 114–21; reprinted by permission of George Braziller, Inc.

The Sixties

A P/A Symposium on the State
of Architecture: Part I

We're living in an era of new space demands, new things which are so fresh and unfamiliar that most minds are unable to direct them in a way which gives an imagery of a truer way. And the fact that we have such wonderful resourcefulness to boot—no limits—produces naturally a kind of individual approach rather than a stylistic approach to architecture. I tend to think that it's a true thing that exists now, but I say this: it isn't a happy thing. It produces a great deal of permissiveness, and the result is really chaotic because those who are incapable imagine they have the privilege of also having that permissiveness. The whole thing is a mess of copying and recopying and wrong attitudes and misinterpretations of things very well considered, like the Le Corbusier and Mies things.

Architecture has a certain nature. One may question that it has a nature: I believe it does. You can't just pick up and say, "I'm going to do my own little doodles on my own piece of canvas": this is a very important expenditure even for the greatest of corporations; it's an act that has a definite social connotation. It has a responsibility, because its existence is not a temporal one, and my feeling has always been—"always" meaning the last two years—that we must strengthen our institutions in whatever way architecture, as the individual expressions of men, can strengthen our institutions. In what way can we strengthen the institutions we live among—of government, of health, and so on? Does this individualism in architecture, which now seems to be permitted an unprecedented existence—an architecture where men are given freedom to express themselves in a way that, stylistically, is apparently uncontrolled, undirected, and unmotivated—help these institutions? Will it help future generations to understand what we did, and will they believe that we performed an act of a new freedom, the likes of which we still can't define, or will they consider it irresponsibility? That is the crux of the question—not whether it's good or bad.

I would try to defend the chaos in this respect: within the limitations of such a material as stone there was a fundamental rhythm; you had to conclude with columns at certain intervals which, even if you knew nothing about architecture very profoundly, made a kind of architecture. When you looked at it you said, "By God, isn't that pretty nice." In it was built a kind of rhythm that you couldn't help. Today you can span 100 feet; the column is so distant from the other column that rhythm doesn't exist any more. And other qualities have changed: you don't feel the music of it; you don't feel the judgment of it. Is it architecture or is it not? Somehow if it's clean and looks new, it satisfies everybody. And what may be called an architectural quality, distinguished from a building quality, is not registered or recognizable. It's due to the fact that our masters, who are conducting our lives in a way, are men who work entirely differently from each other—and therein lies what you may call the chaotic condition. If the four masters—or five, or six—worked like each other, then you would say that in this situation there would be a kind of built-in sense of what personal variations could exist within the premises of form. But since this is not true of the masters, how can you expect it to be true of their pupils? And so, what has been produced in the minds of the most sensitive men (those who have really opened our eyes architecturally) was sought from many points of view. It seems to me, knowing nature a little bit, that various points of view are still there, and many more points of view can be there, and that this is a primitive beginning of what later may turn out to be a more directed point of view.

"The Sixties: A P/A Symposium on the State of Architecture: Part I," reprinted with permission from *Progressive Architecture*, March 1961, unnumbered pages.

Louis I. Kahn

A discussion recorded in Louis I. Kahn's Philadelphia office in February, 1961

American Consulate: Luanda, Portuguese Angola

KAHN: One of the things which impressed me very much during my stay in Luanda was the marked glare in the atmosphere . . . when you were on the interior of any building, looking at a window was unbearable because of the glare. The dark walls framing the brilliant light outside made you very uncomfortable. The tendency was to look away from the window. Another thing that impressed me was the importance of breeze . . . the importance of breeze in carrying away the warm air that accumulated around the building. And I thought wouldn't it be good if one could express . . . find an architectural expression for the problems of glare without adding devices to a window . . . but rather by developing a warm architecture . . . which somehow tells the story of the problems of glare. Some of the buildings used piece work, grillwork . . . wood or masonry grillwork in front of windows. This was unsatisfactory because of what it did . . . because the wall itself was dark against the light; it gave you just a multiple pattern of glare . . . little pin points . . . little diamond points of glare against the dark ribs of the grillwork. And that tended to be unsatisfactory. I noticed that buildings which were very close to windows—were very pleasant to look at from the windows. I also noticed that when people worked in the sun—and many of them did—the native population people—when they worked, they usually faced the wall and not the open country or the open street. Indoors, they would turn their chair toward the wall and do whatever they were doing by getting the light indirectly from the wall to their work. That gave me the thought of a wall a small distance in front of every window as a kind of indigenous architectural sense. Now, placing a wall in front of a window would cut the view and that is not pleasant. One doesn't feel like having the view cut away, so I thought of placing openings in the wall; the wall then becomes part of the window. When that wall got the light—even the direct sunlight—it would modify the glare. So therefore I thought of the beauty of ruins . . . the absence of frames . . . of things which nothing lives behind . . . and so I thought of wrapping ruins around buildings; you might say encasing a building in a ruin so that you look through the wall which had its apertures by accident. But, in this case, you'd want to formalize these openings, and I felt this would be an answer to the glare problem. I wanted to incorporate this into the architecture instead of it being a device placed next to a window to correct the window desires . . . I don't want to say window desires . . . window desires is not the way to put it. I should say: desire for light, but still an active fighting of the glare. Another thing that impressed me: I saw some buildings that were conscious of the heat generated by roofs. They had large areas in the roof . . . large separations between the ceiling and the roof . . . small openings which were visible from the outside in which the breeze could come in to ventilate the areas in the ceiling and roof planes. And I thought how wonderful it would be if one could separate the sun problems from the rain problems. And it came to mind to have a sun roof purely for the sun and another roof purely for the rain. I placed them six feet away from each other so that one could maintain the rain roof . . . which was the important roof to maintain because the sun roof could take care of itself . . . it being a loose roof, one in which the rain can go through. It can never become a problem, you see, except for minor repairs. The sun roof naturally wanted to be made as light as possible . . . because it should be in a way a gossamer . . . something which is just there as an interceptor . . . and I thought of the insulation . . . that the actual sun roof might become the insulation so I would eliminate insulation on the rain roof entirely . . . have no air space except for what you get from the separation between the two roofs, the rain roof and the sun roof. Now there were other thoughts which came to my mind, outside of plan, outside of any aesthetic notions I may have had to begin with about how I build the building. I felt the building should have a restful, a reposeful character, and not be particularly aggravated in contour. I wanted very much—as has always been my desire—to demonstrate to the man on the street a way of life . . . so when he sees a building as he passes it he feels as though . . . "Yes, this building represents or presents a civic story to me of my relation to this building. I expect a dignified building for a dignified activity of man." But those were feelings about a sense of appropriateness which may have come from learning and from other things but are not really deeply fundamental. They are aesthetic considerations and aesthetics are, of course, the laws of art. You learn them by seeing a lot and by being told a lot and by sensing a lot, but the other things come out of the very characteristics of the air, and of light . . . very simple everlasting presences that should constantly talk to you in architecture. You cannot forget that light of a certain character has to do with that which distinguishes the architecture of one region from that of another. Even if you took the demands of a company for their identification in one country or another, you couldn't build a prototype as a kind of business principle, rather than as a building principle. You would have to give not so much a building but a vision, an image. But the image must change from one region to another because the requirements of an area are different in one place or another. The integrity of a building could be one stamp of identity with a company, the excellence of performance could be one . . . certainly their sign could be . . . but when you take the very same building, a prototype, an actual duplication, and place it anywhere regardless of the area . . . this would be a ridiculous building. I also realized that natural ventilation was an important thing to consider in these buildings because of the state of mechanical ability; the repair of air-conditioning systems or plumbing systems was something that would take a long time to develop in this country . . . you can't just import devices without regard to their future performance. But even if you were to have good mechanical maintenance for air conditioning and the other modern devices which control your environment, the protection against the sun and glare and the channeling of wind is still important so as not to impose too much load on the air conditioning. So a non-air-conditioned building can look just the same really as an air-conditioned building except that the windows would change. In Luanda you can just have slats—you don't need any glass at all. You just allow the breeze to come through and you control it with your louvers. But, when you have an air-conditioned building, you've got to have glazing—you've got to contain it . . . you don't want to condition the whole atmosphere. So I felt I was not doing the wrong thing by making the building look like a non-air-conditioned building except for the glazing.

EDITOR: Is it or isn't it air conditioned?

KAHN: This is an air-conditioned building. Only, you must figure that it could at times be one in which the air conditioning would not be functioning. There will be some louvers and operating windows in there anyhow so you can get some ventilation in case the thing goes bad.

The glare walls are designed to present a nonbearing wall. You feel the openings are done with the idea of giving you a sympathetic place in which to view your . . . whatever you want to see. I feel, offhand, that they're now a little too large, that they can be made smaller. It's only that I still haven't developed a kind of sense in lieu of experience to tell me whether they're large or small. I haven't developed this because they must be tried . . . probably anyone could have greater caution . . . I think they can actually be smaller than those indicated. I feel the openings should be smaller because you can have a side view anyway . . . you always have a side view. You can look out and see everything you want. But here you have a controlled view and it can actually be smaller than I have indicated. I feel this is a good approach to architecture . . . a true approach to architecture . . . in that you're constantly aware of the natural forces and trying to restate and to re-establish a way of life in architecture. So a building really aspires to something, and it answers very much a way of life. But, this aspiration has to be constantly renewed and reborn and what is presented by the art of building or the art of painting or sculpture is in light of new techniques. The new techniques will help you . . . it brings before you new measurable means of doing that which your aspiration calls for and that's how you view technique: as a measurable means of expressing closer and closer the desire and the existence will of aspirations.

From the main thoroughfares I developed an entrance court which is really a parking space for the chancellery and the house . . . the residence. I used trees to divide areas of parking and to shade the parking, too . . . right in the street itself. This much of the street would be paved with limestone . . . a material prevalent in Angola. This answers many of the problems which are unsolved in some of these consular buildings . . . I'm not saying it very well . . . let me just say it in different words . . . I'm conscious of this thing for a moment. The government board of architectural review liked the scheme very much because they saw a sense of privacy in the parking . . . in that the paving is different from the usual run of paving . . . which seemed like an ordinary consideration, but they didn't think it was ordinary because it gave a kind of gate . . . a court entrance to these two buildings. The chancellery is surrounded by a play of pool areas which empty one into the other; the upper pool empties into this lower pool and the lower pool empties into a pool at a still lower level . . . and that keeps the water running into this pool . . . which is very essential to water use in these areas. And practically the entire landscaping ideal on the chancellery side is the pool and the various terraces sitting in the environment, a rather stark environment. On the other side you get an environment of green . . . though it's not indicated on the plot plan, this will be a green area, a treed area . . . whereas this will be (the chancellery area) rather an untreed area with the court itself giving shade and direction to the parking and entrance. The residence is treated in the same way as far as the recognition of glare and the recognition of the sun roof. The four courts on the interior of the residence give interior light and afford a positioning of the columns which hold the sun roof. This shows, of course, a lower story . . . and you notice that it has a continuous walkway under the building. I feel that in bringing the rain roof and the sun roof away from each other I was telling the man on the street his way of life. I was explaining the atmospheric conditions of wind, the conditions of light, the conditions of sun and glare to him. If I used a device—a clever kind of design device—it would only seem like a design to him—something pretty.

I didn't want anything pretty; I wanted to have a clear statement of a way of life. And those two devices I feel very proud of as being strong architectural statements from which other men can make infinitely better statements. These are really crude statements . . . they're actually done with almost the feeling that they should be primitively stated first rather than in high degree of taste. The purpose was to state it in a rather primitive, unknowing, unsophisticated way. And I think that in the arrangement of spaces required, the sense of entrance, and the sense of reception, the plan has again a sense of the appropriateness of such devices . . . or the space feeling that one should have considering the type of building it is. One should have a feeling of entrance and reception not by the way of sign but by its very character and this every architect who is conscious of spaces does one way or the other. And, I think this plan does indicate that. Notice also that the piers that hold the main girders for the sun roof arc completely independent of the rain roof. The rain roof is never pierced. The sun roof rises quite independently out of the architecture, so that at no point do you pierce the rain roof. That accounts for these piers . . . these four sets of piers. The girders go across and the joists—concrete prestressed joists—hold the tiled—the clay-tiled leaves which form the sun tree on the sun roof which covers the entire building all together. You're completely conscious of this because when you enter the building . . . here, for instance . . . this is all open through there . . . the rain roof only follows this little portion here . . . is only this and there and this is all open, so . . . when you come into the building here you sense the entire leaflike structure above . . . they'd be open enough so that the light can come through.

EDITOR: Why is the opening in the pier greater in the lower story than in the upper?

KAHN: There's a lintel that allows me to have a smaller opening above . . . it can distribute the load that way. I wanted it open under there because I want to pass through everything and I pass through this beam in order to get a continuous promenade under the building. I then put the building off the ground . . . it is current practice in these areas to raise all important rooms above grade. Also it gives you a feeling of greater protection . . . in a way the chancellery building of this government function is, in a sense, a fort . . . it's a protective building . . . and the extra floor gives it a kind of extra sense of protection.

EDITOR: The physiological reaction to sitting in darkness and looking to light is a problem like the adjustment of the diaphragm of a camera . . . I was wondering why then this interval—the double window—will ease the adjustment the eye must make. You either know or are hoping that when you do finally—after looking through the void of shade—see the bright area, it will be toned down enough so that your iris can adjust instantaneously without having a painful physiological reaction.

KAHN: Listen to what I think. I say it more this way: when you see this wall in front of you, light framed in a window surrounded in darkness is what causes the glare. That's glare, a glare condition.

EDITOR: It provides a shade of gray between the black and the white.

KAHN: Grills or anything like that—which are prevalent in front of a window like that—give little pin points of light which are very glaring. You needn't see it, you can just draw it.

When these members get smaller and smaller, it's all right again . . . you don't feel it as much. Then you get a great modification of the glare.

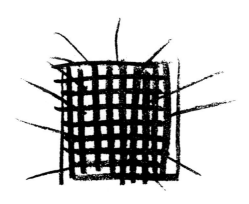

EDITOR: Well this would presumably be easy enough to make a model of . . .

KAHN: Yes, we have made a model of it . . . you can see the difference. You put a large bulb—a 500-watt bulb—in front of you and you can see plenty of glare right close to it. And as soon as you move that thing (the model of the light wall) in front of the bulb it's completely different. You saw the difference right away.

EDITOR: This shape begins to recall . . . almost an eye . . .

KAHN: It does in a way, yes. Of course, I use it as a device to get some grace into a boxlike building. The requirements being so little—I mean the building is so small— the desire to breathe something into it was there too. You have this privilege, this device, you see. You can go overboard very, very easily—you can make something frivolous in a second. I don't know that's even good—I just feel it's good—somebody said it looks African, which was awful. That reminds me—Yamasaki, who said that he was doing a building in Iran says he likes the idea. I've used this device recently very, very often. These are beautiful windows. I think it's well to play not so much on the completeness of the design . . . after all . . . everybody's problem is different and this is only how I designed something. It's one of the reasons why I also think that the completeness of the drawings is not terribly important; I believe it is more important to just simply state something fragmentarily in order not to say: I like the design, I don't like the design. This way it becomes easily a part of the architectural mind without the minor likes and dislikes . . . one can judge it another way . . . and then from this many people can do better. I think that . . . that design is a very personal thing. But I feel that these other things are not really personal . . . it's just simply a sense of architecture, you see, which you feel you want to install within the framework of this, your work.

Goldberg House: Rydal, Pennsylvania

EDITOR: The obvious question is: why couldn't this wall be continued and then you frame from here to there? (That is, have solid corners.)

KAHN: Because that really is the way it works and there is a desire to respect the fact that a building can end up . . . that the ends of a building are different from a prescribed thing like this.

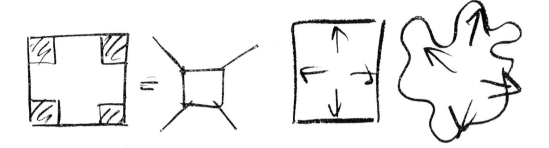

You start with this but sometimes the interior wants to move out and break the walls out. And you hold it in because of the preconceived shape that you have chosen. And that discovery . . . that the diagonal can be something to which you can frame . . .

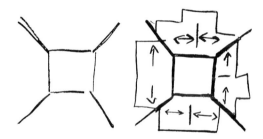

that it can be a kind of circumstantial ending . . . which this is because if I had more money, I probably would have come up with a little bit more. It's purely circumstantial. I felt this was rather a discovery in the desires of interiors—interior spaces . . . a house is a building which is extremely sensitive to internal need. In this satisfaction there was an existence *will* of some kind . . . but there was an *existence* will for this house not to be disciplined within a geometric shape.

EDITOR: You've wound up with a much bigger periphery than, say, a square . . . you could obviously juggle these parts and wind up with a full square . . . it can be done. But the point to me is this: that in this particular configuration you have a circulation ring to which each room relates—all except the living room—by way of the passage through the functions . . . as a sort of buffer zone . . . the major rooms then take their needed configurations independently of each other. If you had filled in the corners or made it a regular volume it would not have been, it seems to me, nearly as clear a relationship as when you shove these things out.

KAHN: In an ordinary square you always have the problem of these ends which are hard to reach. You must penetrate this (the "functional" areas) to come to the spaces—the final spaces being what they will be. You penetrate this to come to this—and so this—these become servant areas and these areas served. The servant areas also serve as insulation . . . they insulate you from room to room.

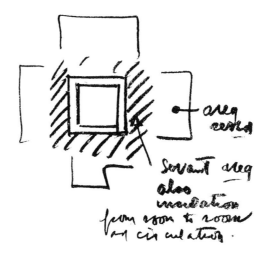

EDITOR: Also from room to circulation.

KAHN: From room to room and from room to circulation.

EDITOR: Aren't the inner servant spaces always skylighted and the others lit from the outside?

KAHN: Yes, I'll draw it for you.

EDITOR: The artist copying his own drawing out of the *Architect's Yearbook* for *Perspecta*.

LOUIS I. KAHN

KAHN: What could be better? Do you want a tree?

EDITOR: How about the light now?

KAHN: All spaces need natural light. I can write that in if you like.

EDITOR: For a house—or period?

KAHN: I would say all spaces need natural light . . . all spaces worthy of being called a space need natural light. Artificial light is only a single little moment in light . . . and natural light is the full of the moon and it just makes a difference.

EDITOR: So doesn't this imply a tautology . . . in saying that you define a space as something which does have natural light.

KAHN: Yes, I can't define a space really as a space unless I have natural light. And that because the moods which are created by the time of day and seasons of the year are constantly helping you in evoking that which a space can be if it has natural light and can't be if it doesn't. And artificial light—be it in a gallery, be it even in an auditorium—loses one a great deal. I would like to—sometime—build a theater which has natural light . . . which you later blot out when the show is on. But why must the rehearsal be in a dingy place? Is the rehearsal a play? No—the play is the play and the people see it, not the rehearsal. During the rehearsal the theater should be as pleasant as possible with a different kind of atmosphere. I'm not so sure that a theater should be always artificially lit unless you rehearse somewhere else. With the absence of the people you probably are producing something which is completely artificial, you see, in the sense that you make the same space but with natural light present. I think natural light should be in spaces that you may call spaces. And interestingly enough I think that the way a space is made is almost made with the consciousness of possibilities of light because when you have a column you see, you are saying a column is there because light is possible. A wall does not say it's possible . . . but when you have a column or a vault or an arch, you're saying that light is possible. So therefore the means of making a space already implies that light is coming in . . . and the very choice that you make of the element of structure should be also the choice of the character of light that you may want . . . and that I think is truly an architectural demand.

EDITOR: If it's so dark you can't see the room it can't be a space. Like the inside of a refrigerator with the light off.

131

KAHN: Is not a space . . .

EDITOR: When you open the door and the light goes on it is a space . . . if it's natural light.

KAHN: If it's natural light . . . Some of the darkrooms which are used in laboratories . . . they always tell you . . . the doctor will always tell you "Well, there's one place where we don't need a view out . . . I don't mean a darkroom . . . I mean to say a coldroom where they have experiments. But you usually find that it is the man in charge of a project who says that while some student who is working for him is suffering . . . who has to do without light. He can't tell whether there's a bird outside, or if it's snowing or raining. When I got to talking to some of the underlings I soon found that they were very unhappy without a window so they could look out at something.

Unitarian Church: Rochester, New York

EDITOR: When you were in New Haven you touched on the various stages you'd gone through . . .

KAHN: Let's put these four plans down. The idea which I sketched on the board before the congregation was my first reaction to what may be a direction in the building of a Unitarian Church. Having heard the minister give a sense of the Unitarian aspirations, it occurred to me that the sanctuary is merely the center of questions and that the school—which was constantly emphasized—was that which raises the question—the spirit of the question—were inseparable. And so, when I spoke, before the congregation . . . they had a blackboard on the platform . . . I drew this diagram:
A square, the sanctuary, and a circle around the square which was the containment of an ambulatory. The ambulatory I felt necessary because the Unitarian Church is made up of people who have had previous beliefs—they still have beliefs but they're simply beliefs of a different kind . . . they were Catholics and they were Jews and they were Protestants. I don't know much about religious ways except that I feel religion. So I drew the ambulatory to respect the fact that what is being said or what is felt in a sanctuary was not necessarily something you have to participate in. And so you could walk and feel free to walk away from what is being said. And then I placed a corridor next to it—around it—which served the school which was really the walls of the entire area . . . so the school became the walls which surrounded the question. The first plan was almost a literal translation of the form drawing as I would call it: form

7 Mmm Drawing,
NOT A DESIGN

drawing—that which represented, which presented inseparable parts of what you may call a Unitarian center or Unitarian place. Although I did not know the specific requirements—I knew them in general. I felt that a direct, almost primitive statement was the way to begin . . . rather than a statement that already had many expressions of experience . . . which may modify so strictly translated a form as in this diagram. It was modified somewhat: the exterior became a square, the interior corridors were round, and the sanctuary was still square. The four corners became larger rooms— they were immediately questioned because four larger rooms had to have four purposes. They couldn't have equal purposes very well because they were positioned entirely too—where the positions were too important. I tried to argue that they could be classrooms like any other classrooms—there are large classrooms and small classrooms. But this was a congregation which didn't have endless resources and money and they questioned everything that I put down. In dealing with the committees which were formed from various activity interests: the committee for the nursery, committee on nursing, committee on entertainment, committee on religious activities, etc., I developed their sense of program as I developed drawings. At one point they insisted that the sanctuary must be separated from the school—that was a terrible blow to me. All this form that I thought was really inherent to what you might call an inexperienced ritual—or rather a ritual which is not established, but a ritual which is rather inspired— could not then state its shape and dimension to follow the ritual. Therefore I thought: the closeness of all parts was a better expression than that which already separated us from the two—in which you can say a school is a different thing than a sanctuary. And so I felt that it was something more than just a primitive statement of this, the beginning statement you might say which can make a Unitarian Church. Dividing may be just doing lip service to the many other activities of man, and imitating how others have made their churches which have a different kind of sense of ritual than this one has. And so at one point I had to simply show the auditorium as a separate thing—but I did this only in diagram, not in actual plan. I never could be forced to make a plan which satisfied this. I resisted making any kind of plan. I wouldn't have done it. But I did at one point draw what it would look like roughly on a piece of paper, a sanctuary in one instance connected with the school square, the school area.

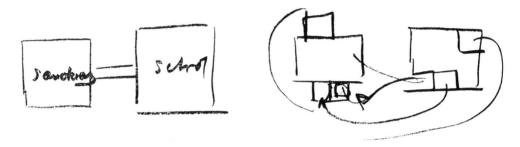

I asked questions about the sanctuary: what do you do after services are over? They say they have a coffee hour; they discuss the things that were talked about in the auditorium. They felt that it would be very good to have a kitchen close to the sanctuary. So I took a piece out of the school block and put it next to the sanctuary. And then they felt another room was necessary next to the kitchen to serve the kitchen. So I placed that and took another piece off of the school. And so it was with other rooms that were necessary, placing them around the sanctuary.

And pretty soon they all began to realize that we were back where I had started. It had to be that way because of the very nature of the activities, and I sensed right from the beginning that these things had to be close. I realized they didn't know what school really was; that a school was an adult room as well as a schoolroom for children. They wanted a kitchen, they wanted a sewing room . . . they didn't want a Chapel— somebody said it would be nice to have a chapel—any one of these rooms could become a chapel . . . such an indefiniteness as to what would be the actual space requirements of a ritual which is not established. With an unestablished ritual I felt that the most resourceful expression was not making distinctions, not making strong distinctions except distinctions of function—because it's a noisy thing on the exterior and a quiet thing on the inside. This also proved to be economically good because the interior required little heating and it's proving to be a very economical building. Now in the development of the various plans: the first plan is a literal expression of the form-drawing. A form-drawing—as opposed to a design. But because of the demands of the various committees and the drive for the naming of every room, the accounting for the need of every room, the first plan fell apart because the corners could not be justified; that is, the balance of rooms on the four corners... The various grades... school grades: kindergarten, junior classes, and senior classes... wanted to be grouped together. And so all plans that follow give in to the design demands of the various committees and, of course, the limit of financing which disallow extra rooms, prevented the development of a clear geometric form on the exterior of the building. At first there was a feeling of losing a great deal by this... and a formalization of these rooms on the exterior... which is expressed by this drawing in that rooms were kept as much as possible the same size so we could develop a structural system with some inherent unity in the system.

EDITOR: At this stage (# 3) it was still a series of cells...

KAHN: Yes, and they still had little things over them, but it was losing itself there.

EDITOR: Well, they're all different sizes...

KAHN: Some of them are...

EDITOR: Should the cell be say—from here to here?

KAHN: No, from here to here.

EDITOR: Then they'd all be odd-sized...

KAHN: It's just another development, a plan—which has not yet lost all these other earmarks—from the more formalistic stage which preceded it...

KAHN: And the next one (stage # 4) is this... and there the smaller rooms were getting larger... there were just constant changes, that's all I can tell you. I don't know what else I can tell you. At this point I felt this is the big change here: before the window's flat, here the windows punched out of the walls. We felt the starkness of light again, learning also to be conscious of glare every time... whether it's the glare in Rochester or glare in Luanda, it still was one realization... if you looked at a Renaissance building with a... or rather a building in which a window has been highly accentuated architecturally—with its... well like this, for instance:
    You have a window that's made this way... this pediment and a window of this

nature . . . this is not a very good detail at all . . . this is not a good drawing . . . you know what I mean: a window that's made in this form—windows framed into the opening . . .

This was very good because it allowed the light that came in on the sides to help again to modify the glare. When you saw light on the side of a wall, it helped you to look and so I felt that it would be well to have a framing of the window and to have blinders on the side of the window to give you a softness so that when you're not looking starkly out . . . when you're in the room off at an angle you can choose to see the light directly or not, depending on the reveal of the window itself. I felt a need to reveal. And this is the beginning of a realization that the reveals are necessary. And this came about also because there was a desire to have some window seats—there's a great feeling that a window seat should be present because there is no telling how the room will be used . . . it adds a friendliness, a hate of comfort and kind of getting away from someone and being alone even in a room where many are present . . . a room which is—its purpose is not settled—but is constantly full of human relationships and nothing starkly in the way of purpose . . . one that has a flexible purpose. I felt this window seat had a lot of meaning and it struck me as a demand of several people in the committee . . . this window seat had a lot of meaning and it became greater and greater in my mind as meaning associated with windows. And that's what this is. There's a true beginning of it in this plan (stage # 4). And it became really well expressed—I would say—in this plan when the windows—instead of being so very prevalent as in this plan—became much more carefully considered (stage # 5). And

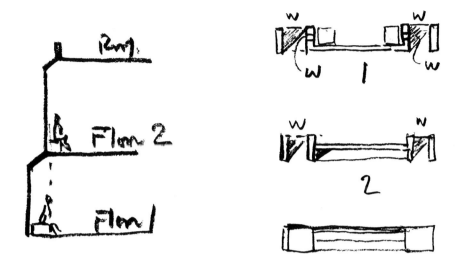

the windows were in a place where really you need them you see . . . and that's what finally resulted . . . this is the final plan . . . not quite the final plan, but pretty much the final plan . . . and these represent the elevation.

For instance, there's a window seat here on the first floor and there is another one on the second floor, but it is not the same configuration as the one on the first floor as the wall recedes inwards . . . In other words it steps in there and forms a window seat which is against the wall rather than in an alcove. In the lower the light in this case is gotten from the side at this joint and above it's gotten at this joint.

It's a play really of wall and variety in the getting of various conditions around the windows which caused one to make these changes. And in some instances this window seat turns into a thing which you don't need at all above and that would not be expressed here. At this stage (# 4) the window seats were equal on two floors— were the same, I mean to say, on the two floors. And . . . what I did was to consider that you back up you might say, a facade to the line of the floor seat. And you back it up to it as though you were just wheeling something up to the facade. But in this case I reconsidered this idea of wheeling to it because these walls can be so much aid in the construction of this space because you get much more . . . you wouldn't need a beam if you actually used these walls in bearing. That was the way I arrived at this whole business . . . by backing it up to this . . . which later became an integral part of stage # 4. A very important development in stage # 5 is this: that above the library, coffeeroom, is a chapel for the school—the school for the students, the pupils. The getting of light below was a problem . . . though one could get light to shape this room

137

above, it was difficult to get light to shape this room below. So I devised four wells for light in the four corners. The light came in above and went down to define this space below. This space being an oblong . . . only two sides in light was not sufficient to express the oblong . . . and therefore I felt that getting the light from above and down a well into the corners of the space gave expression to the form, to the shape, of the room chosen.

EDITOR: When you use light this way, you're using it to define the limits of the room.

KAHN: Yes, I do. I find the limit of the room you actually give . . . I was concerned about the light in this particular room—the others were minor rooms and they get their light from, let's say, from one side—which probably is quite sufficient for the size of the room.

EDITOR: I'm still not clear, sir, about the stepping in of the wall . . .

KAHN: The slab goes to here and this turns, the slab turns down to support this. And this turns down this way and the window seat is here. It avoids the development of a continuous roof line . . . it takes the boxed-in windows that reach all the way up to the corners of the rooms—and frees them as elements.

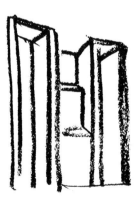

Actually one of the elevations is drawn incorrectly, the roof line is behind the window. Yes . . . you see . . . that should be out because that should really be free standing. The idea is to develop really quite frankly a silhouette.

EDITOR: But the end result is that the stepped wall begins to look like a buttress . . .

138

KAHN: No, I don't think so . . . this is just a seat.

EDITOR: No, I mean the inner part—the stepped part does.

KAHN: Yes, well it might—of course, it might . . . This is really, you might say, a way of playing with the walls to give you a variety of impressions on the interior. It may look like a buttress, yes. That may be its criticism, if you like.

EDITOR: I wasn't implying anything one way or the other . . .

KAHN: No . . . it makes it look like one. It's a way of controlling what you want below and above.

   Colin Wilson said that when he was down here you were working on a new way of spanning the center part . . . he said something about three-legged tables . . .

KAHN: (Discussing stage 5) You get your light from the four corners . . . four columns here and this is a concrete wall here. And off this concrete wall is cantilevered the roof. And this wall also holds these slabs which intersect—the beams are out—I've taken the beams away . . . but you get the light. I think we have the sections through it . . .

   Also, there is an isometric . . .

   This is a terribly, terribly difficult drawing . . . you've got to see the inside looking out . . . . . . Now this, interestingly enough . . . this, acoustically is good (referring to the roof of central area). The turning of the slab upward . . . and these are good for reverberations . . . that you would get in the music. One of the corrections which the acoustical engineers have made is that they'd like us to make this slightly longer . . . this slightly down so that you've got more of a unity in the space and so that you don't get the separation of the two . . .

   These spaces and those spaces . . . in form . . . it's a very interesting truth . . .

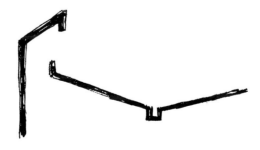

EDITOR: The angularity on the outside which will then be picked up with the horns.

KAHN: . . . there were many more developments than this, by the way, because I had, at one point, four umbrellas with a column here, there, and there and there, an umbrella here, an umbrella there and there and an umbrella here. That was very nice—in fact, the one that represents this thing here with the four domes over it was really . . . I gave up the idea because I hated the idea of the columns on the side . . . and I had to admit also that the columns on the side were encumbering. However, the umbrella scheme with the column inside and the things going off the umbrella was really a truer expression of that construction than the other . . . of being supported on beams at this point. I thought this was still necessary . . . up until the very end . . . until recently I found they were not necessary. A sense of structure . . . that's something I still have to learn a lot about—I have it but I don't. I have other things too that interfere with each other. I have the usual artful fainting spells, you know.

I derived the lighting of the big room—actually it's the same problem—from the small . . . but I couldn't really use the same construction that I did everywhere else . . . it became too important . . . in the hierarchy of spaces it became too important . . . this plan is strangely reminiscent of something which is derivitive. You know, it's funny. This plan looks very much as the older Saarinen did it.

It looks somewhat like it and it came with very little consideration of this . . . it came by backing a façade to it, various ways which were brought to it and then the rightness of it . . . as you felt the rightness of it is what established it.

It's very Gothic, isn't it? Does that bother you? I like it myself.

"Louis I. Kahn," reprinted from *Perspecta 7: The Yale Architectural Journal*, 1961, pp. 9–18.

Architecture-Fitting and Befitting

An excerpt from panel discussions sponsored by Architectural League and FORUM

"I believe we design too quickly without realizing what characterizes one thing from another in form. The realm of spaces which characterizes a schoolhouse is not the realm of spaces which is a city hall. . . .

"I believe that modern cities need a distinction between the aqueduct architecture and the architecture of the activities of man, because the buildings we build are really indicative of what the activities of man need in the way of space. . . . I believe both architectures must be separated from each other, because they are not the same architecture. One is a tough, kickable architecture, and the other is delicate—could be gossamer, in our present technology, could be completely remarkable. And if we knew the distinction, I think it would become even more remarkable, because we would not place that building out of context, but would place it in relation to the tough architecture. . . .

"Growth is only possible if you can refer to something around which you can grow. The oyster needs that in order to produce a pearl. You've got to have something there from which you can understand which way you're going. . . .

"But right now each architecture has blindness around it on all sides, hoping the other architecture does not exist. . . . They're all sitting there really just hoping for things to gather around them which would be equally as respectable. It won't be—unless you set something of an anchoring course of logic in this movement and give it a great architecture—not just a commonplace, 'good-enough' architecture."

"Architecture—Fitting and Befitting," from *Architectural Forum*, vol. CXIV, June 1961, p. 88; © 1961 BPI Communications, Inc., used with permission.

The Nature of Nature

Seminar discussions at Cranbrook Academy of Art

Built into us is a reverence for the elements, for water, for light, for air—a deep reverence for the animal world and the green world. But, like everything which is deeply rooted in feeling and a part of our psychic existence, it does not come forward easily. There are times when we feel strongly, but the simple matter of doing daily chores and solving daily problems keeps us away from the feelings about such simple, wonderful, motivating things.

Design is a circumstantial act. It is a battle with the nature of man, with the nature of nature, with the laws of nature, with the rules of man, and with principles. One must see all this to put it into being. Design is a material thing. It makes dimensions. It makes sizes. Form is a realization of the difference between one thing and another, a realization of what characterizes it. Form is not design, not a shape, not a dimension. It is not a material thing.

In other words, form is really *what* and design is *how*.

Find the form and from it many designs can come—many notions and many personal acts. Design is a personal act, it is how you see it. But the principles, the unique characteristics, are something which do not belong to you at all. They belong to the activity of man of which you happen to be a part and which you must discover. In planning, the central business district or housing areas are nothing but question marks. What are they, really? Where is the beginning? What is the nature of the place for living, or of the place where business is conducted?

We must look back into the nature of man and the laws of nature. We will find very good answers there. We will find selfishness, hate, love, sincerity—all these things. We will find what is called "good and bad" and we must account for it. Don't say you don't want any "bad." You will have it, whether you want it or not. It is in the nature of man.

There are wonderful things in the nature of man which can be brought out, if you think of design in a fundamental way. Empathy, for instance, is a realization of in-common-ness—that which is true of all men. In-common-ness is not just common place. It is a kind of transcendency, commonness in transcendence. It is where you and I become "thou," instead of just I.

This is not accomplished by a committee or by many people. It is the work of a single person right from the start and supported with unquestioning enthusiasm because it is so true to existence itself.

In city planning, connection is very important to me. Not passage, not going from place to place, but simply places, areas which are treated as events in the plan and which give a feeling of connecting one thing to another, a feeling of belonging to everything in the city. A square can do this. Well-placed squares provide a sense of connection between one part of town and another.

This does not mean that a passage does not provide connection. But it is often confused by planners. Going from place to place you need established reference points from which you can sense the city in a certain way, in a certain aspect, a certain point of view. It makes you more loyal to the city. You can be a participant in the city only if there are logical and very strong statements in regard to movement and institutions of which you are conscious.

The architect should give spaces to an institution which evoke new meaning for it. Our institutions need spaces which will evoke a greater sense of dignity, a greater sense of loyalty to the institution and its relationships. For institutions are establishments of responsible civic living. The architect should think of new institutions as reflecting the things which are deeply ingrained in the nature of man and which, when expressed more fully, can make a city a city. And one can put new life into existing

THE NATURE OF NATURE

institutions by giving them other spaces, by creating new connections and by re-defining everything: buildings, streets, lighting, traffic lights, gateways, entrances—everything the city needs to make the passerby understand the way of living in a city.

To put garages under buildings and to sort of hide them, or to wrap a nice little candy bar around them, or a nice grill, it may appear as though some things has been done. But, actually nothing has been done. It only confuses everybody as to the way of living in a city.

To prevent things from being done in an ugly manner, or in a manner which tends to deteriorate the original motives, our principles must be so true and real that they cannot be easily destroyed.

This applies to planning. It is finding the devices which obey the laws of nature and bringing them into consciousness. The architect must think of his responsibility—his responsibility to create something which is always true to the nature in man and to the laws of nature, and which is conscious of water, of air, of light, of the animal world, and the green world.

PATRICK QUINN: To what degree can we give such values as loyalty to a city which elicit from the people part of their innate fiber?

KAHN: It depends on the level of the important planner. If he is a doodler, a designer, a red, green, blue pencil man, I am afraid, nothing will happen. If he realizes the really wonderful natures of people and thinks of all men and what their motivations are, it can be done. I don't think the city will disappear some day. It won't, because it is a place which expresses the various aspects of man, the many points of view of man, how man is really varied. It starts with things that are indestructable, not patterns. Our present way of living puts us in close touch with distant points, it makes a fundamental beginning somehow different from what it was before. We must ask ourselves, "What is the first beginning, what is the first loyalty, around which you can expect the others to come?" Today it is Levittown. It is the planned community, and it is nonsense, because back of it is nothing but profit.

JOHN H. JACOB (Arizona State University): One of the great problems in our cities today is the values people have and our children will have, and we are often told these are materialistic ones. I wonder if we can identify what, in terms of our environment, has contributed to this and what we might do to change these for our children?

143

KAHN: Your question should be the subject of a new conference. It is the only question that makes, to me, any sense. All the others are devices answerable to this question.

"The Nature of Nature," reprinted with permission from *The Journal of Architectural Education*, vol. XVI, no. 3, Autumn 1961, pp. 95–97.

A Statement

A paper delivered at the International Design Conference, Aspen, Colorado, 1962

Life to me is existence with a psyche; and death is existence without the psyche; but both are existence. I think of the psyche as being a kind of prevalence—not a single soul in each of us—but rather a prevalence from which each one of us always borrows a part. This applies to every living thing, be it a flower, be it a microbe, or be it a man or an animal. Every living thing. And I feel that this psyche is made of immeasurable aura, and that physical nature is made of that which lends itself to the measurement. I think that the psyche prevails over the entire universe. It demands an instrument of expression which it cannot hope to have in some other area of the universe. I am sure that this very psyche hammers at the door of the sun and says, "Give me an instrument here upon which I can express love, hate, nobility"—all the qualities which are, in my opinion, completely immeasurable.

The instrument is made by nature—physical nature, a harmony of systems in which the laws do not act in an isolated way, but act in a kind of interplay which we know as order. Man isolates the law and makes every good use of it. But it must not be assumed that the law, when gotten by the tail this way, is very happy except when it is in relation to other laws where its real life actually exists.

When I hear a scientist speak in categorical terms of what he has discovered, I feel that as he grows older, he will change his categorical term into something which is not quite so sure. He discovers that the law is in a degree unchangeable, whereas rule is changeable; you check it off and say, "one down, and so many to go." It isn't quite as simple as that in my mind. Now we are made out of what nature makes of the demand of the psyche for an instrument to play the wonderful song which will

145

never actually be finished. We must take potluck from nature, because nature has no consciousness whatsoever. Nature is not conscious of the sunset; nature is not conscious that the sunset is beautiful. As a matter of fact, if a painter were to faithfully duplicate the sunset, the sunset would laugh at him and say, "I'll make a better one tomorrow." But if man paints a sunset as a reaction and his product says to the young man, "I'll have a good time tonight," and to the older man. "I haven't got long to live," then nature is very jealous, because it cannot do this. Nature is unconscious, but the psyche is conscious, demands life, and gives life. Nature makes the instruments which makes life possible. It will not make the instrument unless the desire for life is there.

Wonder in us is—you might say—a record of the way we were made. It is a well, which is completely full of all the things you will ever learn; because nature, in making things, records every step of its making. It is, one may call it, a seed. But it's understood much more if you realize that in wonder lies the source of all that we'll ever learn or feel. Knowledge which is derived from wonder is unhappy unless it relates itself to other knowledge. And this relation of knowledge to knowledge is what you might call a sense of order; a sense of the position of this knowledge in relation to other things around. When we get a sense of order—not just knowledge or information—then we are very happy. We wink at wonder and say, "How am I doing, wonder?" Because wonder is activated by this knowledge, and better still, by this sense of order. And wonder becomes more reachable, more full of that of which we were made.

From wonder we can also derive the position of that which is intangible; because you cannot measure love; you cannot measure hate; you cannot measure nobility—they're completely unmeasurable things. We may, though, come to points where we know the nature of man sufficiently to know there is a commonness in all of man, because man is man, all over. I don't believe that if you can think of a soul belonging to one man, it is different from another soul. I think all souls are alike, because they are first of all, unmeasurable; and secondly, they are gathered from all of earth. But what is different is the instrument. Nature, being an unconscious thing, cannot make the same instrument again, as we do in factories. Nature cannot, because the moment, at another moment in time, is a different thing entirely to nature. Nature is the interplay of these laws; any one time is not the same as any other. It's a kind of readjustment of equilibrium. When you come about, when you are born, you are not the same person as any other—you are a singularity, as an instrument, but not as a soul.

Nature is the instrument maker. Nothing can be made without nature. In fact, you might say that nature is the workshop of God. With a sense of order, and with the greatest moment in feeling, the feeling of religion in general, combined with the high moment in thought, which is philosophy—you get the area of realization; you realize something. This realization is very true somehow, but still you cannot describe it. This is a great moment for the scientist as well as the artist. The artist feels with expression; the scientist does not feel with expression. The scientist (through his realization) goes excitingly to find again the real definition or position of the law in order. And he works without his feelings at that moment, but through experience, and from realization, which is just full of feeling. At that moment he must be completely objective. And men who speak objectively, speak truly as scientists—not necessarily as creative men but as scientists. Scientists, who are interested in the law and finding the relationship of one law to another, find that the nature of man is already in a different kind of working than science. When a man works in biology, he is nervously concerned only with the laws, the physical laws of nature because his concern is so much with that which is undefinable; that which motivated the making of life altogether. And so, he must surrender the excitement of this for the moment in order to discover better means, tools, to evaluate if not measure the commonness of man biologically, psychologically and any other way. So you see, the scientist, I believe, is concerned with measures and with the nature of nature.

The artist is concerned with expressions, but he starts with the same sense of realization as the scientist does. And here it might be well to say that the difference between a creative man and an artist is that a creative man is one who brings about the new image. He sees a new point of view. From this new point of view he sees different things. And through this point of view, which others are not in possession of, he sees and makes images which are different. The artist is one who senses from this image. He senses the meaning of a new point of view. I can draw a circle on the blackboard, to show what I mean about that. If I can be so arbitrary, I will say what I have drawn is the realm of architecture. Of course, it isn't. We know this is not the realm of architecture, but it has limits, we know that. We know that an architect is not a sculptor, and he's not a painter. Because a painter can paint people upside down. A painter can make people fly in the air, he can paint doorways smaller than people. A sculptor can convey the futility of war by making a piece of sculpture of a cannon with square wheels. But an architect must use round wheels, and he must make doors bigger than people. He is not the same man; his realm is different. I make this circle of what I call the realm of architecture. If we see architecture from this point of view today, the creative man sees it differently. From the same realm, the same architecture, the same eternal qualities which make architecture architecture. And he makes an image, and this image is seen by men today. This image reflects another point of view. Men immediately see that the realm of architecture has grown to be more rich; the walls, the limits are more understood. The creative man makes this image; the artist works towards the beauty of this point of view.

Now this brings us to what is realization. Realization is really realization in form, not in design. Realization has no shape or dimension. It is simply a coming to a deep, revealing understanding in which the sense of order and the sense of dream, of religion, becomes the transference of I into thou. A man does not live a philosophy—he lives what he lives; but he gives philosophy as though it didn't belong to him, because he can't live the philosophy that he senses. From this sense of order and sense of dream come realization. Realization in form. Now form, in my opinion, has no shape or dimension; form is merely a realization of the difference between one thing and another—that which has its own characteristic. A circle is not a triangle, though tautologically it may be the same thing. It isn't the same thing in form. It has characteristics for rather inseparable parts. If you take one thing away, the form is destroyed. Each part must be accountable to the other. This is realization in form. When the scientist realizes this, he can work for years and years and years on this realization, making many designs, many experiments, many extensions of this realization.

Dr. Salk calls men who work towards extension in this light "biological engineers." But the biologist he visualizes he would like to have in his Institute is one who recognizes the immeasurable as well as the measurable. To think that men can really put down a statement saying, "We now know what hope is when we can measure it." I believe this is not so. I believe the unmeasurable will always remain unmeasurable. I believe also that if you continue to think this way, even the unmeasurable will become much closer to you, because you recognize that you'll never get it by the tail. You'll know it much more that way than you will by assuming that you'll ever know it.

In this same way, I believe that you'll never really measure nature, unless we extend for years and years our wonder source, the well, which tells the whole story of how we were made. Now design is the exercise or the putting into being of that which you realize is form. I will give a familiar example, because I can't think for the moment of another: if you think in terms of a spoon, you think in terms of a container and an arm. If you take the container away you have a dagger. If you take the arm away, you have a cup. Together they are a spoon. But spoon is not a spoon; spoon is form. A spoon is made out of silver, out of wood, or paper—when it becomes a spoon, that's design. The realization, spoon. Form. Spoon is not design. This can be extended to buildings as well as it can to everything we make. Take the example, for instance, of that which can come together and that which can be separated. I had a problem for a carborundum factory. If you know what a carborundum factory is, it's a pretty terrible place to work because the dust is very bad. The whole architecture should be shaped to take care of a human working in such an atmosphere. Therefore, it's a completely hooded kind of architecture in which the dust is gathered before it ever reaches the room. That's what the building should look like, although I don't know of any carborundum factory that looks that way. If I were given the assignment, I would do it that way: if you consider, from the present standpoint of architectural thinking, the placement of a cafeteria in this plant, there are many architects who would assume that you merely have to assign it a certain corner of this temple for carborundum making. And this is definitely wrong, because a cafeteria does not contribute to carborundum and carborundum doesn't contribute to the cafeteria. It should be outside of this building; maybe a little Pompeiian house, next to the modern factory would be more appropriate than to try and integrate both. Because form-wise they do not come together: they mean nothing to each other. The realization of this separation, and the realization which does come together, is unexplored in our architecture.

This brings me to law and rule, which is my present concern—not that my architecture changes radically, because at present it isn't changing at all. Law cannot be changed. Law is there. You may not understand it fully, but it's there. Always there. Rule always should be considered as on trial. Rule is just made from realizations of feeling and the law. And when more is known of the law at certain times, then the rule must automatically change. Think of the wonderful discoveries of science today, and think of how much our architecture is at a standstill. I believe our architecture looks like Renaissance buildings, simply in new materials. I do not think it looks like modern buildings to me. It's all because the rules have really not been changed.

When we think of our cities for a moment, we can review again the new knowledge we have, the new sense of order we have, in relation to water, to light, to air, to movement. Just think of law and rule in this sense. If I get in front of a truck—the truck is hard; I'm soft—I'm a dead duck. I disobeyed the law. The rule is the red light and the green light. When I am driving a car. I resent the red light, the rule. I like to drive right through it. But I think of my own child, and I obey the rule.

The law is relentless; it has no feeling; but the rule has. Think of cities that have reservoirs miles away from where the water is used. Why do we have to use drinking water for air-conditioning plants, and drinking water to feed fountains that don't need filtered water? And why must we clean streets with filtered water? Why can't we have an architecture of water that goes through the town easily, recognized in deference to the very precious water? The order of movement today is based on an extension of the horse and buggy. You feel as though the manure has just been swept away. There has been no thought given to the motor car whatsoever. The same streets serve the motor car as served the horse, which was a pedestrian. The hitching post is really the garage, but the garage is a piece of real estate which should be part of the design of the street, it should be the extension of the street. The garage, therefore, is really a round-up street, and must be made part of the design of the street. The streets must be completely redone in the center of town. Why must you rip up a street and put in a new line every time you have to repair or improve services for comfort and control of environment? We dig them up every time as though they were the Appian Way. Why isn't there a building in which a room is dedicated for piping only? The dead center of the city, where those mistakes are most unprofitable, should be completely redone. In the center of town the streets should become buildings. This should be interplayed with a sense of movement which does not tax local streets for nonlocal traffic. There should be a system of viaducts which encase an area which can reclaim the local streets for their own use, and it should be made so this viaduct has a ground floor of shops and usable area. A model which I did for the Graham Foundation recently, and which I presented to Mr. Entenza, showed the scheme. This is finding new rules out of realizations of law.

In the Salk project again. I am developing walls around buildings to take care of the glare. I do not think that venetian blinds and curtains and all kinds of window devices are architectural. They are department-store stuff and don't belong to architecture. The architect must find an architecture out of the glare, out of the wind, from which these shapes and dimensions are derived. And these glare walls are based on a very simple principle, which I got out of observation when I was in Africa, where the glare is very startling. There the people worked with their backs against the sun, and they got the light off walls near where they worked. Their buildings are close together, and their windows look into walls. They modify the glare, by looking at something that is in light. These walls I'm developing for the Salk Center in San Diego are in recognition of this discovery of the law of light, from which I have made a rule for myself in the design of the building.

Recently I was asked to design a town in Israel. Unfortunately I could not go to convey my ideas. But I thought of the desert being reshaped in mounds, which would contain reservoirs. And these mounds would be so placed against the winds that they would help in creating venturi which now are just flowing freely, not being controlled. And that a village be built around a venturi principle of air so that the air would be guided through small avenues and large receivers. The shape of the streets will follow the need which the buildings have there. This would not be applicable in Germany. Some of the buildings which are built in Israel today, follow the rules set down by German architects—good rules for Germany, but not good rules for Israel. This indigenous architecture is, I think, the great excitement of architecture.

In a dormitory I'm doing for Bryn Mawr College, I had a feeling that the dining room, living room, reception rooms and entrance were different, in every respect, from the sleeping quarters. And I kept the sleeping quarters apart from these rooms, believing that I was expressing that one was different from another. But I discovered my mistake. I realized that a person sleeping in a room felt well about his house if he knew the dining room was downstairs. The same way with the entrance to the building. The sense of hospitality, or reception, of getting together must be part of the fabric of the house itself. I changed, much to my delight, the whole conception, and I made these spaces part of the fabric of the other spaces. To me, this is realization in form.

Now if I had just looked at it as design, as I did before, I would have been led to something which may look well, but which had no power to convey one very wonderful thing about architecture. Because architecture really is a world within a world. When you build a piece of architecture, you build a kind of location for an activity of man which is, let's say, different from another activity of man, even though it may be in the same general realm of activity.

One of the most wonderful buildings in the world which conveys its ideas is the Pantheon. The Pantheon is really a world within a world. The client, Hadrian, and the architect, whom I don't know the name of, saw the demand of this pantheonic requirement of no religion, no set ritual, only inspired ritual. He saw the round building, and a very large building. I imagine that he probably thought the building should be at least 300 feet in diameter; he changed his mind because there were no craftsmen who would make such a building, and it was out of the stream of economy. Economy meaning here that there's no man around to do it. I don't mean money—I don't mean budget—I mean economy. And so the Pantheon is now a hundred and some feet in diameter. The dome, the first real dome made, was conceived with a window to the sky. Not because of ethereal reasons, but because it's the least distracting, the one that is most transcending. And there is a demand from saying nothing specific, no direction; that's what form says to you, feeling and philosophy. It says no direction to this . . . no oblong . . . a square not satisfying here . . . too far and away at the corners. The round building is something which is irrefutable as an expression of a world within a world.

Now architecture—if you think of it in terms of school—also probably began with a man under a tree who didn't know he was a teacher, talking to a few who didn't know they were pupils. They listened to this man, and thought it was wonderful that he existed, and that they would like to have their children and their children's children listen to such a man. Of course, that was in the nature of man impossible. School then became a room, and then an institution. Read a program today from the institutions called schools, and what do you get? You get a program that sounds like this: There should be a nine-foot fence around the school; there should be corridors, probably nine feet wide because statistically this is supposed to be enough. These, being cor-. ridors, are possibly the best place to have the air-conditioning return system and lockers.

In this environment you go to your classrooms, which, by reason of the fact that all classrooms have 30 pupils in them, are all alike. You have perfect air conditioning, ventilation and light—this is always given. And the cafeteria can be in the basement, because actually you don't spend much time there. This is the kind of a program you get from the School Board.

Now I think the first act of the architect is to change this; to change the program for what is good for the institution, for the continuation of the institution of learning. Man has established that for which he feels an inner need to know, to relate knowledge to himself. And that school is as much a part of him as though it actually grew with him. That's really what an institution is. It's an extension of man and his needs. And this must be made greater and greater by the architect. He must refuse the program, he must change the client's program—which reads in the form of areas—into spaces. He must change corridors into galleries: he must change lobbies into places of entrance; he must change budgets into economy. Architectural space is a space within which you read how the space is made; within the space, the columns, the beams, and the stones are in the space itself. A great span must have nothing in it, but that which is captured by the span. And the decision of the structure of the span is also a decision in light. A column next to a column is an expression of opening and light. A vault is a choice in character of light. You shouldn't open one room to the other to find out how the space is made. Within the space itself is the structure of that space. That makes architecture different from building, just building. All building is not architecture.

"A Statement by Louis I. Kahn," reprinted with permission from *Arts and Architecture*, vol. 81, no. 5, May 1964, pp. 18-19, 33.

Our Changing Environment

A panel discussion with John Konwenhoven, Dwight Macdonald, Ralph Ellison, Louis I. Kahn, Jose Chavez Morado, and Paolo Soleri moderated by Eric Larrabee

While one person may see inspiration in things as they are, another may see deplorable situations. This is why I think it is imperative to speak of them. I don't believe that one is wrong and the other is right, but I will try to say something about the inspirations within us, which motivate us to continue. There is inspiration to live, to question, to learn, and to express.

There is no distinction in my mind between an artist and a craftsman. A craftsman is not a craftsman unless he is an artist, and an artist is not an artist unless he is really a craftsman. There is possibly a distinction that we can make about the creative man. He is the one who brings about a new image. He is able to see from a different point of view. The artist, I think, is in everyone, because the inspiration to express is in everyone. It is in the nature of man. However, these inspirations are often badly used and their expressions, badly invented. The automobile is an excellent example, being probably the most instrumental factor in causing our world to look like the inside of a wastebasket. Still, it also represents man as he actually is. He is dissatisfied with his lot, physically. He wants to live forever, and what happens—he dies.

I don't believe that society makes the man. I believe that man makes the society, and we must wait for certain men to arrive who have a tremendous grasp of everything—all the parts. This has nothing to do with knowledge, because knowledge is not within us, but is really a kind of unwritten book outside of us. We are such singularities that we can say truthfully that we know nothing. What we take out of this book of knowledge we judge by our sense, whether or not it belongs to order or to the nature of man. Only when it answers all the questions at once have we the right to say we know something. That is why I don't hold much with evaluating circum-stantial things. Today, I would rely only on the inspirations that are really within us, and these are tremendous. They are completely unsated, as are our desires, for it is impossible to satisfy either.

The only thing I feel you can do in the making of something is to be yourself. By imitation you destroy the wonderful gift of being a singularity. The craftsman is the maker, and the art of his craftsmanship is the poetry of his expression. I think everything that we make must be usable as a lesson. We must teach and inspire with our work in order that others may emerge as singularities. The man with the mark of the individual is the maker of society. Mozart made society, and a great architect like Le Corbusier is making society today. A collective effort would not do it. But from the lessons of Le Corbusier one sets up the inspirations of man. Individuals get a direction in what they do.

Art is the making of a life. Nature only expects you to obey the laws of nature. If you get in front of a truck, you are soft and the truck is hard, and you're a dead duck. There is no sympathy for you whatsoever. And the patterns that are made by the interplay of the laws of nature, which work in unison not in isolation, will make wonderful designs, but they are unconscious designs. We make conscious designs because we can choose at random, as an author does in building a story that has its own life. Craft objects, such as the spoon, the hatchet, a piece of silverware, a piece of crockery, a work of architecture, a book, must, to be called works of man or expressions of man, contain the presence of a life.

"Our Changing Environment," reprinted from *The First World Congress of Craftsmen*, June 1964, reprinted with permission from The Louis I. Kahn Collection, University of Pennsylvania and Pennsylvania Historical and Museum Commission.

Talks with Students

Talk at Rice University, 1964

About a month ago, I was working late in my office,
as is my custom,
and a man working with me said,

'I would like to ask you a question
which has been on my mind for a long while . . .
How would you describe this epoch?'

This man is a Hungarian, who came to this country
when the Russians entered Hungary.
I pondered his question because, somehow, it fascinates me
to answer questions to which I do not know the answer.

But I had just been reading in the New York Times Magazine
of the things that had been going on in California.
I had visited California, and I went through Berkeley,
and I noticed the size of the revolution,
and the great promises of the machine, and I felt,
as I had read recently,
that there were poets who were trying to write poems
without words.

I sat for at least ten minutes,
without moving,
reviewing in my mind all these things,
and finally I said to Gabor,

'What is the shadow of white light?'

Gabor has a habit of repeating what you say,
'White light . . . white light . . . I don't know.'
And I said, 'Black.
Don't be afraid, because white light does not exist,
nor does black shadow exist.'

I think that it is a time of our sun on trial,
of all our institutions on trial.

I was brought up when the sunlight was yellow,
and the shadow was blue.
But I see it clearly as being white light, and black shadow.
Yet this is nothing alarming, because I believe that there will come
a fresh yellow, and a beautiful blue,
and that the revolution will bring forth a new sense of wonder.

Only from wonder can come our new institutions . . .
they certainly cannot come from analysis.

And I said, 'You know, Gabor,
if I could think what I would do, other than architecture,
it would be to write the new fairy tale,
because from the fairy tale came the airplane, and the locomotive,
and the wonderful instruments of our minds . . .
it all came from wonder.'

This occurred at a time
when I was to give three consecutive talks at Princeton.
I had no title for the talks,
and I was being badgered by the secretary
to give the titles for Princeton publicity.
After that night of the discussion with Gabor, I knew the titles.
(How rewarding it is to have a person who is concerned
about everything, not just little things.)

Gabor is so concerned.
In fact, he is so in love with the meaning
of 'word' itself that he would compare on equal terms
a piece of sculpture by Phidias
and a word.
He considers a word as having two qualities.
One is the measurable quality, which is its everyday use,
and the other is the marvel of its existence altogether,
which is an unmeasurable quality.

So I knew the titles of my talks at Princeton.
The first, I called,
'Architecture: The White Light and the Black Shadow.'
The second, I called,
'Architecture: The Institutions of Man.'
And the third, I called,
'Architecture: The Incredible.'

In the realm of the incredible stands the marvel
of the emergence of the column.
Out of the wall grew the column.

The wall did well for man.
In its thickness and its strength
it protected him against destruction.
But soon, the will to look out
made man make a hole in the wall,
and the wall was very pained, and said,
'What are you doing to me?
I protected you; I made you feel secure—
and now you put a hole through me!'
And man said, *'But I will look out!*
I see wonderful things,
and I want to look out.'
And the wall still felt very sad.

Later, man didn't just hack a hole through the wall,
but made a discerning opening, one trimmed with fine stone,
and he put a lintel over the opening.
And, soon, the wall felt pretty well.

The order of making the wall brought about
an order of wall making which included the opening.
Then came the column,
which was an automatic kind of order,
making that which was opening,
and that which was not opening.
A rhythm of openings was then decided by the wall itself,
which was then no longer a wall.
but a series of columns and openings.
Such realizations come out of nothing in nature.
They come out of a mysterious
kind of sense that man has
to express those wonders of the soul
which demand expression.

The reason for living is to express . . .
to express hate . . . to express love . . .
to express integrity and ability . . .
all intangible things.
The mind is the soul,

and the brain is the instrument from which
we derive our singularity, and from which we gather attitude.

A story by Gogol could be a story of the mountain,
the child, and the serpent.
It could be *chosen* this way.
Nature does not *choose* . . . it simply unravels its laws,
and everything is designed by the circumstantial interplay
where man chooses.
Art involves choice,
and everything that man does, he does in art.

In everything that nature makes,
nature records how it was made.
In the rock is a record of the rock.
In man is a record of how he was made.

When we are conscious of this,
we have a sense of the laws of the universe.
Some can reconstruct the laws of the universe
from just knowing a blade of grass.
Others have to learn many, many things
before they can sense what is necessary
to discover that order which is the universe.

The inspiration to learn comes from the way we live.
Through our conscious being
we sense the role of nature that made us.
Our institutions of learning stem
from the inspiration to learn,
which is a sense of how we were made.
But the institutions of learning
primarily have to do with expressing.
Even the inspiration to live
serves to learn to express.
The institution of religion stems
from the inspiration to question,
which arises from how we were made.

TALKS WITH STUDENTS

I know of no greater service
an architect can make as a professional man
than to sense that every building must serve an institution of man,
whether the institution of government,
of home, of learning,
or of health, or recreation.

One of the great lacks of architecture today
is that these institutions are not being defined,
that they are being taken as given by the programmer,
and made into a building.

I want to give some examples
of what I mean by reprogramming.

In my classwork at the university,
I gave the problem of a monastery to my class,
and I assumed the role of a hermit
who sensed that there should be a society of hermits.
Where do I begin?
How do I sense this society of hermits?
I had no program,
and for two solid weeks, we discussed nature.
(Nature is such a realization, part of being a hermit.)

An Indian girl gave the first remark of significance.
She said, 'I believe that this place should be so that
everything stems from the cell.
From the cell would come the right for the chapel to exist.
From the cell would come the right for the retreat,
and for the workshops to exist.'
Another Indian student
(their minds work in most transcendent ways)
said, 'I very much agree,
but I would like to add
that the refectory must be equal to the chapel,
and the chapel must be equal to the cell,
and the retreat must be equal to the refectory.
None is greater than the other.'

Now the most gifted student in the class was an Englishman.
He submitted a wonderful design
in which he added another element,
a fireplace, which was on the exterior.
Somehow, he felt he could not deny the meaning of fire,
and the warmth and promise of fire.
He also placed the retreat a half mile away from the monastery,
saying that it was an honor for the monastery to have a retreat,
and that an important arm of the monastery
should be given to the retreat.

We called a monk from Pittsburgh
to tell us how wonderful our thinking was.
He was a merry monk, a painter who lived in a great big studio,
and he came to his cell only reluctantly.
He was really ribbing our plans,
especially about the refectory being
a half-mile away from the center.
He said,
'I'd *much* rather have my meals served in bed!'
We were very dejected when he left,
but then we thought,
'Well, he's only a monk—
He doesn't know any better.'

We developed the problem,
and there were some wonderful solutions.
I tell you, it was most rewarding to have the realization
that the solutions did not come from a dead program,
one put to us in so many square feet.
The usual consideration of the nature of the refectory,
and so on, were disregarded.
When we held the jury, Father Roland came,
and he was a staunch supporter
of the most way-out schemes for the monastery,
but the program, as usually given,
was dead.
The original program had no sense of new,
no will to live,

and these students were highly inspired.
Each student gave a different solution,
but all had the feelings of new life, of new element.
I can't describe all to you,
but what started with just a reconsideration
emerged with the power of new beginning,
in which new discoveries could be made in present-day context.

There was another problem I gave at the university,
that of a boy's club . . . a most interesting thing today.
What is a boy's club?
Somehow or other, it was necessary to establish place
and for the people in the class,
the quest for place brought about a sense
that in the neighborhood of the club it would be wonderful
if certain streets could be blocked to destroy movement,
the disinterested movement, through them.
It would make it impractical to go through,
and would give those streets to which traffic was detrimental
a new life.
These intersections were made into little plazas,
and, somehow or other, the boys' club looked
as though it were possible there.
Merely by the simple imposition,
streets became parking places—
or even play spaces—
the way it used to be.

I know when I was a kid
we used to throw the football out of a first-floor window.
We never went to a play space; the play space began immediately.
Play was inspired, not organized.

During our discussion about the nature of a boys' club,
one student came out and said,
'I think a boys' club is a barn.'
Another student, kind of chagrinned
because he hadn't thought first that it was a barn,

said, 'No, I think it is a hut.'
(That certainly wasn't a great contribution.)

The same Gabor, who attends the class,
says nothing unless he is called upon.
We were already in the third week of deliberation
on the nature of a boys' club.
I said to Gabor, 'What do you think a boys' club is?'

He said, 'I think a boys' club is a *from* place.
It is not a *to* place, but a *from* place.
It is a place which in spirit must be *from where*
you go, not *to where* you go.'

It's immense, when we think of the white light and the black shadow.
Why this revolution?
It is because people are somehow confronted with things,
and are suddenly distrustful of the institutions of man.
From the revolution will come more wonderful things,
and, more simply, a redefinition of things.

Is a school a *to* place or a *from* place?
It's a question I haven't quite decided,
but it is an awful thing to ask yourself.
When you plan a school, do you say that
you will have seven seminar rooms . . .
or is it something that somehow has the quality
of being a place in which you are inspired?
To somehow talk there,
and to receive a kind of feeling of talk?
Could there be those spaces which have a fireplace?
There could be a gallery, instead of a corridor.
The gallery is really the classroom of the students,
where the boy who didn't quite get what the teacher said
could talk to another boy,
a boy who seems to have a different kind of ear,
and they both could understand

The monastery which I am doing
has an entrance place which happens to be a gate.

It is decorated in the invitation of all religions,
something which is now being started.
But they are given place only at the gate,
because the sanctity of the monastery must be kept.

In the Salk Institute for Biological Studies,
when Salk came to my office and asked me to build a laboratory
the program was very simple.
He said, 'How many square feet do you have
in the medical towers of Pennsylvania University?'
I said it was 100,000.

He said, 'There is one thing which I would like
to be able to accomplish.
I would like to invite Picasso to the laboratory.'
He was implying, of course, that in science,
concerned with measurement,
there is this will of the least living thing to be itself.
The microbe wants to be a microbe
(for some ungodly reason),
and the rose wants to be a rose,
and man wants to be man . . .
to express . . .
A certain tendency, a certain attitude,
a certain something which moves in one direction
rather than in another kept hammering away at nature
to provide the instruments which made this possible.
The great desire to express was sensed by Salk, the scientist.
The scientist, snugly isolated from all other mentalities,
needed more than anything the presence of the unmeasurable,
which is the realm of the artist.

It is the language of God.

Science finds what is already there,
but the artist makes that which is not there.

This consideration changed the Salk Institute
from a plain building like the one at the University of Pennsylvania
to one which demanded a place of meeting

which was in every bit as big as a laboratory.

It was the place of the art lobby,
that is to say, the place of arts and letters.
It was a place where one had his meal,
because I don't know of any greater seminar
than the dining room.
There was a gymnasium.

There was a place for the fellows who were not in science.
There was a place for the director.
There were rooms that had no names,
like the entrance hall, which had no name.
It was the biggest room,
but it was not designated in any way.
People could go around it, too;
they didn't have to go *through* it.
But the entrance hall was a place
where you could have a banquet if you wanted to.
You know how you don't want to go into a great baronial hall
where you must say hello to someone you don't want to,
and this is so with scientists.
Scientists are so wrapped up in the fear
that somebody a little distance away
is doing exactly the same thing they are doing.
This kills them.

All these provisions and considerations are programming.
(If you want to call it programming.)
But programming is too dull a word.
This is the realization of the nature of a realm of spaces
where it is good to do a certain thing.
Now you say there are some spaces
you know should be flexible.
Of course there are some spaces which should be flexible,
but there are also some which should be completely inflexible.
They should be just sheer inspiration . . .
just the place to be,
the place which does not change,

except for the people who go in and out.
It is the kind of place that you enter many times,
but only after fifty years you say,
'Gee, did you notice this . . . did you notice that?'
It is an inspiring total,
not just detail, not just a little gadget
that keeps shouting at you.
It is something that is just a kind of heaven,
a kind of environment of spaces,
which is terribly important to me.
A building is a world within a world,
Buildings that personify places of worship,
or of home,
or of other institutions of man,
must be true to their nature.

It is this thought which must live;
if it dies, architecture is dead.

Many hope architecture is dead,
because they want to take over.
But they don't have the encompassing ability, I'm afraid.
So many people are prone to place too much trust
in the machine today.
They must never divorce the machine from architecture,
which is the greatest power they have.

Next, we may have a city without architecture,
which will be no city.

I believe there are unexplored areas of planning.
I believe that if you just hand it over to the architects,
everything will be fine.
However, there are unexplored architectures in the city . . .
the architecture of order is unexplored.
Why must we have very distant reservoirs
that carry parts great distances?
Why are there not points
where great intersections of movement
give continuity?

Though for other civic needs
we need not be so tight minded,
we must somehow give immediate attention to water,
because water is becoming more and more precious.
There must be some kind of order to water;
the water that is the fountain
and the water that is in the air-conditioning plant
need not be the same water that we drink.

I am to build a town in India, or at least so I am told,
and I think that the most prominent architecture there
will be the water towers.
The water towers will be centered at the points of civic service.
There would be water towers, possibly,
at the intersection of roads.
I could also find there the police station, the fire station.
This place will not be a building . . .
It will simply be an extension of the road.
The movement just sort of winds itself into an airplane . . .
my intersection could be a place where you catch your plane.

I think Eero Saarinen's solution at Dulles Airport
is a beautiful solution of a place of entrance.
Maybe the traffic is not the same
because the pattern is not the same,
but there is the sense that you arrive somewhere,
and that you get there all the services,
and you go to the place in a car made for that purpose.
Dulles Airport is so far superior to these airports
in which each company has its own little house.
In these airports you're trapped.
It's really a conspiracy.
They give no grace to man, and he feels so helpless.
He is here when he should be somewhere else.

We were talking earlier this afternoon
of the three aspects of teaching architecture.
Actually, I believe that I do not really teach architecture,

but that I teach myself.
These, however, are the three aspects:

The first aspect is *professional*. As a professional
you have the obligation of learning your conduct
in all relationships . . . in institutional relationships,
and in your relationships with men who entrust you with work.
In this regard, you must know the distinction
between science and technology.
The rules of aesthetics also constitute professional knowledge.
As a professional, you are obliged to translate
the program of a client into that of the spaces of the institution
this building is to serve. You might say it is a space-order,
or a space-realm of this activity of man
which is your professional responsibility.
A man should not take the program and simply give it to the client
as though he were filling a doctor's prescription.

Another aspect is training a man to *express himself*.
This is his own prerogative. He must be given the meaning
of philosophy, the meaning of belief, the meaning of faith.
He must know the other arts. I use examples which I maybe
have used too many times, but the architect
must realize his prerogative. He must know that a painter
can turn people upside down, if he wants to, because the painter
does not have to answer to the laws of gravity.
The painter can make doorways smaller than people. He can make
skies black in the daytime. He can make birds that can't fly.
He can make dogs that can't run, because he is a painter.
He can paint red where he sees blue.
The sculptor can place square wheels on a cannon
to express the futility of war.

An architect must use round wheels,
and he must make his doorways bigger than people.
But architects must learn that they have other rights . . .
their own rights.
To learn this, to understand this,
is giving the man the tools for making the incredible,

that which nature cannot make.
The tools make a psychological validity, not just a physical validity,
because man, unlike nature,
has choice.

The third aspect you must learn is
that *architecture really does not exist.*
Only a work of architecture exists.
Architecture does exist in the mind.
A man who does a work of architecture does it
as an offering to the spirit of architecture . . . a spirit
which knows no style, knows no techniques, no method.
It just waits for that which presents itself.
There is architecture, and it is the embodiment of the unmeasurable.
Can you measure the Parthenon?
No. This is sheer murder.
Can you measure the Pantheon, that wonderful building
which satisfies the institutions of man?

When Hadrian thought of the Pantheon, he wanted a place
where anyone could come to worship.
How marvellous is this solution.

It is a nondirectional building, not even a square,
which would give, somehow, directions and points at the corner.
There was no chance to say that there is a shrine here,
or *there*. No.
The light from above is such that
you can't get near it.
You just can't stand under it;
it almost cuts you like a knife . . .
and you want to stay away from it.

What a terrific architectural solution.
This should be an inspiration for all architects,
such a building,
so conceived.

What will architecture be like fifty years from now,
and what can we anticipate?

You cannot anticipate.

It reminds me of a story . . . I was asked by the General
Electric Company to help them design spacecraft,
and I was cleared by the FBI for this.
I had all the work I could do on my hands,
but I was able to talk about spacecraft anyway.
I met a group of scientists at a very long table.
They were a very colorful-looking lot,
pipe-smoking and begrizzled with mustaches.
They looked odd, like people who were not ordinary
in any way.

One person put an illustration on the table, and said,
'Mr. Kahn, we want to show you what a spacecraft will look like
fifty years from now.' It was an excellent drawing,
a beautiful drawing, of people floating in space,
and of a very handsome, complicated-looking instrument
floating in space. You feel the humiliation of this.
You feel the other guy knows something
of which you know nothing, with this bright guy showing
and saying.

'This is what a spacecraft will look like fifty years from now.'
I said immediately, 'It will not look like that.'

And they moved their chairs closer to the table
and they said, 'How do you know?'
I said it was simple . . .

If you know what a thing will look like fifty years from now,
you can do it now.
But you don't know, because the way that a thing will be
fifty years from now is what it will be.

There are certain natures which will always be true.
What a thing will look like will not be the same,
but that which it is answering will be the same.
It is a world within a world;
that is what it will always be.
When you have an enclosure, it will be different

from what it is outside.
And it will be so because its nature is such.

I think that there are men today who are prepared
to make things look entirely different from the way they
look now,
if only they had the opportunity to do so.
But there is not the opportunity,
because there is not the existent will of this thing
floating around.
You take the drawings of Ledoux, which are very interesting.
Ledoux has this feeling of what a town is like,
of what a city is like, but he projected this,
and 'town' didn't actually look that way at all,
and that was not so many years ago.
He imagined this.

When a man sets out to project something for the future,
it may turn out to be a very amusing bit of history,
because it will be only what can be made now.
But, actually, there are men today who can make what is an image.
It is what is possible today, not what will be the forerunner
of what things will be tomorrow.
Tomorrow you cannot predict,
because tomorrow is based on circumstance,
and circumstance is both unpredictable and continuous.

The very secret of Cartier-Bresson's art is that he looks
for the *critical moment*, as he puts it.
This is like saying that in circumstance,
which is both continuous and unpredictable,
he sets the stage for it.
He knows what will happen here,
but he waits and waits for it.
I know when he was taking photographs of me some years back
that I used to enter the drafting room,
not knowing he was there.
He was in a corner somewhere;
perhaps he had waited for hours in a corner,
and I didn't know he was waiting for me.

I used to go around the room while he was waiting for me
to stop at a certain board.
And I did stop, too,
because the board was occupied by a beautiful Chinese girl,
that's why.
I went over to the board and I started to draw,
and I heard the camera go clickclickclick.
He was ready, you see;
he was waiting for the very moment,
but he was setting the stage for it.
He was a marvellous photographer.
He dealt with that subject, you see. In fact, I learned very much
about the meaning of one art and another through him,
just by making the understanding that his art was different
only because he was giving the circumstance.

To what do you relate the fine aspects of your problems?

I really look for the nature of something.
When I am doing the school,
I would try to solve it by 'school,'
rather than 'a school.'
First, there is the aspect of why 'school' is different
from something else. I never read a program literally.
This is a circumstantial thing.
How much money you have, and where it is to be,
and the number of things you need
have nothing to do with the nature of a problem.
So you look into the nature, and then you are
confronted with the program.
Look at the nature of it, and you see in the program
that you want . . . a library, for instance.
The first thing that is done is the rewriting of the program.
Now this must be accompanied by something which interprets it.
Your program alone would not mean anything,
because you are dealing with spaces.
So you would send back your sketches which encompass
your thought about what the nature of it is.

Invariably, more spaces are required
because every program written by a nonarchitect
is bound to be a copy of some other school
or some other building.

It's like writing to Picasso and saying,
'I want my portrait painted . . .
I want two eyes in it . . .
and one nose . . .
and only one mouth, please.'
You can't do that, because you're talking about the artist.
He is not this way. The nature of painting is such that you can make
the skies black in the daytime.
You can make a red dress blue.
You can make doorways smaller than people.
As the painter, you have the prerogative.
If you want a photograph, you get a photographer.

If you want an architect, you deal with spaces . . .
spaces which are inspired . . .
and so you need to reconsider the requirements
for the nature of the environment which inspires the activity
of that institution of man.
You see in a school or an office building, or a church,
or a factory, or a hospital,
an institution of man.

Do you approach your analysis of the site of a building
the same way, and try to understand the nature of the surrounding area

Often the character of it,
the nature of it,
must be explored because it is there.
You just don't plunk a building somewhere
without the influence of what is around it.
There is always a relationship.

What stimulated your design at Dacca?

This is a very broad question,
but since I went through about five or six buildings,
I had about five or six different stimuli.
It is more or less a recognition of a single element. The stimulation
came from the place of assembly. It is a place of transcendence
for political people. In a house of legislation,
you are dealing with circumstantial conditions.

The assembly establishes or modifies the institutions of man.
So I could see the thing right from the start
as the citadel of assembly and the citadel of the institutions of man,
which were opposite, and I symbolized the institutions of man.
(Earlier, I symbolized the institutions of man by making
a school of architecture—a school of art and a school of science.
Disciplines are different, completely different,
although they were both made by man.
One is truly objective,
whereas the other is truly subjective.)
And then there are buildings which are called
the place of well-being,
where one begins more and more to consider the body
as the most precious instrument,
and to know it, and to honor it.

My design at Dacca is inspired, actually,
by the Baths of Caracalla, but much extended.
The residual spaces of this building are an amphitheater.
This is residual space, a space that is found, a court.
Around in there are gardens, and in the body of the building,
which is the amphitheater, interiors,
and in the interiors are levels of gardens,
and places which honor the athlete, and places
which honor the knowledge of how you were made.
All these are places of well-being, and places for rest,
and places where one gets advice about how to live forever . . .
and so that is what inspired the design.

I made a mosque an entrance.
I was setting the nature of it,
because I noticed that the people prayed five times a day.

In the program there was a note which said
that there should be a prayer room of 3,000 square feet,
and a closet to hold rugs; that was the program.

I made them a mosque which was 30,000 square feet,
and the prayer rugs were always on the floor.
And that became the entrance,
that is to say, the mosque became the entrance.
When I presented this to the authorities,
they accepted it right away.

*Do you feel that with large urban problems, with five or six
architects trying to solve specific areas, it is valid for an architect
to seek and express inner nature as the dominant understanding
when there is the large scale which requires an outer nature?*

Actually, the inner space justifies the outer space,
even though you may give one portion to civic needs.
I think the advantage is that one man can do it.
I don't think a committee can set the nature;
one man does it.
What this one man does is not design the thing.
He simply programs it, you might say.
He gives it its nature.

One man can do this, and not do the building.
If you separate this thing without saying its nature,
you have nothing which holds together.
It holds together physically, but in spirit, very little.
As times goes on, that which this building really needs
to express itself
is absent.
You see, when you go into the department of, say, city planning,
it should show the promise of the city as you enter.
It may be a great hall, in which the city shows its aspiration,
and conveys it to the public.
If you took the program as given, you are saying that a city hall is,
after all, only an office building now.
Then a great loss would occur.
The nature is to inspire, and to give inspiration is

probably too strong an expression.
I would say that you present your aspiration,
something in which you believe,
something which you are not afraid to expose.
We are trying to say something which is better than an elevator,
and a lobby, and a door with a name on it that says,
'City Planning Commission,' and then a counter,
and a secretary,
and a spittoon.
If you think of the city, you think of the realm of spaces,
because actually, one must think of the city as
having a *treasury* of spaces.
Do you think you can relegate this
to any architect who gets a commission?

No—there are some who can think in this manner,
and some who cannot.
And it cannot be done by committee,
or you would be voted down.
You would be voted down by every inferior person . . .
'This is not necessary . . . too much money . . .' This or that.
But it blocks the presentation of a potentiality.
So if you entrust to a man the nature of each
institution of man which wants to express itself,
how do you see these buildings?

One man, not a committee, is there to try to make it exist.
Therefore, how they make it must be that a man's work appears,
and then you know what is worthy, and what is not.
It belongs in the fold of social influence,
because expression was possible.
An emergence comes from that,
and then society comes from that.
From society, you would get nothing but finality.

Considering form and design—is one the maker of the other?

Form has no shape or dimension.
Form merely has a nature, a characteristic.
It has inseparable parts.

175

If you take one part away, form is gone.

That's form.
Design is a translation of this into being.
Form has existence, but it doesn't have presence,
and design is towards presence.

But existence does have mental existence,
so you design to make things tangible.
If you make what could be called a form drawing,
a drawing which somehow shows the nature of something,
you can show this.

When asked by the minister how I would make a Unitarian Church,
I merely went to the board and told him,
without having known one before.
But I didn't make an architectural drawing.
I made a form drawing, a drawing which indicates
the nature of something and something else.
I can show you what the drawing is like.
I said here is an ambulatory,
and here is a corridor, and here is a school.

The ambulatory is for the man who is not so sure.
'I want to think it over. I don't want to
be in the church yet.'
He might be a Catholic, or a Jew, or a Protestant,
you see, and he only goes to the Unitarian Church when he
feels he wants to listen, and thus, the ambulatory.
This is a form drawing.
It shows the nature.

'Would you comment on the education of an architect,
and how to achieve the integration of craft and design?
If you were head of an undergraduate school, how would
you begin the training of architects?'

I think that one method can be quite as good as another.
I would say it this way:
You have professional obligations in all buildings,
since you are dealing with other men and their various interests.

You must know the obligations of dealing with money problems,
that clients have the cost of buildings, the paying of bills,
specific space requirements, and so on.
You must know obligations like this, and understand the supervision,
the honesty, that must be there to see that
the man is given the full value.
We have the profession, but there is a man,
and there is a spirit.
To teach the man, one is in the realm of philosophy,
in the realm of belief, in the realm of the other arts.

The forms of expression are here . . .
this is not expression; this is preparation
for what you must know.
Your obligations as a professional are those of a man
who is entrusted to do a work which is of interest for the people,
for, after all, an architect doesn't dish it out of his pocket.

Also, I would say there is the obligation of proper programming.
In the professional, I would say that what we were talking
about finding the nature of something is here.
The architect finds in his building a certain nature
which belongs to a certain activity of man.

If I were a musician, and I were the first person to invent the waltz,
the waltz doesn't belong to me at all,
because anyone can write a waltz—
once I say that there is a nature of musical environment
which is based on three-four time.

Does that mean that I own the waltz?
I don't own the waltz
any more than the man who found oxygen owns oxygen.
It was simply that one finds a certain nature,
and as a professional, we must find that certain nature.
Our profession is shabby
only because we do not change the programming.
If you change that programming,
you release wonderful forces
because the individual then never makes

the mistake of making something which just pleases himself.
You please society in your programming,
not in the way you do your lousy building.
The architect trains himself in expression which is true.
It is the spirit of architecture
which says that architecture does not exist at all . . .
that's what the spirit says.
It knows no style, no method.

It is ready for anything.
And so the man must develop the humility
of *offering* something,
an offering to architecture.
An architect is part of the treasury of architecture
in which the Parthenon belongs,
the Pantheon belongs,
in which the great lyceums during the Renaissance belong.
All these things belong to architecture and make it richer;
they are offerings, you see.

Now I think this is a kind of basis of teaching.
And this has to do with design, or paintings,
or sculpture, whatever you do.
It is your personal expression.
It is not only technology.
It is the rewriting of programming so that architecture
can be *detected*, you see, and it is not just a manipulation of areas.
In merely manipulating areas, there is nothing
which belongs to the architect, even though he may contribute
to the makings, like a guy who writes a very fine specification.
But that still doesn't make him a good architect.
It makes him a good professional, but not a good architect—right?

In any school which makes clear this difference,
the method
will also
be clear.

*In programming for our building for the School of Architecture at
Rice, we found that such elements as the library, the slide col-*

*lections, the lecture center, and the history of art area could be
a bridge between painting, sculpture, graphic arts, and architecture. We felt that this bridge would influence the form of the
building, and create an interchange which is very important to
the educational process. Would you discuss this, and perhaps talk
about what you feel to be the essence of architectural education?*

I cannot talk about specific problems,
but I can talk about buildings in general,
and in what way they become particular.
What you said about a bridge
and about the seeming relationships between
one department and another
might be very interesting to talk about,
but I can't do it hurriedly.
I've got to think about it,
to satisfy your thoughts.

Suppose you had a great kind of alley,
or gallery, and walked through this gallery,
and connected to this gallery are the schools
which are associated in the fine arts,
be it history, sculpture, architecture, or painting,
and you saw people at work, in all these classes.
It was designed so that you felt always as though
you were walking through a place where people are at work.

Then I present another way of looking at it,
say as a court, and you enter this court.
You see buildings in this court,
and one is designated as painting,
one as sculpture, another as architecture, as history.
In one, you rub against the presence of the classes.
In the other, you can choose to go in if you want to.
Now, without asking you which is better,
which is a very unfair question,
let me tell you what I think is better.
I think the latter is the greater by far.

In the halls that you go through,
you will absorb by some osmosis . . . you will see things.
If you can choose to go there, even if you never do,
you can get more out of that arrangement than you can of the other.
There is something that has to do with the feeling of association
which is remote, rather than direct,
and the remote association has a longer life and love.

So it is the court.
The court is the meeting place of the mind,
as well as the physical meeting place.
Even if you walk through it in the rain,
it is the fact that you are associated with it in spirit
greater than your actual association.

So I have asked the question
and answered it too, haven't I?
That's the best way of giving an examination that I know.
You get the best mark and everything.

You make the bridge and invent it.
The bridge is not physical;
It has to be in spirit, though; its lasting quality depends on it.
Now there are other reasons as well.
We must not assume that every teacher is really a teacher,
because he can be a teacher only in name.
You cannot depend on something that is frozen
in this architectural arrangement . . .
where actually the connection can be made in far reaching ways.
One does not assume that even a good student
can become a successful practitioner,
or that a teacher is necessarily a good teacher.
One who is just beginning to sense things
may emerge to be the best teacher.

Now we take each element in a school of architecture,
and compose these elements.

One of the most important that I know,
since art involves the eyes, involves vision and the mind.
You see it through association and in other ways.
You can close your eyes and see a philosophic realization.
You can see it in a way that you can listen to it,
something philosophic you can see . . . with your mind.

You are passing things that dangle before your eyes,
and they tempt you in a way to stop your mind.
But there are things that happened a long time ago
that have been done with great love,
and are just a wonder in general.

As for the library, in a school of architecture
the library is not a place in which
you are thumbing through the files and catalogues
and discovering a book.
Architects have hardly any patience with a catalogue.
An architect invariably gets disgusted
with the first block of the library, which is the catalogue.
You know this yourself.
Now, if you had a library where you just had broad tables . . .
very broad . . . not just how big is a table . . .
Maybe table is court, not just table, but sort of a flat court
upon which books lie, and these books are open.
They are planned very, very cleverly by the librarian
to open at pages that humiliate you with the marvellous drawings
things that have been recorded, finished and spread before you,
buildings that are magnificent.
If a teacher could make comment on these books,
so a seminar is spontaneous, this would be marvellous.
And so you have a library which has just long tables,
and plenty of room to sit to one side with a pad and pencil,
and the books are out in the middle.
You can look through them, but you can't take them out.

They are simply there to invite you to the lesson of the library.

The library is really just a classroom, and you can make it so,
and looking at this element, 'library' is different from *library*.
The man who is studying and writing his Ph.D. has his catalogue.
It's there, and it is his religion.

In his catalogue, he might see sparks come out,
which are books,
and the association of the catalogue and the books
is very precious to this man.
He makes a lot of recordings
of the books he is going to swallow up,
and he finally writes what the other fellow wrote,
only in a different way.
But *our* library is very different in the school of architecture,
for you are really treating your minds in a very different way.
Every book is really a very, very personal kind of contact,
a relationship.
You know what I mean.
You've gone through it, and you know what I mean exactly.
The location of the library comes from this nature.
If you put it on the first floor, second floor, third floor,
I think it tests against its nature.
You shouldn't be forced to put people through the library.
It should be just something in its structure which says,
'What a wonderful place to go,' and of course,
the location has much to do with it,
and its convenience has much to do with it,
but essentially, it is its nature which you are after, to convey.
Glare is bad in the library; wall space is important.
Little spaces where you can adjourn with a book
are tremendously important. So you might say
that the world is put before you through the books.
You don't need many . . . you need just the good ones, and there is
no such thing as looking for a book through the catalogue.
You don't just ask for a catalogue book . . .
it would die in the library.

A student of philosophy who is writing his degree

knows how to deal with books that are stacked away.
He learns books in a different way.
The Avery Library at Columbia is not a true architecture library;
you have it on various floors.
It is one of the best libraries of architecture that there is.
They have the best architecture books,
editions that are ancient, but you have to bother to get them, and
the impatience of the man who must see something immediately
is too great . . . he doesn't *read* the thing anyway.
If it is in Latin, it is just the same as if it was in English,
because he will see the pictures.
He will see what he sees, what his mind tells him it is.
Then, when you read it, you probably find something
totally different from that which it is.
What you *think* it is
is absolutely as important as what the man *writes* it is.
It's how you feel it and give service to it,
and how you convey it.
You plan the library as though no library ever existed,
and you say the same things with the classroom.
You know how dirty classrooms get,
and how full of passion the whole room is,
quiet passion, violent passion,
whatever it may be, but the room is full of it,
and you have no patience to clean up anything.
In fact, when the classroom is orderly,
you lose everthing . . . that is to say,
you really don't *find* anything.
So the classroom is not a pretty room,
but it is a room which is *dedicated*,
with light, and plenty of space to work in.
You can't mete out the square foot area for a man's work,
because some people require a great deal of room,
and others require little room.
You've got a series of desks, and you've got to hang
your drawings on the back of your shirts,
if there is no room for anything.
You just have to see a place which is very broad,

and full of light. And there must be high spaces,
because the whole lesson of measurement
and association with dimension must be part of the room.
I think you just feel that you are in a room
that is 60 by 60, and from this you can tell
what a room 80 by 80 would be, because you know
what 60 by 60 is.
You don't have to have that big a room;
your mind can take care of many things.

Man can work in seclusion, but, you know,
when you have an idea, if you're a really good person,
you just can't help telling that idea to somebody else.
You want to share it immediately,
and you don't want to hide it.
In a sense, that's our nature.
If you had stolen that idea,
you would be hated for the rest of your life,
but to convey it is just an urge which everyone has.
You can't help it.
Any one of us, in a sense, is a teacher,
because we want to share that idea, and because
sharing the idea has another meaning.
The other meaning is that you know
its validity through sharing the idea.
The confirmation by one man with a sensitive feeling
of its validity is like getting the approval of a million people.
This would not be true
if you were dealing with a mathematical problem,
but it is true that when the problem has to do
with aesthetics, with art.
If that man is honest, and will tell you what he feels,
then you have a tremendous approval,
that of feelings which strike the soul.
The location of the classroom, of course, is important,
but it will not influence anybody.
I think that the power lies in working on your own.

If it is an inspiring place to work,
don't worry about the campus benefitting by it.
If it is an inspiring place to work, you see,
the greatest service is given to the campus
by its just being there.
There is a point about a meeting,
and there should really be classes, like seminar classes,
and they are mandatory things.
You just don't go out and have a seminar
because the mood strikes.
I do not think that there should be rooms designated for seminars
in a row on a certain floor,
because a seminar is really an inspired thing,
and you hold a seminar like this one,
and you sit around and hold it.
As soon as you make it on the second floor,
with all the seminars lined up, it is no longer a seminar.
There isn't the spontaneity in back of it,
and in this sense I think you might ask,
Shouldn't the school of sociology
and the school of architecture have a meeting?

Yes, there should be a meeting—
if either one is prepared for the other.
If you groom yourselves in the motives and the objectives
of the sociologist,
and you know this before you enter a seminar,
and if the sociologist is willing, also,
to understand the essence and the spirit of architecture,
then the seminar would be tremendously beneficial.
Otherwise, you will have a cockfight.
One would just not understand the other.
Each one would go away thinking 'Well,
he doesn't understand me.'
And the other fellow would say,
'He doesn't understand me.'
I find it so.

Now there is this to consider:
I think the teacher is essentially a man who does not only
know things,
but feels things.
He is the kind of man
who can reconstruct the universe
by just knowing a blade of grass.
That man can bring anybody together.
He can bring a sociologist together
with the archeologist or the metallurgist.
Somehow in him, he has a sense of the laws of the universe.
Because of the way this man was made,
he senses it, and through this sense,
he doesn't say, 'the hell with sociology.'
No . . . he respects all parts.

With such a teacher, the meeting would be wonderful.
It would be a great benefit to the architects,
and also to the sociologist.

I think every building must have a sacred place.
I found what I think is a sacred place
in a theater which I am designing for Fort Wayne, Indiana.
It went through a great deal with that;
I didn't know much about theaters.
I knew dressing rooms had to be,
but as long as I had to know all about dressing rooms,
I knew I would never have been able to do the problem,
because, you see, I didn't know the spirit.
It has come to the point at which
I didn't care how many dressing rooms.
I just knew their position,
and their position could be here,
or could be there, they will tell you,
and you might end up with some space left over,
then, well, we need a few more dressing rooms.
But it is all built around the most incomplete

plans that have been offered to theaters,
because there isn't anyone who is the leader
who can tell you the spirit of one quality or the other.
To look for the spirit and find it is the key, I think,
to serving the realm of spaces known as the theater.
Now I'll tell you the result,
instead of tantalizing you with all kinds of things.

The sacred space here is the place of the actor,
the dressing rooms, the rehearsal room.
The dressing room has its balcony overlooking the stage.
There is a relationship between this and the stage, you see.
As soon as I bunched everything together,
it became a sacred space,
and it wasn't just left-over space.

The stage itself was just like a plaza.
I designed it as a plaza.
If you look at it, there are buildings where people are,
but you look out from here to the plaza.
The traps were made so that you could have seats there,
and the forestage would give you a theater in the round,
the background of which would then be this building.
You wouldn't see it,
but at times you *could* see it.
This was the *sacred place*.
After that, I didn't care how big a lobby it was,
really, just so it was big enough.
It was so important to have found this not
in this dead way, you know, with a sort of debris
of left-over spaces.

This was a real building.
It really was so important to find the idea.
We found the theater's own sacred self,
and that theater came absolutely alive.

It was an honest place, an invitation, you see.

The theater is not a place to say,
'I'm sorry we don't have any seats.'
You must always have seats there,
and that's a common thing a man should recognize.
A man comes early to the forum
and he finds a seat that befits a king,
but there is always a place for the king,
even when he comes late.
We are here, and there is a gallery here,
and it all has a very distinct kind of architecture.
I have used brick arches, and I have used the same old stuff,
because it's absolutely magnificent.
Why shouldn't I use it . . . the old stuff?
What I am using here is just an order
which is completely clear.
It's not phony, and it costs less.
I could make the same theater, if I wanted to, in the
damndest beautiful concrete structure,
but I have no fascination for it.
What I'm interested in is to build this . . .
if I build this . . . I know that I have revived a theater.
The presence of this architecture is a fact . . .
and now,
when this lights up,
the theater is complete.
The theater is sort of held togther,
and that is the religious place.

What is the sacred place in a school of architecture?
It could be the lobby,
but it could also be the place where you gather together
for reaction.
Reaction to your work means approval of millions,
even though only a few are present.
It's the kind of thing in which you learn that what you present
you can believe in, and that is a tremendous thing.
So you call it a jury room, if you like, but it is a room

where you meet, where classes all meet,
for a kind of review of an experience in doing a building . . .
starting with a piece of white paper.

It could be the most valuable lesson to call on people
and get some reactions—
maybe violent reactions from persons of certain beliefs.
You don't have to take their marks, you see.
Marks are the teachers' concern.
I think to have this person who comes in
give you a mark
would be asking him too much.
He is reacting, and his reactions shouldn't be marked.

I am against marks in juries.
I really think it shouldn't be considered just a grading session.
If a teacher says a man could enter the jury,
that's the end.
I think a student shouldn't stand there
shaking like a leaf,
before people he doesn't know, and say his piece,
after he has worked all night, and maybe two nights ahead.
He is nervous as a cat, and he gives it his best,
so I think a jury should never have a mark.
The jury should just be a place where you know
you are not going to be called down.
You're just going to get a spirit,
and the atmosphere should be cheerful.

Around this, I think, you can build a school.
You have so many rooms.
The rooms can have rough walls; it doesn't matter.
You can pin things up any place you want to.
You can throw paint on the floor.
The classroom can be like a Jackson Pollock,
but when you come to the jury room—no.

There should be something wonderful about it.
It should be a place where you can have tea . . .
and it should always be a friendly room.
It's always a sanctuary, you see.
It is not a room where you sit around
as if you are on trial.
If is just a great room.
It is the sacred space in the school of architecture.

"Talks with Students," reprinted with permission from *Architecture at Rice 26*, ed. Peter C. Papademetriou, 1964, pp.1–53.

Louis I. Kahn with students in Venice, 1969.

1965

Remarks

I'm scared stiff of people who look at things from the money angle. I had to meet some of them the other day at Fort Wayne in connection with an art center I'm doing there—a small Lincoln Center. The project is to locate the separate organizations. It contains a full-fledged philharmonic orchestra (that's really remarkable for a population of 180,000), a civic theater and, distinguished from it, a theater in the round, an art school, school of music, school of dance, dormitory, an art museum, and a historical exhibit. All this is to be in one bundle on one piece of land, and I had to say what it would cost. This is a very ticklish situation for me because I wanted them to want the project first, and then to talk about cost.

I was armed with just one fact: that the square-foot areas which they required (which, of course, had nothing to do with cubage) were equal to what areas I developed in the design. This was nothing short of a miracle: most architects, not excluding me, exceed their square-foot areas and have various reasons for justifying it. In this case, however, all the member organizations had written their programs individually, and they had a reasonable cushion in there for contingent areas. Such realism to begin with made it possible for me, in the composing, to equal the required area. And I was armed then with accepted area, though not the cost. Except, yes, I had the costs: I knew they exceeded very much the costs that this committee had in mind.

I presented the plans to them in as inviting a way as I possibly could, described the new philharmonic especially so that they could never refuse its existence, and did the same with the other buildings. Then, when they asked me how much it would cost, I said, "Well, gentlemen, I must first introduce the fact that the area which you have asked me to have is the same as the area on my plans." They said, "Well, all right, but how much does it cost?" I said, "Well, it will cost twenty million dollars."

They had in mind something like two and a half million dollars as the initial expenditure, but the way the buildings became interdependent made it seem quite impossible to begin meaningful choice with such a low amount. I waited for a reaction. I felt the quiet shock the new figure caused and one man did venture to say, "Well, Mr. Kahn, we only expected to spend two and a half million dollars. What can we get for two and a half million?" I said, "Nothing. If you had asked me six months ago what you could get for two and a half million, I'd have said you'd have gotten two and a half million dollars worth; but as you see it presented now, there is an entity present: the philharmonic is dependent upon the art school, the art school on the civic theater, the civic theater on the ballet, and so forth." And it is so: the plan is so made that you feel one building is dependent on the other. I said, "After all, what was the purpose of coming here? Was it to make a convenient arrangement, or was it to make something with an extra quality? I've found the extra quality," I said, "which makes the coming together more than what they are when the buildings are separated from each other. Therefore, for two and a half million dollars you would probably get the hind leg of a donkey and a tail, but you wouldn't get the donkey."

After a little bit of a wait one man asked me, "Well, suppose we simply said to you we want an art school built; it's part of other buildings which we're going to build, but now we want to build only the art school. Could you have done it without an elaborate program including all the buildings?" I said, "Yes, I could have done that, but you would have a mosquito and not a donkey." Well, they had a donkey in their minds—half a donkey, not even half a donkey—and a mosquito (a whole thing which they didn't want, of course), and that was it. Finally, one said (because they did like the entity, and they realized that there was something about the entity which was not the same as having each organization represented in its own way), "Well, I can see, Mr. Kahn, I can see spending ten million dollars, but I can't see spending twenty million." Of course, at that point I realized that I was having an easier time than I had anticipated. Then it was the time to be generous, and I said, "Well, I will try everything possible to pare down expenses and pare down costs, but you realize that you have to give up something in order to do this; and, for the moment I can't promise anything because I, myself, think that this entity is now hard to destroy."

For if you sense something which is a coming of a now-accepted thing in man's way of life, which is expressed in a realm of spaces or in a form which is different from any other form, once that happens you cannot take parts away because every part is answerable to the other. Form is of that nature. Form is that which deals with inseparable parts. If you take one thing away you don't have the whole thing, and nothing is ever really fully answerable to that which man wants to accept as part of his way of life unless all its parts are together.

I was really happy to have realized why I was so ready to give up the whole commission if they wouldn't build it all; or rather to feel that all could be built even if it had to be done in steps (as it was done in many wonderful enterprises of man, where the belief was so strong and it was understood so clearly that if you took one part away you didn't have—and everybody understood that you did not have—the entire thing). And I said, "At this moment, I realize something I've never realized before: that there are actually two realities that an architect deals with: he deals with the reality of belief and the reality of means." For example, I now read Goethe (which I had a very hard time reading before), and I find there is wonder in it. He calls his autobiography truth and poetry. This is a wonderful realization of life and the course of living. Though he reported what happened to him, he always avoided confining it to the circumstantial, or what happened, but reflected on its meaning, which transcended his own life. And this I think was marvellous. When you read it, you feel the objectivity and you feel the restraint that he gives you in regard to that which you may get too sentimental about, because he knows it only affects him and shouldn't be imposed on you. If you're reading it, you shouldn't listen to him; you should listen to that which belongs to eternity.

That was wonderful, I thought, and that is really art. It isn't you that you're making. It isn't just a question of believing something yourself, because the reality you believe isn't your belief, it's the belief of everyone: you are simply the radar of this belief. You are the custodian of a belief that comes to you because, as an architect, you are in possession of those powers that sense the psychological entity of something. You're making something that belongs to all of us, otherwise you are really producing very little or almost nothing—if not really nothing. Of course that tells you that almost everybody fails, and it's quite true.

But I don't think that Mozart was a failure, do you? And don't you think Mozart makes a society? Did society make Mozart? No. It's the man, the man only, not a committee, not a mob—nothing makes anything but a man, a single, single, man. This is so true again of Goethe. (I'm only reading Goethe now because I have a great reverence for a person who loved Goethe, and because I love this person I had to read it.) Before this I struggled to read *Faust* page by page. I met Faust for the first time and discovered a wonderful thing: that Gretchen was more soul than body, that Faust was a balance between body and soul, and that Mephistopheles was really all body, the body of man. He had no soul. Two people can't have the same sense of soul. The singularity is a soul and a body, though I believe that soul is a prevalence and that soul is the same in all, no different in anyone. The only difference is the instrument, our body, through which we express desire, love, hate, integrity, all the unmeasurable qualities of soul. Isn't it really true that only a singularity discovers the essence of the nature of man, and, in turn, an institute of man, not several people? So don't think that by research you'll discover anything—let's say, by collaborating with somebody. Either you will be able to reach only the kind of understanding in which you are the custodian of something which you discovered as being true, or you will never discover it. I met a person the other day who had never had an education, and that person, without question, has a remarkable mind—one that needs but a single, tiny fragment of knowledge in order to piece together the most fantastic sense of order. And why should that be so very, very peculiar? After all, the Greeks didn't have the knowledge that we have now, and look what marvellous things they did, only because the mind was highly respected. Somehow or other, because of frugality, because you haven't got so many things to choose from, you begin to think of how gloriously you can express, with the little you have, the nature of man's strivings to express his will to live.

I really felt very religiously attached to this idea of belief because I realized that many things are done with only the reality of the means employed, with no belief behind it. The whole reality isn't there without the reality of belief. When men do large redevelopment projects, there's no belief behind them. The means are available, even the design devices that make them look beautiful, but there's nothing that you feel is somehow a light which shines on the emergence of a new institution of man, which makes him feel a refreshed will to live. This comes from meaning being answerable to a belief. Such a feeling must be in back of it, not just to make something which is pleasant instead of something which is dull: that is no great achievement. Everything that an architect does is first of all answerable to an institution of man before it becomes a building. You don't know what the building is, really, unless you have a belief behind the building, a belief in its identity in the way of life of man. Every architect's first act is that of either revitalizing a prevailing belief or finding a new belief which is just in the air somehow. Why must we assume that there cannot be other things so marvellous as the emergence of the first monastery, for which there was no precedence whatsoever? It was just simply that some man realized that a certain realm of spaces represents a deep desire on the part of man to express the inexpressible in a certain activity of man called a monastery. It's really nothing short of remarkable that a time comes in the history of man when something is established which everybody supports as though it were always eternally so.

And at this point it would be well to speak about the difference between the eternal and the universal. That which is universal is really just what deals with the physical. But that which is eternal is a kind of completely new essence that nonconscious nature does not understand or know about, whereas man is the conscious desire that exists in nature. And I believe that because of this dichotomy, nature will change because of the presence of man, because man is of dream, and what nature gives him as instrument is not enough. He wants much more.

Architecture is what nature cannot make. Nature cannot make anything that man makes. Man takes nature—the means of making a thing—and isolates its laws. Nature does not do this because nature works in harmony of laws, which we call order. It never works in isolation. But man works with this isolation, so whatever he makes is really quite minor, you might say, compared to what is really wanting to be expressed by the desire and the spirit of man. Man is always greater than his works. He could never, with his instrumentation, bring out that which is completely full.

And another thing I feel very strongly: that if a belief always carries with it a great deal of sophistication, I'm afraid it's the limited interpretation of it: one does not know so much about the belief as to make it always fully aware and beautiful. One has to sort of sense it must exist first, and at best it must be called at later times archaic—something which didn't quite express itself in all its beauty, but had such power of existence that others did not change its spirit but worked toward its emergence in beauty. And I believe that beauty somehow sits in that light of being something we work toward. It's a selectivity. It's something which has to do with a completeness of the harmony of a presence.

Second (Legislative) Capital
Dacca, Pakistan

I was given an extensive program of buildings: the assembly; the supreme court; hostels; schools; a stadium; the diplomatic enclave; the living sector; market; all to be placed on a thousand acres of flat land subject to flood. I kept thinking of how these buildings may be grouped and what would cause them to take their place on the land. On the night of the third day, I fell out of bed with a thought which is still the prevailing idea of the plan. This came simply from the realization that assembly is of a transcendent nature. Men came to assemble to touch the spirit of community, and I felt that this must be expressible. Observing the way of religion in the life of the Pakistani, I thought that a mosque woven into the space fabric of the assembly would reflect this feeling. It was presumptuous to assume this right. How did I know that it would fit their way of life. But this assumption took possession.

Also, the program required the design of a hotel for ministers, their secretaries, and the members of the assembly. But this requirement became in my mind a corollary to the assembly and I thought immediately that it should be transformed from the connotations of a hotel to that of studies in a garden on a lake. In my mind the Supreme Court was the test of the acts of legislation against the philosophic view of the nature of man. The three became inseparable in the thinking of the transcendent nature of assembly.

I couldn't wait until morning in my anxiety to relate these thoughts to Kafiluddin Ahmad who is in charge of this project. In the morning I was there at nine o'clock sharp and told him about the symbolic importance of the mosque; I got no immediate response, no reaction. But he got on the phone and talked to several ministers. After he had spoken for some while, he turned to me and said, "Professor Kahn, I think you have something there." I felt enormous confidence that the plan could have form. "But," he said, "you will have a problem with the Chief Justice of the Supreme Court because he doesn't want the court next to the assembly."

We saw Chief Justice the next day, and we were greeted with the usual tea and biscuits. He said: "I know why you're here—the grapevine is very well developed in Pakistan. You're barking up the wrong tree, because I will not be a part of this assembly group. I will go to the provincial capital site near the provincial high court where the lawyers are, and I think I will feel much more at home there." I turned to him and said, "Mr. Chief Justice, is this your decision alone or is it also the decision of the judges who will follow you? Let me explain to you what I intend to compose." And I made my first sketch on paper of the assembly with the mosque on the lake. I added the hostels framing this lake. I told him how I felt about the transcendent meaning of assembly. After a moment's thought he took the pencil out of my hand and placed a mark representing the supreme court in a position where I would have placed it myself, on the other side of the mosque, and he said: "The mosque is sufficient insulation from the men of the assembly."

I was very happy that the motivations of religious thought were communicable. It was not belief, not design, not pattern, but the essence from which an institution could emerge which revealed the true receptivity of his mind.

The relationship of the assembly, mosque, supreme court, and hostels in their interplay psychologically is what expresses a nature. The Institution of Assembly could lose its strength if the sympathetic parts were dispersed. The inspirations of each would also be left incompletely expressed.

In the first sketch of the mosque I indicated four minarets. The meaning of mosque with assembly was then inseparable and a necessary image; and I used the most obvious and borrowed terms. Now the question of the nature 'Mosque' related to 'Assembly' has questioned the need for minarets. At one time in design the mosque was a pyramid, the peak of which was a minaret. Now it is the Mosque Entrance to the Assembly, but the question of its form for a long time remained.

Because this is delta country buildings are placed on mounds to protect them from flood. The ground for the mounds comes from the digging of lakes and ponds. I employed the shape of the lake, too, as a discipline of location and boundary. The triangular lake was meant to encompass the hostels and the assembly and to act as a dimensional control.

The assembly, hostels, and supreme court belong to the Citadel of the Assembly and their interrelated nature suggest a completeness causing other buildings to take their distance. Whether I've even arrived at the proper expression of assembly or not I don't know, but I've also said this: the acts of assembly are the makings of the intellectual institutions of man. That made me realize that the buildings of the program other than those related to the Assembly belong to the Citadel of the Institutions which I place on axis and facing the Citadel of the Assembly.

In us
Inspiration to express
Inspiration to question
Inspiration to learn
Inspiration to live
These bring to man his institutions.

The architect is the maker of their spaces.

The mind, the body, the arts bring to light these inspirations.

The mind, brain and psyche, sensor of the universe
and of eternity in joy of wonder with question
"why anything?"

The body is life; none without the psyche. Its
beauty, grace, and strength should be coveted and
honored by the man and by society. Art is the
language of the spirit. To create is the sense
realization of the psyche and obedience to the
laws of nature.

The institutions are the houses of the inspirations.
Schools, libraries, laboratories, gymnasia. The
architect considers the inspiration before he can
accept the dictates of a space desired. He asks
himself what is the nature of one that distinguishes

*itself from another. When he senses the difference,
he is in touch with its form. Form inspires design.*

It occurred to me in thinking about the meaning of institutions that the prime institution stems from the inspiration to live, which has remained meekly expressed in the institutions of man. It is an inspiration for building I hope to sense, the form of which could lead to new explosions of programs and designs expressing the beauty of physical well-being. It would be a place of baths, exercise and meeting. It is the place where the athlete is honored and a man strives for physical perfection. I have in mind an environment of spaces far reaching in richness and delight. The responsibility of a country to its people in regard to their physical well-being is certainly as important as the culture of the mind and the regulation of commerce. This institution of physical well-being is suggested as a building position harboring a stadium, the body of which will contain the rooms of meeting, baths, exercise, and their gardens, and flanked by a school of science and a school of art. Also composed with these buildings is a block of satellite institutions and commercial services. This block is the anchor of the dwelling places which is being recomposed out of an old village with its mounds and depressions already established. I spoke to Mr. Steen Eiler Rasmussen about the deliberate separation of the two citadels and he has inspired me to look into this decision and sense whether the two can be brought together and have a greater meaning than the meaning of looking across the separating park at each other. I felt that their being separate was good, living on different planes of inspiration. But Mr. Rasmussen knows the beginnings of towns in their essence so beautifully that I feel that this plan needs a thorough review before I can feel confident about the belief which is in back of it.

What I'm trying to do is establish a belief out of a philosophy I can turn over to Pakistan, so that whatever they do is always answerable to it. I feel as though this plan which was made weeks after I saw the program has strength. Does it have all the ingredients? If only one is lacking it will disintegrate. This is my problem. Mr. Rasmussen described it to me with little sketches conveying the life and the beauty of the bazaar; which limited by dimensions, expresses so beautifully the power of architecture which could give self-containment to an inspired way of life: it becomes the making of a world within a world. In the same way, in this thousand-acre reservation, one should feel its particular character in all the parts.

In the assembly I have introduced a light-giving element to the interior of the plan. If you see a series of columns you can say that the choice of columns is a choice in light. The columns as solids frame the spaces of light. Now think of it just in reverse and think that the columns are hollow and much bigger and that their walls can themselves give light, then the voids are rooms, and the column is the maker of light and can take on complex shapes and be the supporter of spaces and give light to spaces. I am working to develop the element to such an extent that it becomes a poetic entity which has its own beauty outside of its place in the composition. In this way it becomes analogous to the solid column I mentioned above as a giver of light. The problem of an element in a composition appears again in the making of the anti-glare porches for the hostels. In this element it is recognized that the light be on the inside of the porch as well as the outside. If you have light (not necessarily sunlight) on the interior, the contrast between the darkness of the solids and the brightness of the openings is not great and, therefore, you do not feel the glare. The staggering of porches as the building rises offers the chance to get light into the porch, but a sliver of light is needed to give the presence of light to the interior. The sun is unwelcome. So far I have only half solved the problem. I am stating it, but I have not solved it. The various explorations I have made of possible openings, some reminiscent of the past, are not really concrete forms although I think some of them are much more so than others.

Since the first program was given to me, and since these remarks were first spoken, addenda have arrived which changed the proportions of the accommodations on either side of the lake. Study given to the breeze and the sun has reoriented buildings on the lake causing new groupings though the direction of the original lines are retained. The esplanade has grown into an entrance garden reducing the lake. Many of the sketches are intended to answer the order of geometry which will become a dimensioning system. The transformation from its rule to a freer play will be a constant course of study. Balance not symmetry. (June 1964)

The Decision

The uniqueness of a country united in spirit and culture, yet separated geographically, found an inspiring solution. The determination to close the physical gap between the East and West wing of Pakistan created the unprecedented idea of a Capital in two locations, each vested with interrelated responsibilities. The Government of Field Marshal Ayub Khan took this historic decision to establish the Second Capital of Pakistan at Dacca during the Governor's conference at Nathiagali on the 12th and 13th June 1959.

The Site

The site for the Second Capital at Dacca was decided by a Committee headed by the Governor of East Pakistan. This Committee selected Tejgaon Farm area for the Second Capital and recommended 200 acres of land for its site. During development of the programming of land for the various functions appropriate to the Capital, it was found that the 200 acres were grossly insufficient to express its nature. Land requirement for these uses, as approximated by the Pakistan Public Works Department, proved to be in sympathy with the vision and knowledge of the Architect, which indicated 1,000 acres as the minimum requirement to meet the present and future needs. After more than two years of efforts by the Central Ministry of Works, the Provincial Government agreed to allot 840 acres as the site for construction of the Second Capital. The original conception can now have the space to express itself. The minor condition of delay in acquisition of the 90 acres to be occupied for another two years by the Agriculture Department should not affect the planning stages and the constant demand for sites by interested parties.

Master Plan

The Master Plan is conceived as a clearly defined Reservation within the city of Dacca encompassing the Government buildings and its related buildings in the setting of gardens, waterways and fountains, interconnected with roads and walks. The plan is anchored by the conception of a major north and south axis. On one end is the Citadel of the Assembly and on the other end is the Citadel of Institutions, which are separated by an area of land designated as the Public Park. Other land uses are devoted to houses, their gardens, social needs for men and their families. A portion of land will be developed for higher residential buildings, including residences and offices for Consularies. Physical conditions of this region, particularly of the site, demand that a positive design attitude must be developed for the conditions of sun, wind, weather, rains, and floods. The tradition is the making of lakes to obtain fill to make mounds for roads, directing the drainage and raising the building locations above water problems. Land allocations are greatly influenced by the above and other development requirements.

Architecture of the Capital

The Architectural image of the Assembly Building grows out of the conception to hold a strong essential form to give particular shape to the varying interior needs, expressing them on the exterior. The image is that of a many-faceted precious stone, constructed in concrete and marble. The architecture of the Hostels with deep protecting porches is the same as that of the Assembly. Conceived as studies and their gardens they are placed looking toward the Assembly, forming a triangular composition. The lake in which the buildings are reflected and the interweaving of lesser lakes, fountains, and gardens, holds the entire composition in balance.

Other buildings related to the lake or on the grounds contiguous will be of masonry construction following the principles of architecture, which respect the influence of indigenous conditions and from which all architecture gets its beginnings.

The National Assembly

The interior of the Assembly Building is divided into three zones. The Central zone is the area of the Assembly. The middle zone provides inner circulations, ties together the galleries of the people and the press, gives access to Committee rooms and the Library. The outer zone is the area of the offices, Party Rooms, Lounges, Tea Rooms and Restaurant, the Garden Entrance, and the Entrance of the Mosque.

The levels of the floors of the offices have been arranged to give privacy of movement to the Speaker and the Members of the Assembly, Ministers and Secretaries. The Assembly Chamber, 100 feet high, is an amphitheater of 300 individual seats arranged in pairs. Each of the present members will occupy a double seat, which in the future will be assigned to two members. A ring of seats on the periphery is provided to accommodate a Joint Session of the three Legislative Assemblies. To the right of the Speaker is the President's box, to the left the Speaker's box, and flanking them, the Distinguished Visitors Gallery and the Gallery for High Officials.

From the entrance Lobbies of the Members of the Assembly radiate the aisles leading to their seats. Two of these aisles enter the Division Lobbies.

Five balconies in the Middle Zone above the Assembly level are the Public Galleries. The Press Galleries are nearest the Speaker.

Deep beams and light modifying vaults form the ceiling of the Assembly Chamber. Wall Tapestries inspired by the Spectrum and the Crescent and Star will, together with the ceiling elements, give acoustical quality. The Assembly Chamber will be carpeted. The desks, tables, platforms, canopies, and galleries will be of the finest cabinet construction. All public and other areas of hard use will have marble skirting and marble floors designed to suit the geometry of the space. Nonstructural partitions are of panelled teak.

The Middle Zone of the Assembly Building is composed of eight Light and Air Courts to light all interior spaces, except the Assembly Chamber, with shielded natural light and ventilation and is the source of fresh air for the air-conditioning system. The Outer Zone is protected from glare, rain, and sun by deep garden porches harboring the windows of the outer zone which are also designed with this idea of physical protection.

LOUIS I. KAHN 1965

Fine Arts Center
Fort Wayne, Indiana

I think I won't speak much about individual things, but you may sense in a general way, what I'm striving to do. The main purpose is to try to get a single entrance for all the activities—the philharmonic; the civic theater; the art school; art gallery; dormitories—and to produce, if possible, an entrance which is not the accepted entrance but one which sees a door as greeting a car. In the first scheme there is an entrance doorway which is a garage. I thought of a covered street on one side of which were the art center buildings and on the other a car building. But I had to give up the idea. If you consider what it should cost to park a car, you've got to first begin by saying it's worth 10¢, and then when you say you can't get it for 10¢, clients say, well, maybe we can spend 11¢, and from 11¢ you must go to $1,500 which it does cost. Then it's not worth it any more. It's not worth any more than 10¢ because a parked car is a dead thing, and so to glorify it is, for me, like glorifying nothing. How do we do it? Well, I don't really know how to do it, but I believe that 10¢ should be about as much glory as you should see in it. So, that's why I gave up, because I really couldn't believe in it.

Then I thought further of the meaning of a place of assembly like a philharmonic hall. If you were to realize a philharmonic hall, you would say that the music is only partly important; décolleté is important; seeing a person and becoming entranced is also important. And, you know the man who is going to speak about music very profusely is the man who was asleep through the entire concert. But it's all part, is it not, of the nature of going to a concert? So is seeing the entire hall—not to be forced by its shape to look at it from under a balcony, not just to hear music, but to feel the entire chamber—because being in the chamber is like living in the violin. The chamber itself is an instrument. If you think a great deal about such a place, you can come to the realization that you are making a musical instrument containing people.

Mikveh Israel Synagogue
Philadelphia

The spaces are enclosed by window rooms 20 feet in diameter connected by walled passages. These window room elements have glazed openings on one exterior side and larger unglazed arched openings facing the interior. These rooms of light surrounding the synagogue chamber serve as an ambulatory and are the high places

202

for women. These window rooms prevail in the composition of the entrance chamber and the chapel across the way. In the community building, light is given to the interior by exterior roofless rooms born out of the same idea which, incidentally, gave rise to the plans at Dacca.

The windows on the outside do not support the building; what supports the building, as you can see on the plan, are the spaces between the windows. The windows could never be a support because of their shape. I chose to support the roof between the windows where a clear definition can be made between a column, a beam and a wall. A column means a beam; a wall says a multitude of beams or a slab. They're different things.

In the model, the open spaces which make the window rooms independent of the structure are made too wide; but they are important to give light to the round shapes. The light from the exterior captured in the interior room of the window is seen from the synagogue chamber as free of glare. The whole idea comes from realizing that contrast of walls in darkness against openings in light renders interior shapes illegible and turns the eyes away.

The Indian Institute of Business Management
Ahmedabad, India

The plan comes from my feelings of monastery. The idea of the seminar classroom and its meaning of "to learn" extended to the dormitories comes from the Harvard Business School. The unity of the teaching building, dormitories and teachers' houses— each its own nature, yet each near the other—was the problem I gave myself. The lake between student and teacher is one way of distance with little dimension. When I found this way, the dormitories tended, psychologically, to break away from the school, though it has no appreciable distance from it.

A work of art is the making of a life. The architect chooses and arranges to express in spaces environment and in relationships man's institutions. There is art if the desire for and the beauty of the institution is filled.

Orientation to wind and shade from sun has given architectural elements to the composition. My arrangements with the Indian school is to design one project employing the staff of architects and engineers of the National Institute of Design in Ahmedabad. Mr. Doshi, wonderful architect of India, sees to the architectural interpretations in India when I am not there. I am still not clear about the orientation problems, but Doshi is coming from India and will explain.

When Doshi came, he found it was best to flip the whole complex over in the opposite orientation. (June 1964)

The first designs of the dormitories were composed as houses for 60 student. each with two stories of rooms above open, connecting porches on the ground. The end bays of each house toward the lake step ten feet to a level four feet above the water, giving a two-story house-clubroom facing the lake. This became the space of invitation vested in each house and adding to the interhospitality in spirit embodied in the seminar idea of exchange among students and teachers. The dormitory rooms, in groups of ten, are arranged around a stairway and tearoom hall. In this way, corridors are avoided, favoring the making of rooms which contribute to the central idea, calling for plan and residual spaces for casual and seminar study. The tearoom entrance and positioning of the stair and washroom serve to protect the rooms from sun and glare without obstructing the essential through breeze.

The houses are oriented to the wind, all walls parallel with its direction. They are placed diagonally around a court to enclose the court and retain the strictness demanded by the orientation. If you have a square in which everything is normally answerable to a square, you find that two sides are oriented improperly. By taking the diagonal you form odd conditions, but you do answer, you can conquer this geometry if you want to. And you must relentlessly look at orientation as something that you give to people because it is desperately needed. That's the basis of these diagonal shapes.

In the school building, you notice I introduced a light well. I think it is somewhat superior to the device I invented for Luanda, because there I put a wall up to shade the sun and modify glare, and here the solution is an integral part. The construction of the building is better as well because you have less span to deal with and the windows are not on the exterior where you don't want them. This is a reverse bay window, you might say.

The inner court will be shielded during certain ceremonies by a large canopy spanning eighty feet. What gave me the courage to do this was the architectural provisions made in the courtyards of the Akbar Palace at Lahore for the same purpose.

You know the people in India make wonderful cloth and they have stretched even greater distances with it. This court is different from things I have conceived before. It gives such joy to be the one to discover a beautiful way of life that belonged to another civilization.

You notice I made all these buildings answerable to each other even though the scale of the house and the dormitory and the school is so different. The material of brick bearing walls and piers with concrete floors is retained throughout the larger spans giving rise to arches and buttresses, the more modest spaces simple slabs on walls. Consistent with the order of brick construction and the introduction of concrete, the concrete combines with the characteristics of brick in the making of the flat arches. In the houses, where there is not sufficient dimensional expanse to use a full arch, concrete restraining tension beams are introduced to counter the thrust of the flat arches.

The fullness of light, protected, the fullness of air, so welcome, are always present as the basis for architectural shapes. I was impressed with the need for air when I happened, with twenty other people, in the palace in Lahore, where the guide showed us the ingenuity of craftsmen who had covered an entire room with multicolored mirrored mosaics. To demonstrate the mystery of the reflections, he closed all the doors and lit a match. The light of the single match gave multiple and unpredictable effects but two people fainted for lack of air in the short moment that the room was shut off from the breeze. In that time, in that room, you felt that nothing is more interesting than air.

Adele Levy Memorial Playground
New York City (with Isamu Noguchi)

I did not speak in terms of architecture. He did not speak in terms of sculpture. Both of us felt the building as a contour; not one contour but an interplay of contours so folding and so harboring as to make, by such a desire, no claim to architecture, no claim to sculpture.

The shapes are Noguchi's. How to make them, from my point of view, would have to answer to an order of construction. Noguchi has the same sense of order, except that he has no bondage to it. The playground has to satisfy the realm in which I work and has to satisfy the realm of his work.

We agree that a playground building in a park must give itself to the park and its natural characteristics. A building in the familiar sense would assert itself; an interruption of the park. A window, apparent, would give away the needs of a building. This is the reason why light courts are introduced; placed and dimensioned to assure full light to the interior yet not presenting a window to be broken on the outside. Play must be free and uninhibited, spaces to be discovered with shapes not imitative of nature yet unrestrained in their making.

The walls of the castle cannot be thick enough to satisfy the seriousness of defense. The hall— the space within—has faith in the eventual freedom from such security. The needs of light to the interior, the needs of a service room, of a kitchen, of a place away from the central hall, act with courage to justify the making of spaces within the walls, logically placed to feel that security is not lost. This is the pragmatism and also the humanity of the castle. Its life in architecture is inspiring because its statement is clear in spirit and in the bondage of use. A building rising from its foundations is eager to exist. It still doesn't have to serve its intended use. Its spirit of wanting to be is impatient and high, allowing no grass under it. A building built is a building in bondage of use. Its spirit then must call out and remind its user of its will to have been. Isn't it true that sometimes a building being built is of more interest than one that is finished? A building that has become a ruin is again free of the bondage of use. But it is different from when it was being built because it now allows foliage to grow over it, as loving as a father permitting the child to pull at his carefully chosen clothes.

The stark architectural directness of the castle and the musically rhythmic image of the Greek temple combines in my mind a thought about Le Corbusier. I believe Le Corbusier, even in the light of his marvellous revelations in architecture, is just beginning to create his greatest work. I dare to think of a building that he might make, a great block of building, which is cut into from top to bottom in varied places of varied shapes neither forgetting the castle, nor the order of temple, giving light to spaces and passages on the immediate interior and leading to a glorious central and single space, the walls and their light left in faceted planes, the shapes of the record of their making, intermingled with the serenity of light from above.

Salk Institute of Biological Studies
La Jolla, California

The original concept of the three parts which expresses the form of the Salk Institute—the laboratory, the meeting place, the living place—has remained. The acceptance of the separation has made Dr. Salk my most trusted critic.

Two major changes from our collaboration: the two laboratory gardens and four laboratory buildings have become a single garden flanked by two laboratory buildings; the distinction in the construction of the spaces of the laboratories from the spaces for the pipes has become greatly clarified to the point where a far more interesting construction, intended in the beginning to serve this distinction, has given way to a system of construction far less exciting but one that serves more characteristically the intended use.

I realized that two gardens did not combine in the intended meaning. One garden is greater than two because it becomes a place in relation to the laboratories and their studies. Two gardens were just a convenience. But one is really a place; you put meaning into it; you feel loyalty to it.

The laboratories, now under construction, are conceived of as work levels and service levels. Each of the three work levels is related to a garden or to a view of garden. The space above each laboratory is, in reality, a pipe laboratory, nine feet clear, where service men can install equipment relative to experiments and make changes to ducts and piping. This dismisses the apprehension of needing the room to satisfy the mechanical means for experimentation. In the laboratories at Pennsylvania, the vertical services and the expulsion of all unwanted air had its undeniably right position. The horizontal services were in the spaces of the Vierendeel truss and exposed. This answered in one way only: the pipes are visible and accessible but they do gather dust and, in biological studies, this could be a disadvantage. So, in the first scheme for the Salk laboratory, crawl space was provided in a generously deep folded plate construction. This gave an awkward but possible accessibility as well as integral enclosure. Dr. Salk, when his belief in what must constitute the nature of a laboratory space was fully realized, could not turn back to something that was less than what we finally accepted, even though it meant drastic change. I felt the loss of the folded plate construction. My structural engineer was not for change. The mechanical engineer still believes that the folded plate could work. Yet study and new architectural potentialities finally gave rise to everyone's belief in the validity of the last choice.

"Remarks," reprinted from *Perspecta 9/10: The Yale Architectural Journal*, 1965, pp. 304–33.

Louis I. Kahn at a meeting for the Yale Center for British Art, 1971.

Address

5 April, 1966

I would like to just introduce you to some thoughts that I've had recently. One being that everything that nature makes it records, in what it makes, how it was made. In the rock is the record of the making of the rock; in man is the record of the making of him. And in the making, the consciousness of man as contrasted with the non-consciousness nature, sets up in my mind a feeling of dichotomous existence of man and nature. So everything that man makes, nature cannot make. And everything that nature makes, man cannot make. The inspiration that is built in man is the inspiration to live and the inspiration to learn the way we were made. Because all that man really wants to know is how he was made. If he knew this, he would know all the laws of the universe. So learning is a kind of inspiration. The inspiration to express is all of art. It has to do with the seekings of nature to express that which is fundamentally inexpressible. It is impossible to express love, hate, nobility, and integrity. Those qualities which are really, you might say, the *raison d'etre* of man's living. The reason for man's living is to express. And art is his medium. All of science is a servant of art. Science deals with what is; art deals with what is not. But rich in every way, science wants to be expressed and inspired by the feelings of nobility, feelings of integrity, and love. Every building that a man builds I believe is answerable to the institutions of man which he establishes through these inspirations. The inspiration to express is the establishment of all our places of learning. The inspiration to express is that which sets up man's urge to seek shapes and forms which are not in nature. Nature cannot build locomotives, nor build houses. So every building is answerable to an inspiration of man. When a commission comes to an architect, he thinks of the institution it serves and the environment of spaces which expresses one place of man, and another. It is almost the first duty of the architect, you might say, to take a program and to translate its area programs to spaces so that the lobby becomes a place of entrance, the corridor becomes the gallery, and the budget becomes economy. I met an architect in Mexico, Luis Barragan, a landscape architect. His peers tell me he is a land man, and I'll say nothing more about him. He likes wood and a few other things which are just sort of offhand remarks. I've found that he is completely remarkable. A man who does not express himself in many works, in the house I've visited every bit of what the man could do can be seen. His gardens have nothing but a trickle of water, and still are so immense that all the landscaping in the world couldn't equal it. We can't run to a place in his house which wouldn't let up until the ceiling reached thirty feet. We sat down, because it was cold in Mexico, to some gin which he had (fine stuff). We were sitting around just enjoying mere life, and he said to me, "What is tradition?" I sure wasn't prepared for that one but nevertheless was determined (you know I'm a professor so I must answer all questions) and I said, "Yes, my mind goes to London somehow to the Globe Theater and looking in through some opening when Shakespeare did *Much Ado About Nothing*, and people were on the stage in full brigade (it was a full house and Shakespeare was very popular). The first actor who tried to make the first gesture fell into a heap of dust under his costume. The second actor, whose cue it was, had the same thing happen to him. The audience, reacting to the actors, also fell into a heap of dust and so did the men in the gallery. I suddenly realized that everything that lives cannot live again, and any action which has happened cannot be re-acted. Forms simply are still. There was a first act of movement; somehow it disappears. But that which man has done, somehow, doesn't live. So that etching of Shakespeare, his image, lives! An old encrusted mirror in which you cannot see your image any more still lives, and you can anticipate and imagine the image of a beautiful person in it. Man's works belong to eternity. Not men as living things; they go but their works remain." And he felt that even the words that I had said disappear again in the dust, so as it is now. But anticipation was life. If the sun wasn't what you anticipated, then the very razor edge that exists between the moments that have passed really doesn't exist because it's too difficult to calculate. And therefore, though I am not in favor of existentialism of any kind, all that I am really interested in is anticipation.

Now I met somebody in India who said he had a hot idea of how to teach world art. It's very systematic, and all of the artists would be able to communicate with each other on equal terms. I had just about a half a days' time before I left India. I was to have a meeting that night and the next morning I was to leave. But because this man was terribly sweet, a wonderful fellow from Berkeley, I couldn't imagine anything he said could be right. Nevertheless, if he had a measurable way of teaching art, I was interested. I was very equipped with my handy kind of words which I have studied very carefully for such cases, but he was such a terribly sweet man that I did not want to do this. Suddenly I realized that actually I couldn't do with a good answer, the answer just came to me, and I told him what it was. I felt there were three things that had to be taken care of in the teaching of the architect. One is professional (and that had to do with everything that is measurable—however a man can measure things it belongs to the profession), that which had to do with the strength of materials, that which had to do with the way you conduct yourself and the client, the office, statics, science and technology. Also doing the right thing, you might say, make things stand out: The order of brickwork, the order of concrete must be understood, even the aesthetics belonging to it justifies the rules, let's say, of art. But that aspect, the second, was that of teaching a man. In teaching the man, one had to teach what was already in the realm of the unmeasurable, and there it was a question of teaching other arts. It was the distinction also between teaching and instructing. There the teacher entered because the job of the teacher is to teach another man, and that was a different realm entirely. But there was a third realm which is even more important, and that was the spirit of architecture itself. The miracle that man can take upon himself; the responsibility and love for the emergence of the making of a world within a world which is what architecture really is. And it is a very unmeasurable thing. You begin to realize also that a man does not do architecture, but he does a work of architecture as an offering to architecture. Architecture is a spirit that can never be satisfied, and it is completely insatiable. It transcends all styles; there is no such thing as modern since everything belongs to architecture that exists in architecture and has its force. This is the spirit of architecture. Architecture doesn't know about styles. It knows nothing but simply its presence, and it's ready to receive an offering that is true. So man does not do architecture. He does a work of architecture which he offers to architecture. That is true with the sculptor, true with the painter, and even true with the scientist. I say even true with the scientist because I always consider him a servant of art. A servant of expression, because the *raison d'etre* for living is to express.

Now in this light, you take the Salk project. Salk came to me and said, "I want a lecture building at the University." That was before it was occupied, because everybody hates it now (but for other reasons). He asked how many square feet it was. I told him some ninety-one thousand square feet, to be exact, and he said, "That's just what we need because I need ten-thousand square feet; I have ten scientists and they all tell me they need ten-thousand square feet of space." But then he added something to the program when he said, "I want to invite Picasso here!" And that really made a big difference! And my mind went around, why I don't know, to some of those orbiting things. The laboratory became very insignificant, and that was my commission; the laboratory as though it was a meeting house which was the center of the unmeasurable. The science building was not described to discover the unmeasurable. There was almost something dicotyledonous about asking Picasso to be there. It was more usual to think that the man was so much obsessed to becoming a marking of a new institutional sense, something different from what he called the censure of biological engineering which most laboratories are—biological laboratories. It had to respect the fact that somebody else is doing something else and it is just as important to biology as it is to discover certain characteristics (which are endless anyway). The sense of the institution is being made of three inseparable parts.

The meeting house, which was the center of the unmeasurable and was the true address from the human standpoint, of the laboratory. But it gave rise to the idea that the studies of the laboratory are also not the same thing as laboratory space because the laboratory space was so souped up with utilities that a poor little office surrounded by them would completely be swamped by it. And it seemed economically ridiculous to have so much equipment for a little office that contained nothing but a pencil, paper, and a filing cabinet. So the distinction is between the space which is usually the space of the oak table and the rug and pipe, and the place which has everything. One that could change the temperature in ten square feet away from another ten square feet from some kind of ultimate temperature below and above. That sense of the difference between the demands of one space and another are essentially the differences between one institution and another, and the parts of it. I've felt that there is really almost a dicotyledonous relationship between the study and the laboratory because they demanded different things. I came to visit the laboratory people who were going to occupy these places and they were so nervous about the smallest noise they reminded me that what they were mostly annoyed by, when they were in their study (which by the way was only a smidgen of space), was that they were so afraid that some other scientist, somewhere not too far away who probably had no education at all, would supersede him in some kind of experimental discovery. And so the nervousness of the situation was immense. But I realized also that they were all wrong about what they wanted. They wanted everything very close to them, and one person took out his lunch at exactly twelve o'clock, took out a ham sandwich, pushed the microbes aside and ate his sandwich. And I felt it was a pretty good idea to have some place he could go. There was the idea of the meeting house. The meeting house was a place where one can really get away from it all. There isn't such a rush after all, you see, for the mind, if it really is a mind at all, needn't worry about the other mind. Because fundamentally all are singularities; there isn't one alike.

Now in Pakistan, I had a similar problem. I was given a program of about twenty-five pages and that wasn't even a full program since the program was speaking about the assembly building. It said the requirements of the assembly building were something like this: THE ASSEMBLY BUILDING—TEN ACRES. That was the program! And a few other things which were really funny like, "hostels should have closets." Anyway, these were twenty-five pages of very meaty and serious requirements. The third day I was there a fellow with a good idea said why didn't you bring it all together into one unit. And the idea stemmed from this thought; that, after all, an assembly building is a transcendent place. A place, no matter what kind of a rogue you are, when you go into an assembly somehow you may vote for the right thing. Now, I thought that it has transcendent qualities so I observed that the Pakistanis do pray five times each day and very earnestly. So I thought of this preposterous idea of having a mosque attached to the assembly. I thought the mosque should be answerable to the assembly, and the assembly answerable to the mosque.

It was the next morning and I couldn't wait to tell Kafiluddin Ahmad who was then in charge of the project. He called, without much waiting, the President and several ministers in Hindu (didn't understand a word), and he came out to me and said, "Mr. Kahn, I think you have an idea there."

In the program there was some semblance of a prayer hall, which was three thousand square feet, and the instruction was also to have a closet for rugs. But I turned it into thirty thousand square feet, and the first translation of this was a mosque about the size of Hagaster Theater. The point was to emphasize the idea. When I took this thought to the Chief Justice of the Supreme Court, he didn't want to be anywhere near the assembly. He said, "I know why you've come, it's no use. I'm going to make my office near the Provincial Supreme Court because they have the books there, the environment there, all the other judges are there, and I will feel much more happy." So I made a big sketch for the first time of the assembly. I showed the hostels on the lake overlooking the assembly, and the mosque which I attached to the assembly to make part of the entrance to the assembly. When he saw the mosque, he took the pencil out of my hand and placed the Supreme Court where I would have placed it. Then he placed the pencil opposite the entrance where the mosque is and said, "The mosque is insulation enough for me."

The thought of the eminency of trying for that quality, which belongs to itself in whatever it may be, came from the nature of the way of life. I think that if you were to judge the city as if it was an institution of man that the nature of connection is very vital in architecture. The sensitivity of the emergence of new institutions, even out of the old, seems to want to branch from it. The sensitivity to what may be willing to be an institution of man, and the spaces around which it could express itself, are almost a first requirement. All the other things like traffic and water supplies, which have their own architecture, certainly you might say that the architecture of movement is one of its own. It's a kickable architecture compared to the gospel architecture of the institutions of man.

And so it is with the architecture of water which has a most romantic architecture. I am being asked to design a city in India. The first thing I think of is just what is the architecture of water; which is a marvellous architecture. If only I could do that part of it I'd feel so happy compared to doing the buildings which I like to do where it is the framework which gives direction to the states where things can happen. Such as the estates of working, the estates of living, the estates of government, that are really defined by certain surfaces. And how you express these surfaces architecturally is how they have their architecture of light, their architecture of movement, and their architecture of water. All of this has its distinct architecture and are expressed in their own way. Our cities are just making sort of bumblings of real estate and patriotism which have nothing to do with the real expression of making these estates out of an architecture which is just learning to be expressed in all directions. It is a much more wonderful architecture than any I've ever seen in any of the books. All of the things that have been so much are really not adequate for what really can be the expression that is possible.

Now I just want to touch on the difference between design and composition. I think architects should be composers and not designers. They should be composers of elements. The elements are things that are entities in themselves. I was just speaking today about why it was that when you see these buildings at Harvard that are these colonial and Georgian buildings they look good. The things that we do somehow don't quite reach the serenity, the simplicity, and the modesty of those buildings.

I really think its because we are not looking at things elementally. When a real Georgian architect, not the ones at Harvard, took in his hand what was the fireplace before he placed it on the plan, he knew everything about it. It was part of the way of life, and every element of it was known to him. He composed it around the knowledge of the meaning, let's say of the roof, that had something to do with water and snow. When he put a dormer in, he made it out of permission of the roof—he asked the roof first, "I don't want to spoil you, I want to make something there so can you give me permission?" He doesn't make the whole roof over, he simply makes a modest thing for which he makes light, and if he is very ingenious he convinces the roof to put in more. But the point is that it is an element that is related to something, in the same way as scraping your feet of snow when you enter the doorway and fumble with the key. There is this relationship of the door which is not at all but elemental. This is the same as the walk, and the same as the fireplace because you know it so well.

Now of course, you know very well how everyone wants to be responsible and when it comes to putting it (the chimney) above the roof you really stop and say,

"Why did we have to adhere to the building laws?" "Why don't we have little chimneys instead of high chimneys, and why can't we make the roof high enough so you hide the chimney?" All of these things come to your mind because it is not elementally considered. Composition is dealing with element, and design is a matter of working within them so it becomes perfection. Composition to me becomes attitude and it has to do with the recognition of elements.

I would think that if you are dealing with a column you must give it a beam. You cannot have a column without a beam. It is an elemental thing. You can't have a column and a slab. If you have a column and a slab, you know the slab has a beam inside of it. That consciousness will cause less serious errors in the making of architecture, because how many times do you frame a beam into the side of the column instead of above it? All of those things are, in my opinion, very poor acts of architecture.

With this introduction, I would like to show you a few slides and tell you in what way I tried to capture things in the commissions that I have gotten. This is the Salk project. You know this is the laboratory space. The studies are here, and they are in the garden away from the laboratories. I purposely took them away out of the realization that the study was not in the laboratory. Now if the laboratory wanted a study, that is all right. There is nothing wrong with that, but this provides the opportunity to move away from it out of the realization that this needed space is taken over by the laboratory space which is so very well equipped. There is nothing mandatory about it, but it sets the framework. The meeting house also is where even the rooms are made so. There is no great dining hall to eat in, but there are little places where you might meet people that you want to meet, rather than try to make some sort of dodge for those you don't want to meet. That is also true of the library and the director's house. They are spaced in the middle where you have my mark which is named nothing, but is a place where you actually can have a banquet. Because there an unknown space which is big enough for a banquet has little to do with the everyday use of a place where you eat. With a religious place here, a meeting hall here, I set up these elements and this is a little village for those who want to be very close to the laboratories. Many want to practically live in the laboratories themselves. They have to for biological experiments where many of them have to be very close. So it is their nature to have this; it is not just a cute idea to make people comfortable. The scientists do want everything including a "double-tendor" or something like that. Now I have two schemes for the laboratories, and the first one I fought for very strongly. I lost the battle, and I'm very glad I did because the next scheme was so much more resourceful.

This shows the upper and lower levels of the garden. Dr. Salk thought of the idea that there should be no study opposite a laboratory, but there should be a garden opposite a laboratory so the study should not be visible to the scientist. One scientist should not feel the feet of another over him. So therefore, the portico separates one study below from the study above. That is how sensitive he became to the premises which I myself set. I was always sliding away, because our society makes us slide away. But he didn't let me when he said, "Spend money" (which I certainly did!).

It shows the laboratories are made so that the laboratory is one here, but the actual surface of the laboratory was in itself a laboratory where you can go in and store many of the experiments which are really refrigerator storage of an endless number of experiments. This clears the laboratory and you are guaranteed by this way always of a clearing where you can make changes. And here you can serve and also store. You see, there the study is opposite the pipe space, but there it's opposite the portico, and opposite the kind of runway and the garden below. This is purely Salk's insistence. I was going to give him capacity. Three studies with one over the other. How economical! He said, "No, how wrong!" And he was certainly right.

This shows the relation of the laboratory to the studies. The studies have one idea which I am not sure was such a good idea, but every study had to look out to the sea. This idea of Salk's I tried to work out with the garden between it.

These are the studies, and this is the plaza. It contains no trees, it just connects both. I always had trees here and I said it had to be the garden—a main garden just obsessed me. I could never draw it with gardens, I could never make a model where I put a garden in. But still my mind said garden, garden, garden. I invited Barragan, because I was so impressed with his gardens, to come and see this place. And he turned to me after he saw the place, and touching the concrete which he loved very much, "You are going to hate me, but there should be no tree here." And he was so right. He released you from the bondage of the tree, so much that I couldn't see it any other way. And so now I say it has no trees, and it is not going to have any. Even the irrigation which I had here ready for the trees now has to be justified as a drainage system of the plaza. And I think I have a pretty good scheme for it, so it looks just fine. The color of the concrete is a kind of almost silium color. It is a color of rose.

These are the back buildings where all the turrets and services are. This again does not interfere with the laboratory space. It is completely clear, and has nothing to obstruct it. This stair goes down into the lower garden.

There are travertine walks, which with concrete, look extremely well. I had, in fact, intended to make it slate because it would look well as a contrast. I couldn't afford slate. It cost more than travertine in California, and luckily concrete is much more the material. The judgment was bad and the economy was right.

This shows the entrance into the lower garden, and these are pools which are not yet filled with water that cascade down to this little sitting place here. This I intended of course to landscape, and this portion will be landscapes and so will this plowed part here. But the plaza now, in my mind, is completely blank. It was a very good lesson that Barragan taught me. He said the reason why the plaza should be there is because it adds another facade; the facade that looks to the sky. I thought that was beautiful, he was so convincing!

This slide shows the character of concrete which has been untouched. All the forms are made out of four by twelve plywood, and at the joints the concrete bleeds out. This gives the opportunity for the concrete to be relaxed in its forming itself; not to be restrained in any way at the points where it cannot be restrained. Allowing it to go through actually perfected the concrete at the joints, and all corners were made specially, so that they made all three sides removable. The corners were never raw, they were always straight.

These are some of the examples of mechanical space which leads into the laboratory and are some pipe spaces. These are all air intake areas. And these are the studies in front. I think the tone now, the concrete and the wood, blends together much as this black and white photograph does.

All of the places which allow water to come out were done in lead. All these holes were plugged with lead. The lead and the concrete and the travertine are about the only materials really used. All, I think, sympathetic to each other.

Every bit of the form work was designed; nothing left to the contractor. Here it shows what the effect of the bleeding of the concrete can do. In a certain light, these are all accentuated. The corners are quite true.

Here is a meeting place which has not yet been started, and is hoped to. I just wanted to demonstrate a thought. It came to me in Africa. It is that of a building within a building. Also in other places where the light is protected and which refutes, in my opinion, the need for the brise-soleil which is too close to the building and causes heat to enter the building. Whereas, if you have a building outside of a building and it has no roof, then the interior which is the round thing has a chance to look out. Because it has light on the interior of the wall, the glare is eliminated because there is no contrast.

This slide illustrates the principle of this. This is the exterior wall around a lot of paper-thin concrete which has flanges to express and also to make a very thin non-supporting structure. And behind this are the windows of the dining halls which are on three levels.

The interior looking out to a modified lighted wall and a glare outside. This, I'm sure, will cause the room not to need curtains or any other such devices. It is architectural and not brought in as an appurtenance that can be later defiled and possibly misused.

ADDRESS

Now here is the Plan of Dacca and what I've shown you here is changed from the hostels which were supposed to be hotel rooms for ministers, secretaries, members of the assembly, and judges, to studies in a garden on a lake. I flanked the assembly by the lake. The mosque was here, and at that time it was rather a big thing. The Supreme Court was near the other buildings. This was the center of the institutions because I felt that an assembly really produces the institutions of man. These were just basic institutions which are placed across. This is the legislative center of the capital of Pakistan.

This shows the present state of development with the hostels here and the assembly (some buildings here). Now I've changed the Supreme Court to this location, and here is the library, and here is the secretariat, also the hostels, garden, square, and other institutions. There is a hospital, and a house along here, which are still not started.

This shows the general configurations of the assembly. The requirements are numerous. The search for the light causes these shapes to exist. The center area is also fitted out with the means of keeping light inward on the interior areas.

It indicates the light search. Even these buildings have a wall in front to shield the light off the office wings. It isn't, in my opinion, the best scheme with just the wall added. But if it can only be made so that it is an integral part, it is indestructable. Of course, in this case you can take the wall away and say you cannot afford it, but if you can make it so that it is tied in with the structure you must be able to afford it. Again it is a weakness in my opinion.

The plan of the assembly is a mosque here which turns slightly to the west. I made it differently that way so that you could, in fact, express this differently. The office spaces are on the sides, and here are some lounges and other requirements. The assembly is in the middle. These light wells that come down are really the elements, you might say, that put anything left over into the other spaces. This is elementally thought out.

This is one of the elements I speak about. This is crossed by stairways and other requirements. This makes the opening and the wall to ease themselves into repose. But that is the general idea. And then the stiffening is made also by stairways and other ways that come across on the interior. This concrete is made in five-foot pours with a marble insert every five feet, and this covers the point of termination of the pour, and also acts as a wash on the outside (there are three hundred inches of rain there) every five feet on the building. This is so the building does not get damp throughout from the water that is above. Every five feet determines its own water stop. That is the general theory behind the making of the concrete. It also works with their economy and their way of pouring concrete because they have no machines.

They just have a swarm of bees, people, and you don't see what the work has been during the day until they leave! For this reason they are also using sticks instead of vibrators. The idea of controlling the length of pour was part of the design.

Here is the plan of Ahmedabad School of Business Management which is patterned school-wise after the School of Business Management at Harvard. Here is the school, here are the dormitories, here is the lake, the teachers' houses and the servant houses. Most of these are existing trees that are just groves of mango. The dormitories are really houses which have no corridors. They have an entrance with other facilities in a little corner. They enter a triangular place which is a tearoom, and from the tearoom you enter your room. It's studying the principle of the school being case-study minded: no lectures, the lectures are just inspired out of case studies. All the dormitories are also places where people can meet.

So the dormitories and the school are really one: they are not separated. It is within the University of Gujarat which is around this place. Everything is relentlessly adhered to the direction of the wind. Nothing is given in to that importance.

This is what it looks like. I want to introduce you to an idea here. This is a brick and concrete order. It is a composite order in which the brick and the concrete are acting together, in not only the floors, but also in flat arches which are restrained by concrete members. It extends the idea of concrete entering the brickwork. I understand that today there is much work on walls and concrete combining to make structures. It is more consciously done, and I think there could be a composite brick and concrete order established as I tried to do here with these restraining members. I have some sketches which show more about this. Now, these buttress areas are backs of arches. Each dormitory room is actually distinguished by its own construction. It is my belief that structure is the beginning of life, and that structure is already a decision in life. When the walls were thick and an opening was made through the wall for the first time, the wall cried and said, "What are you doing to me. I am a wall and I am protecting you. Why are you making an opening?" The man hesitatingly complained about this complaint and said, "I must look out. I feel as though I've got enough protection." And the wall was very dissatisfied until the opening was made to discern them, and became part of the order of the wall. The stones were more discerningly made, and the windows were placed over it. The wall was very happy that it could have something other than just itself included in what its powers were. And then came the column. The column was really the beginning of architecture in my opinion, because it made a very distinct picture of what is light, and what is not light. And so, the rhythm of light and no light given by the column gave also birth to the arch, the vault, and all other devices which came out of the realization that you can have a support which is designated, instead of something that you rob or just simply modify by some aesthetic notion at the moment. It is with this feeling too, that I believe that you can't make a big space and then divide it into little pieces. You make a big space when you have a big space, and the effort of the big space calls for a big effort. And a small space only calls for a little effort. I am not so sure that I hold to the law of space. I think it really is not truly architecture. And I am not so sure that the architect's duty really is to build all the buildings in the world, but just build their fifty percent if they can do that effectively, and I don't think they can. I think the effective part of it is probably one percent, and they are the guides to what builders should do. Whatever the architect indicates should be the inspiration for the builder. An architect who has too much work proves to himself that he is unable to do it. It takes too much thought, and there are too few of us. Going back to this, I would like to extend the idea of the order which is behind this which was a brick and concrete order.

This is unfortunately very black, and you can see they are made from photographs. There are large openings here. I made these large openings because there are earthquake conditions, and actually the arch below is just as important as the arch above. You have a gravity force, but you also have a force this way. I thought that was expressed. I tried to carry it out, and I think I showed many weaknesses in places where I couldn't find the answer.

Some of the arches of experimentation I've left in the gardens of the houses so that one can use them as playgrounds. And there are quite a number of experiments I had to make because the attitude towards brickwork was very low in India. It is really a mud attitude; it was mud to begin with and had to end up so. And believe me the brick is quite good if only you put one brick over the other. It is quite as simple as this. So I sat around with a great big hat and learned to chew words like "aurgoodo" like say "that is good."

The way the building is made is manifested on the exterior by some of these arches. This arch is actually the way you build this exterior wall. I could have chosen to have a wall just to take over as a wall, but no, I chose to show the arch, and then fill the arch. It was the teacher working and it taught me not to argue with the teacher.

This shows fairly clearly the workmanship which is rough, but I think very acceptable. These are all cast in place. I wanted a brick cast, but they couldn't do it. You can't lift one of those things, and it must be placed in position.

I have this because I thought it would remind you of a Greek Temple, which is a good thing to be reminded of. I have every feeling that Le Corbusier really wanted to build a new Parthenon. I feel at least also that he thinks in terms of the Greek architecture. He thinks in terms of material. I would never have thought of material first. I'd think of the nature of something, see the emergence of what kind of institution it would be. But how right it is to think about material! How right to have found that the material inspires. Certainly a monument that is thought of in concrete and then thought of also as carving names in concrete is completely insensitive. You would have chips of pebbles flying in your face when you carve the statements of a great president. Then also if you'd asked the President if he would like to carve it he would say, "Certainly not! I want to think it over and maybe write it differently."

The next slide indicates something of the reversed arch. Because Leonardo in his sketch book says, "In the remedy for earthquakes you reverse the arches." I found this book, I must say, after I thought of this, but nevertheless it was very heartwarming to see this wonderful page.

Here is the one that shows the arches much deeper than the ones above.

Thank you very much.

"Address by Louis I. Kahn," reprinted with permission from the *Boston Society of Architects Journal*, no. 1, 1967, pp. 7–20.

Louis I. Kahn in Morocco, 1968.

Louis I. Kahn in Nepal, 1972.

Statements on Architecture

From a talk given at the Politecnico in Milan, January 1967

I want first to begin by saying that architecture does not exist.
What does exist is a work of architecture. And a work is an offering to architecture
in the hope that this work can become part of the treasury of architecture.
All building is not architecture.
One of the most important aids in the work that I do comes from the realization
that any building belongs to some institution of man.
And I have the greatest reverence for those inspirations from which the
establishment of institutions came and from the beauty of the architecture
interpretations. But we solved it from it.
Think of one glorious expression which was inspired by Hadrian. Hadrian wanted
a place where everyone could worship equally. The Pantheon was the result.
How wonderful the interpretation which gave us a circular building from which one
could not derive a formalistic ritual. And how so genius was the tracing of the only
opening to the sky.
I must relate you an experience in my conduct of school recently.
The problem was a monastery.
We began by assuming that no monastery existed up to now.
I was a hermit who had the idea of socializing elements, of bringing them together
into a single self-complement.
We had to forget the word monk, the word refectory, the word chapel, the cell. For
two weeks we did nothing. Then an Indian girl said: I believe the cell is the most
important element of this community and that the cell gives the right for the chapel

LOUIS. I. KAHN 1967

to exist, and the chapel gives the right for the refectory to exist, and the refectory gets its right from the cell, and that the retreat is also given by the cell and that the workshops are all made by right of the cell.

Another non-Catholic, also an Indian, said I agree with Menah.

But, he said, I want to add another important realization, and that is that the cell must be equal to the chapel, the chapel is equal to the refectory and the refectory is equal to the retreat, every part is equal to the other, one is not better than the precedent or than another.

The designs of these two Indian students, I must say, were rather inferior but the inspiration of their talk was certainly a great guide to the class.

The most brilliant student, an Englishman, produced a marvellous design in which he invented new elements. One was the necessity for a fireplace which dominated the monastery. And he also traced the refectory a half a mile away from the center and in the wake of the retreat, saying that it was such an honor for the retreat to be near the monastery, for an important arm of the monastery had to be given to it.

I am sure that if a program of requirements was given first in this problem, no such thought will come to the class.

The nucleus of the very beginning monastery was not a loss but new realizations came to it by reconsidering the spirit of the monastery.

It is for this reason my interest in this nucleus, in form realization, form meaning, the realization of inseparable parts of something.

It is for this reason also that I came to the realization that in doing the Magistery Chamber of the capital of Pakistan—I had to introduce a mask in the entrance.

It is for this same reason that when Dr. Salk came to my office and wanted to have a biological laboratory built and when he mentioned that he would like to invite Picasso there, I suddenly had the idea of having a meeting place of the unmeasurable and the science laboratory was the center of the measurable.

In the monastery which I am doing myself, which is the same monastery of which I gave the problem, I have myself discovered other things which are the contrary to discovery of the class.

For instance I have a gateway building. This gateway is the transition between the inside and the outside, I mean is the center of the Ecumenical Council.

It is not in the program, it comes from the spirit and nature of the problem.

This is why I think it is so important that the architect does not follow the program but simply uses it as the point of departure of quantity, not of quality.

For the same reason that the program is not architecture—it is merely instruction, it is like a prescription by a druggist.

Because in the program there is a lobby which the architect must change to a place of entrance. Corridors must be changed to galleries. Budgets must be changed to economy and areas must be changed to spaces.

The inspirations of man are the beginning of his work.

The mind is the soul, the spirit, and the brain, the brain is purely physical.

That is why a machine will never be able to compose Bach.

The mind is really the center of the unmeasurable, the brain is the center of the measurable.

The soul is the same and all. Every mind is different. Everyone is a singularity.

The inspirations come from the walks through life and through the making of man, the inspiration to live gives a life to all institutions of medicine, of sport, of those manifestations of man that come from the inspiration to live forever.

The program that you get and the translation you make architecturally must come from the spirit of man, not from the program.

The inspiration to learn is the making of all institutions of learning.

The inspiration of question is probably the center of all philosophy, and religion.

The inspiration to express, which I think is the most powerful inspiration, is the center of all art.

And art is the language of God.

Structure is the maker of light.

A square building is constructed like a square and its light must give evidence to the square.

An oblong must be constructed like an oblong.

Same with the circular, same with the building which is more fluid and still must find its instruction internally in its making which is actually geometric.

I just want to tell you one more story.

It's about a man in my office who doesn't do any work.

But I gladly pay him because he helps me think.

Once in class—and he attended class—in explaining that structure is the maker of light I introduced the idea of the beauty of the Greek columns in relation to each other and I said the column was no light—the space was light.

But the column feels strong not inside—the column—but outside the column.

And more and more the column wants to feel its strength outside and it leaves a hollow inside, more and more, and it becomes conscious of the hollow.

And if you magnify this thought the column gets bigger and bigger and bigger, and the periphery gets thinner and thinner and inside is a court.

And this was the basis of the design for the Capitol in Pakistan.

One day I walked into the elevator and I found him in there—he is about six foot five—and he didn't see me, he had his hands like this, thinking, you see, and I walked in like a crumbled piece of paper under him.

When we walked out, both of us, to the same floor, he said: oh!—he saw me.

And then I walked—my room is next to the elevator—so that he put his whole frame inside the door while I sat at my table and—as if he were in the other room somehow, he is so tall, you see—he wanted to say may I come in, you see. I said sit down. He said to me: Professor, I've been thinking: is the interior of the column hope?

I knew it wasn't hope, though I made believe that I was thinking about it. I looked down to the window and I tumbled with some papers.

And I said: would you accept inspiration?

He said yes.

And it is what I am trying to say only—is that everything that you use is under scrutiny, there is nothing finished. And the door is open, very open, to the realization of wonderful new institutions. And the wonderful way in which they can be made by inspiring composition and inspiring engineering.

"Louis I. Kahn: Statements on Architecture," reprinted with permission from *Zodiac*, vol. 17, 1967, pp. 55–57.

Space and Inspirations

Lecture for the symposium "The Conservatory Redefined" at the New England Conservatory, 14 November, 1967.

I sense that this conference is dedicated to the wonders of expression and to the inspirations which bring the urges to express. Inspiration is the feeling of beginning at the threshold where Silence and Light meet: Silence, with its desire to be, and Light, the giver of all presences. This, I believe, is in all living things; in the tree, in the rose, in the microbe. To live is to express. All inspirations serve it. The inspiration to learn comes from the story etched in us of how we were made; and urges us to discover its wonders which encompass unmeasurable desire and measurable law. Institutions of learning must have begun from a commonness of urge that they be established. Here the minds are gathered to offer each singular sense of beginning, one to the other. Expression is honored only as Art, the transcendent language.

He who sees another walk with grace, and aspires to that beauty, feels the commonness of spirit in Art. He feels its validity, yet recognizes its unmeasurableness. Physical validity invites measurement by nature's unconscious unchangeable laws. The record of the rock is in the rock. Each grain of sand is in its exact place, is of the exact size and color. Conscious rule invites constant change to new comprehensive levels of Rule. The laws of nature are in the making of all things. Man's indefinable desire to make a house or to shape a stone or to compose a sonata still must obey the laws of nature in their making.

I think of Form as the realization of a nature, made up of inseparable elements. Form has no presence. Its existence is in the mind. If one of its elements were removed its form would have to change. There are those who believe the machine will eventually take the place of the mind. There would have to be as many machines as there are individuals. Form preceeds Design. It guides its direction for it holds the relation of its elements. Design gives the elements their shape, taking them from their existence in the mind to their tangible presence. In composing, I feel that the elements of the form are always intact, though they may be constantly undergoing the trials of design in giving each its most sympathetic shape. Form is not concluded in presence, for its existence is of psychological nature. Each composer interprets Form singularly. Form, when realized, does not belong to its realizer. Only its interpretation belongs to the artist. Form is like order. Oxygen does not belong to its discoverer. It is my feeling that living things and nonliving things are dichotomous. Yet nature, the giver of all presences, without question or choice, can anticipate desire by the fathomless marvel of its laws; it has given us the instruments to play the song of the soul. But I feel that if all living plants and creatures were to disappear, the sun would still shine and rain still fall. We need Nature, but Nature doesn't need us.

Architecture has no presence, Music has no presence—I mean of course, the spirit of architecture and the spirit of music. Music in this sense, as in Architecture, favors no style, no method, no technology—this spirit is recognized as Truth. What does exist is a work of architecture or a work of music which the artist offers to his art in the sanctuary of all expression, which I like to call the Treasury of the Shadows, lying in that ambiance, Light to Silence, Silence to Light. Light, the giver of presence, casts its shadow which belongs to Light. What is made belongs to Light and to Desire.

In the teaching of Architecture I feel there are three aspects: Professional, Personal, Inspirational. Practice relates to professional responsibilities requiring knowledge, experience, business, regulations, science and technology to make a workable design. The person as an individual looks for the signs of dedication to his art and its nature. He looks for the nature in the painter, the sculptor and the musician, in the movie maker, the printer and in the typist. Here the teacher is distinguished from the instructor. He looks for the expressive powers of his art; Art as the making of a life. It comes from Life.

When a great composition again presents itself, it is as though some one you know well entered the room, someone you still had to see again to know. Because of its unmeasureable qualities, it must be heard and again heard. This, I believe, is the part of education where a man's work should not be judged. And if it is to be criticized, it should inspire constructive criticism. For example, I was asked to write a comment on the work of two eighteenth century architects, Ledoux and Boullée. When their drawings were shown to me for the first time (I mean the original drawings) I was struck by two impressions: of the enormous desire shown by their drawings to express the inspirational motivations of architecture, and of how outrageously out of scale they were with human use. But still they were highly inspiring. They were not projected to satisfy function or living in, but belonged to the challenge against narrow limits. For instance, a Library by Boullée showed a room 150 feet high, books stacked high along its walls. The idea was to hand a book down to the man below, and so on, down to the reader, in a space without a table or chair. It would be very difficult, I think, to turn the first page in such a library. But still it was stupendous as a kind of audacity belonging to architecture.

I wrote an introduction to the catalogue:

> Spirit in will to express
> can make the great sun seem small,
>
> The sun is
> Thus the Universe.
> Did we need Bach
> Bach is
> Thus music is.
> Did we need Boullée
> Did we need Ledoux
> Boullée is
> Ledoux is
> Thus Architecture is.

I walked up a high flight of stairs to my studio which I share with Le Ricolais and Norman Rice at the University of Pennsylvania. I often stop at the intermediate landing where plates are hung showing architecture, painting, and sculpture. Here I met one of the fine teachers of sculpture, Bob Engman, out of Yale, where I too began my teaching. He was standing with his back to me, very sturdy figure indeed—you know him—and I put my elbow on his shoulder and said, "What do you see in this old stuff?"—(pointing to a display of Egyptian sculpture)—and he turned to me with a knowing grin expressing without words its wonder. Then with words "isn't it marvellous . . . such beauty . . . what insight," all words less than his expression. And then I said to him, "Bob I gave thought to two words: Existence and Presence." Art embodies both. The one speaks of the spirit, the other of the tangible.

Architecture can be said to be the thoughtful making of spaces. The Pantheon as a marvellous example of a space projected out of desire to give a place for all worship. It is expressed beautifully as a nondirectional space, where only inspired worship can take place. Ordained ritual would have no place. The ocular opening in the top of the dome is the only light. The light is so strong as to feel its cut.

The domain of Architecture has limit. Within its walls of limit all other activities of man exist, but the emphasis is on Architecture. The domain Business within the walls of its limit has also architecture but the emphasis is on Business. All buildings, therefore, do not belong to Architecture. The Pantheon is an example of what is made in the domain Architecture and not in the domain Market Place. It expresses uninfluenced directions toward the making of its space as an institution of man, as it would direct the making of a place of learning, a place of government, a place of the home, places of well-being, giving them each the space environment aspiring to their dedications. They are places which express what man desires to establish, and give form to a way of life. The inspiration to learn gives rise to all the institutions of learning. The inspirations to express give rise to all places of religion, in which Art is probably the greatest of its languages.

You in music, as we in architecture, are interested in structure. To me the structure is the maker of the light. When I choose an order of structure which calls for column along side of column, it presents a rhythm of no light, light, no light, light, no light, light. A vault, a dome, is also a choice of a character of light. To make a square room is to give it the light which reveals the square in its infinite moods. To get light is not just making a hole in a wall, nor is it the selection of a beam here and there to frame the roof. Architecture creates a feeling of a world within a world, which it gives to the room. Try to think of the outside world when you're in a good room with a good person. All your senses of outside leave you. I'm reminded of a beautiful poem by Rumi, the great Persian who lived in the early thirteenth century. He tells of a Priestess walking through her garden. It is Spring. She stops at the threshold of her house and stands transfixed at the entrance chamber. Her maid-in-waiting comes to her excitedly, saying "Look without, look without, Priestess, and see the wonders God has made." The Priestess answered, "Look within and see God." It's marvellous to realize that a room was ever made. What man makes, nature cannot make, though man uses all the laws of nature to make it. What guides it to be made, the desire to make it, is not in universal nature. Dare I say that it is of Silence, of lightless, darkless desire to be, to express a prevalence of spirit enveloping the Universe.

When I see a plan before me, I see it for the character of the spaces, and their relations. I see it as the structure of the spaces in their light. A musician seeing a work must have immediate sense of its Art. He knows the concept from its design, and from his own sense of psychological order. He senses the inspirations from his own desires.

I feel fusion of the senses. To hear a sound is to see its space. Space has tonality, and I imagine myself composing a space lofty, vaulted, or under a dome, attributing to it a sound character alternating with the tones of a space, narrow and high, with graduating silver, light to darkness. The spaces of architecture in their light make me want to compose a kind of music, imagining a truth from the sense of a fusion of the disciplines and their orders. No space, architecturally, is a space unless it has natural light. Natural light has varied mood of the time of the day and the season of the year. A room in architecture, a space in architecture, needs that life-giving light—light from which we were made. So the silver light and the gold light and the green light and the yellow light are qualities of changeable scale or rule. This quality must inspire music.

I am designing an art museum in Texas. Here I felt that the light in the rooms structured in concrete will have the luminosity of silver. I know that rooms for the paintings and objects that fade should only most modestly be given natural light. The scheme of enclosure of the museum is a succession of cycloid vaults each of a single span 150 feet long and 20 feet wide, each forming the rooms with a narrow slit to the sky, with a mirrored glass shaped to spread natural light on the side of the vault. This light will give a glow of silver to the room without touching the objects directly, yet give the comforting feeling of knowing the time of day. Added to the sky light from the slit over the exhibit rooms, I cut across the vaults, at a right angle, a counterpoint of courts, open to the sky, of calculated dimensions and character, marking them Green Court, Yellow Court, Blue Court, named for the kind of light that I anticipate their proportions, their foliation, or their sky reflections on surfaces, or on water will give.

A student of mine came to my room, which is, by the way, everybody's room, and asked me a question: "How would you describe this area?" I was terribly interested. Reflecting, I said to him, "What is the shadow of white light?" Repeating and reflecting on what I said, "White light white light, the shadow of white light," he whispered, "I don't know." I answered, "It's black. But really there is no such thing as white light, black shadow. I was brought up, of course, when light was 'yellow' and shadow was 'blue.' White light is a way of saying that even the sun is on trial, and certainly all our institutions are on trial."

I feel that in the present revolt against our institutions and ways, that there is no Wonder. Without Wonder the revolt looks only to equality. Wonder motivates Desire toward Need. Demands for equality of means can rise only to the trade of old lamps for new without the genii. I feel when Wonder is, the light will become a brighter yellow and the shadow a brighter blue.

I am trying to find new expressions of old institutions. The institutions of learning, let us say, with which we are so concerned today, probably began with a man under a tree, and around him the listeners to the words of his mind. The marvel of the first classroom never leaves me, and now I approach a problem with the desire for the sense of beginnings. I think we need in all schools reverence for the marvels of the beginnings. At this conference we are to speak on the learning of art. The professional, personal, and spiritual facets of its realms will be presented to us. I feel that ideas presented based on new realizations must be free of the influences of the circumstantial.

And now, I must tell you the last story which is about meeting a man, a wonderful architect of Mexico. As I walked through his house I felt the character of "House"—good for him and good for anyone at anytime during its lifetime. It tells you that the artist only seeks truth and that what is traditional or contemporary has no meaning to the artist. His gardens are conceived as personal places not to be duplicated. It gives one the sense that when a garden is made that all drawings for its making must be destroyed. The garden itself survives as the only authentic reality, which must wait for its maturity to realize the spirit of its creation. Later we gathered in good company and he asked me the question: "What is tradition?" This point was brought up earlier today. For the moment I didn't know how to answer except that I had the desire to answer his question, because his outstanding singularity, induced a generative sense. I said: "Yes, my mind goes to the Globe Theatre in London." Shakespeare had just written *Much Ado About Nothing* which was to be performed there. I imagined myself looking at the play through a hole in the wall of the structure, and was surprised to see that the first actor attempting his part fell as a heap of dust and bones under his costume. To the second actor the same happened, and so to the third and fourth, and the audience reacting also fell as a heap of dust. I realized that circumstance can never be recalled, that what I was seeing then was what I could not see now. And I realized that an old Etruscan mirror out of the sea, in which once a beautiful head was reflected had still with all its encrustation the strength to evoke the image of that beauty. It's what man makes, what he writes, his painting, his music, that remains indestructible. The circumstances of their making is but the mold for casting. This led me to realize what may be Tradition. Whatever happens in the circumstantial course of man's life, he leaves as the most valuable, a golden dust which is the essence of his nature. This dust, if you know this dust, and trust in it, and not in circumstance, then you are really in touch with the spirit of tradition. Maybe then one can say that tradition is what gives you the powers of anticipation from which you know what will last when you create.

Thank you.

"Space and Inspirations," reprinted from *L'Architecture d'Aujourd'hui*, vol. 142, February/March, 1969, pp. 13–16.

Twelve Lines

Spirit in will to express
can make the great sun seem small.

The sun is
Thus the Universe.

Did we need Bach
Bach is
Thus music is.

Did we need Boullée
Did we need Ledoux
Boullée is
Ledoux is
Thus Architecture is.

"Twelve Lines," reprinted with permission from *Visionary Architects: Boullee, Ledoux, Lequieu* (Houston: University of St. Thomas, 1968), p. 5.

1968

Foreword

To see these modest structures and see them again in the mind invokes wonder in what inspires the works of man. If I were asked what I now would choose to be, I would say "to be the creator of the new fairy tales." It is from the sense of the incredible that all man's desire to make and establish comes. The simple structures of shelter seem like the markers of a vastness of the land, a place from which to dream kingdom where the house or the castle is not yet in the mind.

Without historical records, the story of America could come from the primitive desires and inspirations, the feeling or joy, which the endless unexplored land can evoke. The spirit of independence, our unique freedom, the feelings of unmeasured generosity and humble hospitality came from the spirit of the unrestricted spaces of the frontier.

The stone and wood, not bought but found, are used true to the rights one dares to take in gratitude for the gifts of nature. These noble and most ancient materials which in all ages inspired numerous and beautiful variations in the expressions of their orders here were used true to their nature with clarity and economy.

Later, the Architect appears, admiring the work of the unschooled men, sensing in their work their integrity and psychological validity. They now stand in silence, yet stir the fairy tale and tell of life.

Foreword reprinted from Clovis Heimsath, *Pioneer Texas Buildings: A Geometry Lesson* (Austin: University of Texas Press, 1968).

Silence

Architecture has no presence. A work is an offering to the Sanctuary.

The paths of living reveal nature, Man evoking in the singular the powers of anticipation renewing the desire to be to express.

A work is made in the urging sounds of industry and, when the dust settles, the pyramid echoing silence gives the sun its shadow.

In his house, a great window looks out to a garden that has the feeling of a fragment of natural landscape captured out of context by a high wall which itself is completely covered with green. Only a narrow clearing laid with recento, a rhinoceros-hide-looking stone, adjoining this window is paved. No paths, no flowers, just wild wind-blown grass. In the clearing is a very large bowl carved out of the same dark hard stone filled to overflowing with water. A source tipped with a rotted splinter of wood breaks the flow of water, and each drop falls like a silver tear spreading rings of silver over the sides of the great bowl extending their wetness to the paved place. The black stone is the alchemist.

Out of the Odyssey in nature of the stream from the tiniest mountain sources, through the varied grooves of its path in light and shade, he selected the darkest place of its dance on the rocks to sense silver of water in a dark bowl and brought it home to contribute to the sense of silence which, as even in the song, prevails in all his house.

Later in the day we all gathered. Barragan asked me, "What is tradition?" I answered, "My mind goes to the Globe Theater in London. Shakespeare's *Much Ado* was being performed. As the first actor attempted a movement, he collapsed in a heap of dust and bones under his costume. This befell all actors and onlookers in succession. I realize that the course of happening can never return. The circumstances of their making is but a vehicle. Man's way through life and what he makes in his quest for expression reveals his nature, which falls as a golden dust eternal. Those who feel their desires through this dust gain the powers of anticipation, which is the inheritance of tradition."

I asked Barragan to come to La Jolla and help me in the choice of the planting for the garden to the Studies of the Salk Laboratory. When he entered the space he went to the concrete walls and touched them and expressed his love for them, and then said as he looked across the space and towards the sea, "I would not put a tree or blade of grass in this space. This should be a plaza of stone, not a garden." I looked

232

at Dr. Salk and he at me and we both felt this was deeply right. Feeling our approval, he added joyously, "If you make this a plaza, you will gain a facade—a facade to the sky."

Once we had breakfast in Mexico City. We talked about a commission he was just offered to design a religious place in the heart of a large city in Texas. He explained how happy it made him to be offered such a trust, but also how let down he was when he saw the site surrounded by uninspired buildings. "I cannot," said he, "find a beginning. I am afraid that I must refuse." I reminded him of Independence Square which gained its significance from all structures around by simply being four feet above the level of the street and then asked, "If you were able to tear down the buildings on one side, revealing to the religious place a mountain range in the distance, would their silence inspire in you a beginning?"

"Silence," reprinted with permission from *VIA*, vol. 1, 1968, pp. 88–89.

silence lightless darkless
desire to be

light the quiet of all presences
out of law or will

light to silence
silence to light
Inspirations
desire to express
sanctuary of art
treasury of the shadows

Silence and Light

Talk with students at the School of Architecture of the Eidgenossische Technische Hochschule, Zurich, February 12, 1969. This talk officially opened the exhibition of his work.

I'm going to put on the blackboard here what may seem at first to be very esoteric. But I believe that I must do it in order to prime myself. Don't forget that I'm also listening and I have really no prepared talk except that I put a few notes down just to get the scaredness out of me because, you know, this is like a blank piece of paper on which I've got to make a drawing. And so, the drawing is a talk this time, you see. It is wonderful to consider, you know, that you must see so well that you hear too. And sometimes it is well to hear so well that you see too. The senses really can be considered one thing. It all comes together. It is the reason why I constantly refer to music in referring to architecture, because to me there is no great difference—when you dig deep enough in the realm of not doing things but simply thinking what you want to do, all the various ways of expression come to fore. To me, when I see a plan I must see the plan as though it were a symphony, of the realm of spaces in the construction and light. I sort of care less, you see, for the moment whether it works or not. Just so I know that the principles are respected which somehow are eternal about the plan. As soon as I see a plan which tries to sell me spaces without light, I simply reject it with such ease, as though it were not even thoughtfully rejected, because I know that it is wrong. And so, false prophets, like schools that have no natural light, are definitely un-architectural. Those are what I like to call—belong to the marketplace of architecture but not to architecture itself.

So I must put on the board something which I thought of only recently which could be a key to my point of view in regard to all works of art including architecture.

And so, I put this on the board: Silence and Light. Silence is not very, very quiet. It is something which you may say is lightless: darkless. These are all invented words. Darkless—there is no such a word. But why not? Lightless; Darkless. Desire to be; to express. Some can say this is the ambient soul—if you go back beyond and think of something in which light and silence were together and maybe are still together, and separated only for the convenience of argument.

I turn to light, the giver of all Presences: by will; by law. You can say the light, the giver of all presences, is the maker of a material, and the material was made to cast a shadow, and the shadow belongs to the light.

I did not say things yet made here, desire being that quality, that force, unmeasurable force, everything here stems from the unmeasurable. Everything here promises the measurable. Is there a threshold where they meet? Can a threshold be thin enough to be called a threshold in the light of these forces; these phenomena? Everything you make is already too thick. I would even think that a thought is also too thick. But one can say, light to silence, silence to light, has to be a kind of ambient threshold and when this is realized, sensed, there is Inspiration.

Inspiration must already have something of a promise of being able to express that which is only a desire to express, because the evidence of the material making of light gives already a feeling of inspiration. In this inspiration, beside inspiration, there is a place, the Sanctuary of Art, Art being the language of man before French, you know, or German. It says the language of man is art. It stems from something which grows out of the needing, of the desire to be, to express, and the evidence of the promise of the material to do it. The means somehow are there. The Sanctuary of art—sort of the ambience of a man's expressiveness—has an outlet, you might say. It is my belief that we live to express. The whole motivation of presence is to express. And what nature gives us is the instrument of expression which we all know as ourselves, which is like giving the instrument upon which the song of the soul can be played. The sanctuary of art—I'm taking this little lesson to say that it is the treasury of the shadows.

I'm sure there is no such separation. I'm sure that everything began at the same time. There wasn't a time when it was good for one thing or another. It was simply something that began at the same time. And I would say the desire to be, to express, exists in the flowers, in the tree, in the microbe, in the crocodile, in man. Only we don't know how to fathom the consciousness of a rose. Maybe the consciousness of a tree is its feeling of its bending before the wind. I don't know. But I have definite trust that everything that's living has a consciousness of some kind, be it as primitive. I only wish that the first really worthwhile discovery of science would be that it recognizes that the unmeasurable, you see, is what they're really fighting to understand, and the measurable is only a servant of the unmeasurable; that everything that man

235

makes must be fundamentally unmeasurable.

Now, of course if you see that, you wonder how you can make a dime—we call it a dime—but I'll say a franc. It certainly doesn't look to me as though you could make a franc out of that, unless you sell it to *Zodiac*, you know. Well, maybe you can do it; but it is just part of an inner belief that you cannot evaluate a Giotto painting. It defies any analyzation, it defies measurement, because after all, Giotto gave us the prerogatives of painting. He said that to a painter, a doorway can be smaller than a person. But the architect must use a doorway that is bigger than a person. Is he less in art than the other? No. *He just recognizes his realm of expression.* The painter can paint people upside down, as Chagall does, as you know, but he has this prerogative because he's a painter. He's representing nothing; he's presenting everything. It's a presentation of the wide realm of expression which exists in man. A sculptor can make square wheels on a cannon to express the futility of war. Unfortunately, the architect must use round wheels if he wants to bring his stone from place to place. From this, you get the sense of that which tends to be in the marketplace, and that which never reaches the marketplace.

And this is, you might say, the crossroad, the place of realization; a place where one sort of senses, how much there, how much here, is the content. Giotto vibrates in this area, defies time. No time will ever say it's old fashioned. Tremendous discoveries of expression lie in such a great man, as it did in the other great men. The essential quality which I admire most in Einstein is that he was a fiddler. From this he derived much of his sense of the universal—or rather, you might say universal order was something that came to him from his sense of eternity, not from just his mathematical knowledge or the knowledge of science. Why didn't it reach the other fellow if knowledge was there, because it filters through everybody? Knowledge is available. It just happened to be in him, the knowledge of something else, and so it is in every one of us. Knowledge is very specifically something that belongs to each individual in his own way. The book of knowledge has never been written, nor will it ever be written for man. Certainly nature doesn't need it. It's already written for nature.

So let's talk a little bit about a problem that comes to a man as an architect. Suppose you were assigned to say—and what a wonderful commission it would be— what is a university. And, instead of being given a program, saying that a university should be for so many people; the library must have so many books; you have to have so many classrooms; you've got to have a student center; and you have to have schools for the professions;—think in terms of university as though it never happened, as though it isn't here. You have nothing to refer to, just the sense of a place of learning, an undeniable need: *an undeniable desire on the part of all of us that a place be for learning*; something which comes specially to someone who is willing to convey to others what is so special in him, and what becomes special in those who learn—in their own way special—as though a singularity taught singularities, because we're all singularities, and none of us are like the other. So consider a university. I gave this problem to the University of Pennsylvania, to my students. There was no program—well, I said, yes, consider the University of Pennsylvania as probably the seat, because somebody has to have something to put their hat on, so that was the only indication. Now one student—he was a German student—who in a very halting and most modest way said he believes the core of the University is the library, but a specific library. He said it was the central library. He said that the library of the university is like the Acropolis. It is the offering of the mind. And he considered that when you go into the library, and you see these books, you judge them as offerings of the mind. A man motivated not by profit of any kind—just a sense of offering—he writes a book, hoping that it will be published. He's trying to—he's motivated by the sense that he has somewhere in there, whether it is deep, deep in the silence, or whether it is already on the threshold of inspiration. He must be there to write it, and what he draws from here, and what he draws from there, somehow, he motivates his writing a book. And he gets it also from another, beautiful source, and that is through the experience or the Odyssey of a life that goes through the circumstances of living and what falls as important are not the dates or what happened, but in what way he discovered man through the circumstance. It's a golden dust that falls which, if you can put your fingers through, you have the powers of anticipation. The artist feels this when he makes something. He knows that he does it now, but he knows also that it has eternal value. He's not taking circumstances as it happens. He's extracting circumstances from whatever fell which revealed man to him. Tradition is just mounds of these circumstances, you see, the record of which also is a golden dust from which you can extract the nature of man, which is tremendously important if you can anticipate in your work that which will last—that which has the sense of commonness about it. And by commonness, I mean really, the essence of silence is commonness. That's the essence of it. When you see the pyramids now, what you feel is silence. As though the original inspiration of it may have been whatever it is, but the motivation that started that which made the pyramids is nothing but simply remarkable. To have thought of this shape personifying a kind of perfection, the shape of which is not in nature at all, and striving with all this effort, beating people, slaves, to the point of death to make this thing. We see it now with all the circumstances gone, and we see that when the dust is cleared, we see really silence again. So it is with a great work. I see a Giotto painting also with a feeling of silence—as though it came from here, you see—as though it didn't come from any sense of the marketplace. Like, I will make a painting that's worth so much money, you see, or anything of that nature. It came from there.

Going back to the university, then this was a center; it was something about the humanities that was really the university. Another part of it was that of the professions. This was the engagement of man in the various avenues of expression be he a doctor, or a lawyer, or an architect, or a bookkeeper, or a nurse, anything—it was a way of expression. You choose to be a nurse because you want to, you have something that tells you to be a nurse, or something that tells you to be an architect. And the university position has nothing to do with the marketplace. The marketplace has to do with the way that which personifies this profession is practiced by the individual; this is something the university should not be concerned with, except to inspire him in the nature of his profession, and in what way he will, in the end, be the happiest in the exercise of this expression. Problems of the marketplace really do not belong there, because no matter how much you teach it, the tendency will be for the person to find his own way, *because a man does not really learn anything that's not part of himself.* He might try very hard. He may even pass examinations, but he'll never really be a chemist, even if he studies chemistry, unless he's a chemist from the very, very start. And so, therefore, knowledge per se is to me very doubtful, you see. But knowledge taken to prime your way of expression is not; to develop a person's talent is not. Very good. Very wonderful. The place, the realm, within which the talents of people can be exercised.

So the university has nothing to do with the marketplace. It doesn't disdain it, because it gets its support from the marketplace; but it still doesn't teach it, because it's useless to teach it. To prepare you for nature's ways, yes. The laws of nature must be known, because there are three aspects in the teaching. There is a teaching of the professional position's, responsibility to other people which includes the differentiation between science and technology, which are completely different things. And your specific knowledge that you need in statics or acoustics, those are all very necessary things and belong definitely in the realm of teaching, to prepare you for your responsibilities, conducting your office as a responsibility to society—yes, all these things—but there is another responsibility, and that is to *teach the man to be himself,* which is delving into the various talents which can be employed in the profession, not all having to do with design, not all with specification writing, but it somehow—all belongs to it. You're not teaching geniuses, you're just teaching, you know, actually; the nature of the profession, the many facets, you see, among which self-expression can come about. But the most important thing to teach is to know that architecture has no presence. You can't get a hold of architecture. It just has no presence. *Only a work of architecture has presence,* and a work of architecture is presented as an offering to architecture. Architecture has no favorites; it has no preferences in design; it has no preferences for materials; it has no preferences for technology. It just sits there waiting for a work to indicate again to revive the spirit of architecture by its nature, from which people can live for many years.

And so the university is a sanction. The library of the sanction place, then, the places of the professions, the library of these professions are there, hooked up because there is also an offering of the mind, and this is somehow connected with the unit—with the more objective offering of the mind—which is the offering of the sanctuary, the Acropolis. You might say objective or subjective—it doesn't really matter. It's just offering. Now if you consider this, it must be put in mind differentiations of a wonderful kind. It brings in mind the difference between the garden, the court, and a piazza. Because your connections are not going to be just colonnades and that sort of thing, it's going to be mental—the connection. You're going to feel it in some way. But the consciousness of a planner that there is an association, a kind of interrespect between the two is already, guides the hand, you know, in saying it should be here, it should be there, it should be there, you see. Otherwise it becomes merely land-scraping. I call it, you see. Not landscaping: land-scraping. It is really a consciousness, not drawing around trees here and there or stamping them on your plan, you see—I hate that—really I do. So the connection, then, is the realization of what is a garden, what is a court, what is an avenue, what is a piazza. A garden is a very private thing. You would say that the landscape architect, or the architect, or the gardener, who makes a plan for a garden with his fountains and places to sit, and the trees chosen in relation to porticos and so forth, should make the plan as an instruction for something that will grow into being, and once everything is established that will grow into being and it's full, after that he takes this plan and throws it into the fireplace and doesn't keep it as a record, because the next garden he makes must be completely different, because that garden is very, very private and belongs to the individual. It's not a place of invitation, it's a place of part of the expression of living. The court is different. The court is the boy's place. The court is already a place of invitation. I would like to call it the outside-inside space. It is a place which one feels that if he comes to, he can make a choice as to where he goes from there. And a piazza is man's place, much more impersonal, defined like a court. Playing with this so-called architecture of connection, which happens to have no rules, is a consciousness of the involvement of the land and the buildings, their association with the library, and the library. Now there are many things absent. It wasn't sufficient, just the connection. The class was very excited about one aspect which I hinted at, that there must be a place of happening. A place of happening, and you say why can't things happen the way they will. They don't have to. The Agora, for instance, was a place of happening; Agora, the Stoa. The Stoa was made most marvellously. It was made like this. No partitions, just columns, just protection. Things grew in it. Shops became. People met, meet, there. It's shaded.

You present a quality, architectural, no purpose, just a recognition of something which you can't define, but must be built. Today, the general unrest among students should call for this kind of space. You shouldn't try to fight a battle as to who's right and who's wrong, but should create the architectural interpretation of this, which is a place without partitions which will form themselves into partitions some day. So it is a recognition of a place where possibly the student, the administration, and the teacher would meet. It's a club of the university, not the student center, so to speak, but everybody's center, and it sits probably in a green area like this without paths whatsoever, because who knows where you're going. But that's a definite architectural quality. It has the same quality as all religious places, which also just by simple quality of knowing that a stone stands free, that it has something more than just simply singing at random or going through a forest and trying to jump. What is the feeling? It is something in the way of a mysterious decision to make Stonehenge. It's terrific. It's the beginning of architecture. It isn't made out of a handbook, you see. It doesn't start from practical issues. It starts from a kind of feeling that there must be a world within a world. The world where man's mind, you see, somehow becomes sharp. Have you ever said anything significant when you were outside waiting for a bus? Never. You said something significant inside a building, never outside a building. Did you ever say anything significant at a picnic? No. Well, you had a hell of a good time—I realize that, but you didn't say anything that was the mind saying. It was really quiet functioning as humans in the most sparkling, beautiful, amusing way, which is definitely a part of our lives, but it is not necessarily how buildings start. Buildings start as a kind of recognition that there must be a place of concentration where the mind, somehow, is given play. And I make a distinction between mind—and this might be put here too, because it doesn't belong here, but I'll put it here anyway—Mind and Brain. Brain is an instrument given by that fellow over there. Mind is this and the instrument. Somewhere in here is Mind. Mind is the instrument and the soul Brain. Now this is Mind. Brain is—I would say the machines we make now, you see, for calculating, for putting into; I don't know what you call them, these computers—these are brains—never the mind. The mind makes it but it never will really give you anything that brain can do. And the men who really know the instrument will tell you that themselves. It's the men who don't know it who will tell you otherwise. It's like putting a penny in a slot and getting a very wonderful answer worth more than a penny. I'm afraid not.

So they discovered that this was a place of meeting of everyone, a very necessary thing. From this you recognize also that a school of architecture probably starts with a court, surrounded by shops, in which you build and tear down at will. It's a closed court because nobody really likes to show how badly he does things, so it becomes something which amongst your confréres is okay. Outside, not. It's not an exhibition place. There is no admission set for this thing—it's not this—it's closed. From this grow other things, spaces high and low, but it is a kind of area undetermined, spaces undetermined in their light, in various light, in various light, in various heights, and that you move around with a sense of discovering the spaces rather than being named for certain reasons. Actually they're just there and you feel it is a school of architecture because of how much concentration you put into the primitiveness, the fundamental-ness with which you made these spaces. These are all. I think, indication of the tremendous opportunities that exist today in architecture. The discovery of the ele-ments of our institutions which need revival, which need to be bolstered up, which need to be redefined.

Now, in the Congress Building in Venice I built, I am thinking of building a place which is the meeting of the mind and a place where expressions of the meeting of the mind can take place. It is also a place of happening. I don't believe in inviting shows for the Biennale saying, "You come with your exhibit, bring your big packages; bring the things you've done," but rather say, "Come here, meet other people, and by meeting them something will happen to you!"—and it will. Here in the Palazzo dei Congressi they meet to sense each other's mind. In the Biennale they meet to express something—actually, tangibly. It is somehow a place of existence, which I might put here. I'll put it here, existence here, and presence. You see presence is here, existence is here. It exists. You can feel the thought, but it doesn't have presence. When you describe, when you will say. "Oh! It's marvellous! It's beautiful! It's terrific! It's—it's immense!" you are saying words which no university professor understands at all. But when you say, when you see a thing, you say, "Oh, I don't like stone. I think it should be taller. I think it ought to be wider," you are dealing with the measurable, because it is made. So in the work of art there is the measurable and the unmeasurable. When you say "It's terrific," you're talking about the unmeasurable and nobody understands you—and they shouldn't because it is fundamentally unmeasurable.

Now, from this grew other things. It wasn't just the university and the buildings there, which are not yet, have not been made in the university. And there were other buildings—I don't want to mention the whole story. But what grew in it; a realization of the marketplace and the university; and it so turned out that, the university here, the marketplace, there was place between—it happened to be in Philadelphia, the Schuylkill River. City planning couldn't be here, because it is too politically infested. City planning could also not be here because it is too theoretically oriented. So there had to be a place of happening, a place where the marketplace goes to, where the university goes to, both represented—but they are not here and they're not particularly here—and this was a place of happening right here, that was designed by one of the students as a bridge crossing the Schuylkill, and it was a kind of place of auditoria, a place where there were many auditoriums, many that would be the proper ones that selected for the kind of discussion which is a generator of the sense of the institutions of man, which a city planner should be most conscious of—not the traffic; not housing particularly; not any of these things—but fundamentally first, the sense of the institutions of man which yet have not been made and those which are here, but they're very badly in need of change. From this is the true generator of planning, not the other things like traffic. To me it's child's play. Traffic—we can really put it into a machine and find the answer. In a certain way you can. At least a help. Not the real answer, but at least a temporary one.

So there must be found in every city really, a place free of the marketplace, free of the school, which is, in a sense, the nerve center of worthiness, you know; of that which can make a city great, really, because you measure the city, really, not by the excellence of its traffic system, but *why* it has a traffic system because there is worthiness to serve. And this architecture of connection between, let's say, of the whole city, takes direction. The university, you see, and the other schools take direction by the reason of their courts, their gardens, and their avenues, and so forth. The connection is both mental and physical. This institution, I think, is necessary everywhere, because otherwise, nothing will progress, really. The marketplace won't progress, nor will this progress. There must be a ground here which is a kind of—it's a freedom ground at this point. This came out of no program, simply as speculations on the power of architecture to set down that which commands technology; which really writes the program, because after all, if an architect gets a program from a client, he gets an area program. He has to change the areas into spaces, because he's not dealing only with areas. They're spaces: it isn't just feelings. They are feeling; ambience. They are places where you feel something—different. As I said you don't say the same thing in a small space, you see. So a school must have small spaces as well as large spaces, and all classes need not be the same. There's something like a place of learning. Felt so. Taken out of the very essence of your feeling as a person, the various other people to a sense of commonness, which is a tremendous guide to a person's mind.

You say the institutions of man. I don't mean institutions like the establishment. I mean, really, institution being that it's an undeniable desire to have the recognition that man cannot proceed in a society of other men without having certain inspirations that they have—be given a place for their exercise. Actually, the institutions of learning stem from the way we were made. Because nature, in what it makes, it records how it was made. In the rock is the record of the rock, and in man is the record of man. Man, through his consciousness, senses inside of him all the laws of nature, except that his instrument is usually very poor, which he gets from nature, in the way of a brain, and when he mixes it up with his sense, you see, and desire, he finds that there are plenty of obstructions, and he takes years before he senses this himself. But regardless, the quality which he inherited, that part which I say is the golden dust which he does inherit, that which is the nature of man, he inherits, just like his physical being, in this he senses the desire to learn to express. So all learning, you see, stems from the way we were made, only to find out the laws of the universe because it's in you. And so it is with other inspirations which are in us. The sense of physical well-being comes from the desire to live forever: to express. The highest form of expression is art because it's the least definable.

Desire to live—to express. The institutions, therefore, are established, because there is this sense of wanting to learn, and the wanting to learn makes you pay a tax to see that a school is established. Nobody resists this tax because it is in the nature of man that he wants to learn. Sometimes he's beaten out of it because of certain things, like he's scared of, to be in front of a class, he looses his courage because he's slower in becoming free of this thing. That's why I believe that no marking should exist at any school because it's destructive of man. And it's very difficult, well I say, I know it is, but really, if you didn't mark anybody, I think you'd find that your class would become brighter. Actually, it is so because people don't grow equally. I have good experience in this because I was a very poor student, and I somehow managed to get past; but I only learned the things that were taught to me after I got out of school and not during the time, because I was naturally bashful. I didn't want to assert myself, and also I made my lessons three days afterward instead of the day I should. So all these things are just part of the person.

Now another example, let's say, of searching for the nature of the problem: a boy's club, I gave one time as a problem. And the speculation was: what would be the first room that one would make, which would present a boy's club. If I were to take the programs issued by the Association of Boys' Clubs, which has a standard program, or what it is, I would meet this kind of a situation: I would come to the entrance, and then there would be a supervisor who would see to it that you're a boy or a girl. Then you would go through, you see, and then you would be hit by a room that is ping-pong—noise—absolute stress and strain, because it is good to feel, as they said, that the boy must feel that he's now amongst others, you see. And then there are some guidance rooms, so to speak, and also where the older boys can be. Well, it just continues. There is, of course, a swimming pool; there is a gymnasium. But I tell you that many people would never join because of that shock, you see, of being supervised from the start, and they go into a place where you're likely to be pushed. When a boy is delicate and frail and not a fighting sort of person he walks into a gang of enemies. So, the problem was given: what is the first room. One thought that it should be a room with a fireplace: a generous one with much seating around it, and one can take a seat, hopefully that someone would come, you see, and sit by him, or that he had at least a choice not with any strain attached to it. But during the course of the development of the problem, it was found that the best place was a court. You open the door and you're in a court with an arcade around it, but the promise of the kind of room that you'd want to go to all around it. So the man chooses—the boy chooses what room he wants to go into because he's just entering life, so to speak, you see, with others, and the sensitiveness of this is certainly far greater than knowing exactly how a boy's club works. You don't know. And so you make a plan which you don't know, and it's a far superior plan.

I'll now talk about functionalism. I think you can talk about machines being functional; bicycles being functional; beer plants being functional, but not all buildings are functional. Now, they must function, but they function psychologically. There is a psychological function which is a paramount function whether it's a factory or otherwise. Just so people are involved, there must be a place for people. Even an atom-cracking plant must consider that there are people involved in this thing, and there are places for everything, but there is something which has to do with the association of people with it. And that sense, I think, brings about a new era in architecture which doesn't try to make everything be accountable. So, when you are given, as I said, a program by a client in which he gives you how much square-foot area he needs, let's say, for a lobby which he measures by square-foot area, you usually won't have more than three or four people at a time, or maybe ten or twenty. That's where the elevators are, where the stairways are, from which you go upstairs. Now measure, if this were also an entry for a school of architecture, you see how it would fail. But the program reads just the same for a school of architecture as it does for an office building—pretty much the same. It's measured by so many square feet per person; three and a half people per acre—that kind of thing. But actually, you translate the lobby into a place of entrance, and it becomes a very different thing. It is a space of entrance, not a lobby. You change it. You change corridors into galleries because you know their value, you know their tremendous association value when they are a gallery instead of a corridor, and the first thing that must be done of great importance is to make the budget economical, which means worthwhile; which means that you may spend the same amount of money, but the attitude shouldn't be that the money rules what you do. You must find that which is worthy within what is considered for the moment to be a limit, but your duty is also to portray what may increase this limit, in order to bring a worthwhile thing to the client—depending on just how you are made, whether you give in to certain things. But the going through this exercise of portraying what seems to be the nature of something is a very essential thing, I feel, to your eventual powers, which will bring about a new architecture.

Now, I have some other things here, but I cannot speak enough about light because light is so important, because, actually, structure is the maker of light. When you decide on the structure, you're deciding on light. In the old buildings, the columns were an expression of light, no light, light, no light, light, no light, light, you see. The module is also light—no light. The vault stems from it. The dome stems from it, and the same realization that you are releasing light. The orders which you think about when you are, in a sense, determining the elements of design—that is to say, the elements, and how you are considering them in design to be perfected. There is in the design the consideration of the difference between the order of structure and the order of construction. They're two different things. There is an order to construction which brings in the orders of time. They're very much married to each other. The order of structure can make conscious the crane. The crane that can lift twenty-five tons should appear in a specification of present-day architecture which does not appear now. The architect says, "Oh! They're using a crane on my building. Isn't that nice—so they can pick it up more easily," never realizing that the crane is a designer; that you can make something that's twenty-five tons coming to something that's twenty-five tons, and you can make a joint that's so magnificent, because that joint is no little thing. In fact, if you'd put gold into it, you wouldn't be spending too much money, because it's so big. So the realization that joint making, which is the beginning of ornament—because I do believe that the joint is the beginning of ornament—comes into being again, you see. What you can lift as one thing should be something that motivates the whole idea of making a single thing which comes together with another single thing. So in the order of structure you make this decision like I did in Ahmedabad when I said that a beam needs a column. A beam needs a column; a column needs a beam. There is no such thing as a beam on a wall. And if you make the decision which I made, saying that the beam of brick is an arch, therefore, since I did not want to use any concrete beams, and since I was not going to use any columns, it became so natural to use an arch, because it was only part of the wall construction which is characteristic of brick, and I placed everything supported under arches, and invented many things about arches, like big arches which stretch as much as twenty feet, let us say, with a very low thing using restraining members in concrete like this to take the thrust away, bringing the wall very close together, giving a space with that much opening because I made a composite order in which the concrete and the brick will work together. This is a composite order. A sort of sense of structure, a sense of the order of brick, sense of the order of structure, which made this possible. The design goes on and on; speculation of the ways you can do this thing in the most

245

characteristic fantastic ways, because you recognize that structure has an order; that the material has an order; that the construction has an order; the space has an order in the way of the servant spaces and the spaces served; that the light has an order because it has an order in the sense that it is given by structure, and that the consciousness of the orders be felt.

I just remind you in closing, the story of Rumi, a very famous Persian poet, who lived in twelve hundred or so, who writes of a poet; I'm not going to write the poetic language, because I don't read Persian, and also, it's far from me, the words that I read. There was a Priestess who was going through her garden in spring, and of course it was a glorious day. As she went through her garden, observing everything, and came to the threshold of her house, and there she stopped in admiration—standing at the threshold, looking within. And her servant-in-waiting, came over to her, saying "Mistress, Mistress. Look without, and see the wonders that God has created." And the mistress said, "Yes, yes, but look within and see God." In other words, what man has made is very, very manifestation of God. Thank you very much.

"Silence and Light," reprinted from H. Ronner, S. Jhaveni, and A. Vasella, *Louis I. Kahn, Complete Work 1935–1974* (Boulder, Colorado: Westview Press, 1977), pp. 447–49.

Foreword

Prevailance of order
Prevailance of commonness
Being is of order
Desire to be of order is life
To live is to express.

The spare atmosphere of Mars tells us of this prevailance to be;
not of the attitude not of the choice, the vectors to the character
of living forms and shapes.
In outer space the Earth is felt in wonder as if for the first time.
This marble, blue-green and rose, unique in our system makes
us realize that man's work can be like no other.

The builder seeking a beginning is primed by
his feelings of commonness and the inspirations of Nature.

Just a fragment of knowing steers wonder to intuition and
to the acts of expression. In the presence of the mountain
the water the wind the desire to express feels the possible.
The site confirms the possible and encourages agreement
on the beginning in the making of a man's place.
A mere foothold is confident of the settlement,
the first institution of man.

The works of man reveal his nature.

The time of a work holds its own validity from
which the sense of truth can be drawn to inspire
a work of another time.

The city from a simple settlement became the place
of the assembled institutions.

The measure of the greatness of a city must come from
the character of its institutions established by those
sensitive to commonness and dedication to man's desire for
higher levels of expression.

The places of the island the hamlet the mountain
draw us to them for their simple truth.

To leave them for the city must bring
revived faith in new beginning.
A city must ever be greater and greater.

Commonness is the spirit Art
A work of art is an offering to Art.

Architecture: Silence and Light

Let us go back in time to the building of the pyramids. Hear the din of industry in a cloud of dust marking their place. Now we see the pyramids in full presence. There prevails the feeling of Silence, in which is felt man's desire to express. This existed before the first stone was laid.

I note that when a building is being made, free of servitude, its spirit to be is high—no blade of grass can grow in its wake. When the building stands complete and in use, it seems to want to tell you about the adventure of its making. But all the parts locked in servitude make this a story of little interest. When its use is spent and it becomes a ruin, the wonder of its beginning appears again. It feels good to have itself entwined in foliage, once more high in spirit and free of servitude.

I sense Light as the giver of all presences, and material as spent Light. What is made by Light casts a shadow, and the shadow belongs to Light. I sense a Threshold: Light to Silence, Silence to Light—an ambiance of inspiration, in which the desire to be, to express crosses with the possible. The rock, the stream, the wind inspires. We see what is beautiful in the material first in wonder, then in knowing, which in turn is transformed into the expression of beauty that lies in the desire to express. Light to Silence, Silence to Light crosses in the sanctuary of art. Its treasury knows no favorite, knows no style. Truth and rule of commonness, law out of order are the offerings within.

Architecture has no presence but exists as the realization of a spirit. A work of architecture is made as an offering reflecting the nature of that spirit. One can also say that the realms of painting, sculpture, and literature exist in spirit, their natures revealed by works that are unfamiliar. In using the word "unfamiliar," I recognize the singularity of every individual in attitude and talent. But the phenomena of individual realizations of a spirit are only new images of that same spirit. So it is in nature that the diversity of forms evolves from universal order.

Form is the recognition of an integrity of inseparable elements. This is true in both nature and art. In nature validity is nonconscious. Every grain of sand on the beach has a natural color and shape, is of natural weight and in its natural position. It is part of the constant play of equilibria, governed solely by the laws of nature. What man makes must answer to the laws of nature, and is governed in his concepts by rules and choice. The one is measurable. The one is completely unmeasurable. What nature makes, it makes without man, and what man makes, nature cannot make without him.

Nature does not make a house. It cannot make a room. How marvelous that when I am in a room with another the mountains, trees, wind, and rain leave us for the mind, and the room becomes a world in itself. With only one other person one feels generative. The meeting becomes an event. The actor throws aside the lines of his performance. The residue from all his thoughts and experiences meets the other on equal terms. Even now, though I feel I am saying things differently from the way I have said them before, I have thought about them and the idea is therefore not essentially generative. The room, then, is a marvellous thing.

Architecture deals primarily with the making of spaces to serve the institutions of man. In the aura of Silence and Light, the desire to be, to make, to express, recognizes the laws that confirm the possible. Strong, then, is the desire to know, heralding the beginning of the institutions of learning dedicated to discover how we were made. In man is the record of man. Man through his consciousness feels this record, which sparks his desire to learn what nature has given him and what choices he has made to protect himself and his desires in the odyssey of his emergence.

I believe that consciousness is in all life. It is in the rose, in the microbe, in the leaf. Their consciousness is not understandable to us. How much more would we comprehend if we were to uncover their secrets, for then a wider sense of commonness would enter expressions in art, giving the artist greater insight in presenting his offerings answering to the prevailance of order, the prevailance of commonness.

Dissension is out in the open. I do not feel that its roots come from need alone. Dissension stems from desire—desire for what is not yet made, not yet expressed. Need comes from the known. Supplying only what is lacking brings no lasting joy. Did the world need the Fifth Symphony before Beethoven wrote it? Did Beethoven need it? He desired it, and now the world needs it. Desire brings about the new need.

I look at the glancing light on the side of the mountain, which is such a meaningful

Silence to Light

The desire to express

The Threshold

The Inspirations

The Sanctuary of Art

The Treasury of The Shadows

Architecture is the making of a room; an assembly of rooms. The light is the light of that room.
Thoughts exchanged by one and another are not the same in one room as in another.

A street is a room; a community room by agreement Its character from intersection to intersection changes and may be regarded as a number of rooms light, bringing every tiny natural detail to the eye, and teaching us about material and choice in making a building. But do I get less delight out of seeing a brick wall with all its attempts at regularity, its delightful imperfections revealed in natural light? A wall is built in the hope that a light once observed may strike it again in a rare moment in time. How can anyone imagine a building of spaces not seen in natural light? Schools are being built with little or no natural light, supposedly to save on maintenance costs and to assure the teachers of their pupils' undivided attention. The most wonderful aspects of the indoors are the moods that light gives to space. The electric bulb fights the sun. Think of it.

I am reminded of Tolstoy, who deviated from faithlessness to faith without question. In his latter state he deplored the miracles, saying that Christ has radiance without them. They were holding a candle to the sun to see the sun better.

Structure is the maker of light. A column and a column bring light between them. It is darkness-light, darkness-light, darkness-light, darkness-light. In the column we realize a simple and beautiful rhythmic beauty evolved from the primitive wall and its openings. At first, walls were thick. They protected man. He felt the desire for freedom and the promise of the world outside. He made at first a rude opening. Then he explained to the unhappy wall that, in accepting an opening, the wall must now follow a higher order with arches and piers as new and worthy elements. These are the realizations in architecture of Light and Structure. The choice of a square room is also the choice of its light as distinguished from other shapes and their light. Even a room which must be dark needs at least a crack of light to know how dark it is. But architects in planning rooms today have forgotten their faith in natural light. Depending on the touch of a finger to a switch, they are satisfied with static light and forget the endlessly changing qualities of natural light, in which a room is a different room every second of the day.

I spoke of form as the realization of a nature. A shape is an expression of form. Form follows desire as a realization of a dream or a belief. Form tells of inseparable elements. Design is the struggle to develop these elements into shapes compatible with each other, reaching for a wholeness, for a name. Form in the mind of one is not the same as it is in the mind of another. The realization of a nature, form, and shape are not part of the process of design manipulation. In design there are wonderful realizations: the order of structure, the order of construction, the order of time, the order of spaces come into play.

As I see a sheet of music, I realize that the musician sees it to hear. To an architect, the plan is a sheet on which appears the order of the structure of spaces in their light.

The institutions of learning give the architect a program of requirements. These requirements are derived from previous plans which were designed to answer momentary needs. These needs are very far from the original spirit School. The architect must consider the program merely as a guide. The spirit School, in the sense of its conceived commonness, should be considered as though it is being realized for the first time.

Recently my class decided to speculate on the question: what is a university? We had no program. We thought of the nature of a university. Our minds were empty of knowing and full of adventure. One student gave emphasis to the central library as the place of the dedication of the mind. It was suggested also that the libraries of the different professions should be related to the main library by a conscious "Architecture of Connection," since the university's most direct service to the community is the sanctioning of the professions. But we were distressed because we realized that the university is gradually falling into the sphere of the marketplace, competing with other schools for research money and inventing special degrees to attract students. Architecture, for instance, is being separated from urban design and city planning and thus shutting off students with broad natural talents in architecture, who refuse to accept such professional distinctions.

In the marketplace the professions tend to become businesses which suppress individual talent, whose leadership has always been followed. The architect can realize the spirit of his art and the emerging orders only when the problems before him are considered as part of a whole. Relegated to niches of specialization, he will become one of a team, designing parts and giving the world nothing but solutions of immediate needs. He will never be free or experienced enough to guide prevailing desires to inspirations. Although I feel that unique talent cannot be overthrown, it is hurt by being retarded. Talent has to be recognized early to do good work.

In considering the architecture of connection—library to library—my students developed their thoughts about the significant places to be found in the university. The garden became inseparable from the room, the court, the entrance place of invitation, the green, or the great court as the place of the happening.

Dissensions made us think of a place or a structure not yet named for the teacher, the student, and the directors. Like the stoa, it would not be partitioned, and its position on the campus would be on a great lawn with not a path crossing it. The division would be agreed upon later and the lawn modified by the use it evoked.

It was thought that a university has much to gain from the city, which in turn may consider the university as one of its most important institutions. But professional practice is in the marketplace, and the university in sanctioning the professions should be free of it. This brought to our minds the role of the city planner. We realized that there must be a place free of the university and free of the marketplace where both

The one desires To be to express The one Eternity is of two Brothers to be to make The one light Non Luminous The one light Luminous

could meet. The visions of planners meet the political economy of the city. This separate place should be recognized as a new institution of man, equal to the institutions of government, of learning, and of health.

The city is measured by its institutions, and its growth is felt in the works of its leaders who are sensitive to the desires of the people and who want to serve their desire for expression. The studies leading to the emergence of new institutions become the points of departure for planning. Movement plans and redevelopment schemes are merely corrective projects. The known institutions need new vitality, conscious recognition. As an example of current deterioration, think of City Hall, which evolved from the early meeting place on the village green. It is probably the most dishonored building in the city—a place associated with taxes, fees, courts, and jails, where nobody meets. Since the day of the meeting house, the interests of people have become greatly extended and diversified, but there is no place for us to air these interests. A place of auditoria, meeting rooms, and seminars would revive the spirit of representation and give every man a place which he feels is his own city house.

Our inspirations assist us when we clear our senses of known solutions and methods. The realization of a yet unthought-of nature and the elements of its form can stimulate an entirely new point of view about everything. Today we talk about technology as though our minds will be surrendered to the machine. Surely the machine is merely a brain which we get, pot luck, from nature. But a mind capable of realization can inspire a new technology and humiliate the current one.

Teaching is a work. The beginning is dear to the teacher, for he senses what man is from what he accepts and is willing to support. The code of the teacher is often remote from another man's. Because of his desire to tell about his mind, he seeks words that are as close to his codes as possible without losing generativeness. I have used "commonness" instead of "spirit" for that very reason. Spirit is immediately assumed as understood. Commonness makes one think.

Art is the making of a life. When we hear the strains of a familiar musical masterpiece, it is as though a familiar person entered the room. But as you must see him again in order to believe his presence, so must the music be played again so you can remember all that touched you before.

In Mexico I met the architect Barragan. I was impressed by his work because of its closeness to nature. His garden is framed by a high private wall, the land and foliage remaining untouched as he found it. In it is a fountain made by a water source lightly playing over a jagged splinter and, drop for drop, falling in a great bowl of rhinoceros-gray-black stone filled to the brim. Each drop was like a slash of silver making rings of silver reaching for the edge and falling to the ground. The water in the black container was a choice from the path of water as a mountain stream in light, over rocks, and then in deep seclusion where its silver was revealed. He learned about water and selected what he loved most.

His house is not merely a house but house itself. Anyone could feel at home. Its material is traditional, its character eternal. We talked about traditions as though they were mounds of golden dust of man's nature, from which circumstances were distilled out. As man takes his path through experience, he learns about man. Learning falls as golden dust, which if touched gives the power of anticipation. The artist has this power and knows the world even before it began. He expresses himself in terms of psychological validities.

A student once asked, "What is the intuitive sense?" Robert le Ricolais, mathematician, engineer, and scientist, answered, "What made man venture to make the first thing? Surely it was not his knowledge but his sense of validity. But intuition must be fed. I might say that everything must begin with poetry."

"Architecture: Silence and Light," reprinted from Arnold Toynbee et. al., *On the Future of Art* (New York: Viking, Press, 1970), sponsored by the Solomon R. Guggenheim Museum, pp. 20–35.

Louis I. Kahn at the opening of the Kimbell Art Museum in Fort Worth, 1972 (Photo: Robert Shaw).

Not for the Fainthearted

On Drawing

One day, as a small boy, I was copying the portrait of Napoleon. His left eye was giving me trouble. Already I had erased the drawing of it several times. My father lovingly corrected my work. I threw paper and pencil across the room, saying, "Now it's your drawing, not mine." Two cannot make a single drawing. I am sure the most skillful imitation can be detected by the originator. The sheer delight of drawing has its way in the drawing. That also is a quality the imitator can't imitate. The personal abstraction, the rapport between subject and thought also are inimitable.

To an architect the whole world exists in his realm of architecture—when he passes a tree he does not see it as a botanist but relates it to his realm. He would draw this tree as he imagined it grew because he thinks of constructing. All the activities of man are in his realm, relating themselves to his own activity. A few years ago I visited Carcassonne. From the moment I entered the gates, I began to write with drawing, the images which I learned about now presenting themselves to me like realized dreams. I began studiously to memorize in line the proportions and the living details of these great buildings. I spent the whole day in the courts, on the ramparts, and in the towers, diminishing my care about the proper proportions and exact details. At the close of the day I was inventing shapes and placing buildings in different relationships than they were. . . . The sketch book of painter, sculptor, and architect should differ. The painter sketches to paint, the sculptor draws to carve and the architect draws to build.

On Stopping Our Pencils

In Gothic times, architects built in solid stones. Now we can build with hollow stones. The spaces defined by the members of a structure are as important as the members. These spaces range in scale from the voids of an insulation panel, voids for air, lighting, and heat to circulate, to spaces big enough to walk through or live in. The desire to express voids positively in the design of structure is evidenced by the growing interest and work in the development of space frames. The forms being experimented with come from a closer knowledge of nature and the outgrowth of the constant search for order. Design habits leading to the concealment of structure have no place in this implied order. Such habits retard the development of an art. I believe that in architecture, as in all art, the artist instinctively keeps the marks which reveal how a thing was done. The feeling that our present-day architecture needs embellishment stems in part from our tendency to fair joints out of sight, to conceal how parts are put together. Structures should be devised which can harbor the mechanical needs of rooms and spaces. Ceilings with structure furred in tend to erase scale. If we were to train ourselves to draw as we build, from the bottom up, when we do, stopping our pencil to make a mark at the joints of pouring or erecting, ornament would grow out of our love for ducts, conduits, and pipe lines by pasting acoustical material over structure. The sense of structure of the building and how the spaces are served would be lost. The desire to express how it is done would filter through the entire society of building, to architect, engineer, builder, and craftsmen.

On Winking at Chapels

As a problem in architecture, consider a chapel of a university. Is it a space divided for denominations of set ritual or is it a single space for inspired ritual? In search of form for such a chapel, its concept may come from how you think about its undefined nature. To invent a circumstance, let us imagine the feelings of a student of architecture after an inspiring criticism. Full of dedication to his art, he passes the chapel and winks at it; he doesn't go in, he winks at it. This is inspired ritual.

The chapel has a central space which for the moment we won't describe; around it is an ambulatory for those who don't want to enter. Outside the ambulatory is an arcade for those not in the ambulatory; the arcade overlooks a garden for those not in the arcade. The garden has a wall for those who don't enter and merely wink at the chapel.

On the Limits of Architecture

Giotto was a great painter. Because he was an artist he painted the skies black for the daytime and he painted birds that couldn't fly and dogs that couldn't run, and he made men bigger than doorways. A painter has this prerogative. He does not have to answer to the problems of gravity, or represent images as we know them in real life. As a painter he expresses a reaction to Nature, and he teaches us through his eyes and reactions about the nature of man. Again, a sculptor is one who modifies space with objects expressive of his reactions to Nature. Architecture nevertheless has limits. When we touch the invisible walls of its limits, then we know more about what is contained by them. A painter can paint square wheels on a cannon to express the futility of war. A sculptor can carve the same square wheels. But an architect must use round wheels. Though painting and sculpture play a beautiful role in the realm of architecture, just as architecture plays a beautiful role in the realms of painting and sculpture, they do not have the same discipline. One may say that architecture is the thoughtful making of spaces. It is not the filling of areas prescribed by a client. It is the creating of spaces that evoke a feeling for appropriate use.

On Winking at Wonder

Form comes from wonder. Wonder stems from our "in touchness" with how we were made. One senses that nature records the process of what it makes, so that in what it makes there is also the record of how it was made. In touch with this record we are in wonder. This wonder gives rise to knowledge. But knowledge is related to other knowledge and this relation gives a sense of order, a sense of how they interrelate in a harmony that makes all things exist. From knowledge to sense of order we then wink at wonder and say, "How am I doing, wonder?"

On Interplay in Architecture

My medical research building at the University of Pennsylvania incorporates this realization that science laboratories are essentially studios and that the air to be breathed must be separated from stale, waste air. The normal plan for laboratories places the work areas along one side of a central corridor, the other side of which houses the stairs, elevators, animal quarters, ducts, and other facilities. In such a corridor there is mixed together with the air you breathe the outflow of contaminated, dangerous air. The only distinction between one man's work space and that of another is the difference in numbers on their doors. For the university, I designed three studio towers in which each man may work in his own bailiwick. Each studio in these towers has its own escape subtower and exhaust subtower for the release of isotope air, germ-infected air, and noxious gases. A central building around which the three major towers cluster serves as the area for facilities, usually to be found on the opposite side of the corridor in the normal plan. This central building has nostrils for the intake of fresh air located far from the exhaust subtowers for vitiated air. This design, the result of consideration of the unique uses to be made of its spaces and their service requirements, expresses the character of the research laboratory. From what I have said I do not mean to imply a system of thought and work leading to realization from form to design. Design could just as well lead to realization in form. This interplay is the constant excitement of architecture.

On "House" and "A House" and "Home"

Form is *what*. Design is *how*. Form is impersonal, but design belongs to the designer. Design is prescribed by circumstances—how much money there is available, the site, the client, the extent of skill and knowledge. Form has nothing to do with such conditions. In architecture, it is a harmony of spaces good enough for a certain activity of man. Reflect, then, on the abstract characteristics of "house" or "home." "House" stands for the abstract concept of spaces good to live in. "House" is thus a form in the mind, without shape or dimension. "A house," on the other hand, is a conditioned interpretation of living space. This is design. In my opinion, the greatness of an architect depends more on his power to realize that which is "house" than on his ability to design "a house"—something prescribed by circumstances. "Home" is the house and its occupants. It becomes different with each occupant. The client for whom a house is designed states the areas he needs. The architect creates spaces out of these required areas. Such a house, created for a particular family, must, if its design is to reflect trueness to form, have the character of being good for another family.

On the Future of Architecture

The city is made up of institutions—that which has been established and is supportable by all men. Education, government, the home are such institutions. When an architect begins his work, the building he is about to design must present itself as belonging to an institution. Even before satisfying the client's specific needs, the force of the institution in society should be the background of his architectural decisions. I cannot predict the architecture of the future. We can only work within the laws we comprehend now. The architecture will be based on new rules as the system of laws becomes more and more part of a new comprehension of physical order and the nature of man.

On Law and Rules

Man makes rules which are of the laws of nature and of the spirit. Physical nature is of law. The laws of nature work in harmony with each other. Order is this harmony. Without a knowledge of the law, without a feeling for the law, nothing can be made. Nature is the maker of all things, the psyche desires things and challenges nature to make that which expresses the inexpressible, that which cannot be defined, that which has no measure, that which has no substance—love, hate, nobility. Still the psyche wants to express just that and cannot without an instrument. Law is the maker of instruments. The violin—beautiful out of the law, how the upper and lower diaphragm of the violin lends itself to the stresses of a bow, and the vertical strip dividing the two membranes are in a sense a continuous column. Even the sound holes in the upper diaphragm are cut so that little of the continuity of the beam is lost. Law leads to rules. A rule is subject to change, being man-made.

On Things Disliked

I do not like ducts; I do not like pipes. I hate them really thoroughly, but because I hate them so thoroughly, I feel they have to be given their place. If I just hated them and took no care, I think they would invade the building and completely destroy it. I want to correct any notion you may have that I am in love with that kind of thing.

On Designing Schools

Schools began with a man under a tree, a man who did not know he was a teacher, discussing his realization with a few others who did not know they were students. The students reflected on the exchanges between them and how good it was to be in the presence of this man. They wished their sons, also, to listen to such a man. Soon, the needed spaces were erected and the first schools came into existence. The establishment of schools was inevitable because they are part of the desires of man. Our vast systems of education, now vested in institutions, stem from these little schools, but their spirit is now forgotten. The rooms required by our institutions of learning are stereotyped and uninspiring.

The actual classrooms . . . should not follow the usual soldierlike dimensional similarity but should invoke use through their spatial variety, for one of the most wonderful aspects of the spirit of man under the tree is its recognition of the singularity of every man. A teacher or student is not the same with a few, in an intimate room with a fireplace, as in a large high room with many others. And must the cafeteria be in the basement, even if it is not in use so much of the time? Is not the relaxing moment of the meal also a part of learning? A realization of what particularizes the domain of spaces ideal for "school" would make the designing of an institution of learning challenge the architect and awaken in him an awareness of what "school" wants to be, which is the same as saying an awareness of the form: school.

"Not for the Fainthearted," reprinted from *AIA Journal*, vol. 55, no. 6, June 1971, pp. 25–31; reproduced with the permission of The American Institute of Architects, 1735 New York Avenue, Washington, DC 20006.

The Room, the Street, and Human Agreement

1971 American Institute of Architects Gold Medal Award Address

I have some thoughts about the spirit of architecture. I have chosen to talk about the room, the street, and human agreement.

The room is the beginning of architecture. It is the place of the mind. You in the room with its dimensions, its structure, its light respond to its character, its spiritual aura, recognizing that whatever the human proposes and makes becomes a life.

The structure of the room must be evident in the room itself. Structure, I believe, is the giver of light. A square room asks for its own light to read the square. It would expect the light either from above or from its four sides as windows or entrances.

Sensitive is the Pantheon. This nondirectional room dedicated to all religions has its light only from the oculus above, placed to invest the room with inspired ritual without favoritism. The entrance door is its only impurity. So powerful was this realization of appropriate space that even now the room seems to ask for its release to its original freedom.

Of the elements of a room, the window is the most marvellous. The great American poet Wallace Stevens prodded the architect, asking, "What slice of the sun does your building have?" To paraphrase: What slice of the sun enters your room? What range of mood does the light offer from morning to night, from day to day, from season to season and all through the years?

Gratifying and unpredictable are the permissions that the architect has given to the chosen opening, on which patches of sunlight play on the jamb and sill and that enter, move, and disappear.

Stevens seems to tell us that the sun was not aware of its wonder until it struck the side of a building.

Enter your room and know how personal it is, how much you feel its life. In a small room with just another person, what you say may never have been said before. It is different when there is more than just another person. Then, in this little room, the singularity of each is so sensitive that the vectors do not resolve. The meeting becomes a performance instead of an event with everyone saying his lines, saying what has been said many times before.

Still, in a large room, the event is of commonalty. Rapport would take the place of thought. This room we are in now is big, without distinction. The walls are far away. Yet I know if I were to address myself to a chosen person, the walls of the room would come together and the room would become intimate. If I were now reading, the concern would be diction.

If this room were the Baptistry of Florence, its image would have inspired thoughts in the same way as person to person, architect to architect. So sensitive is a room.

The plan is a society of rooms. The rooms relate to each other to strengthen their own unique nature. The auditorium wants to be a violin. Its envelope is the violin case. The society of room is the place where it is good to learn, good to work, good to live.

Open before us is the architect's plan. Next to it is a sheet of music. The architect fleetingly reads his composition as a structure of elements and spaces in their light.

The musician reads with the same overallness. His composition is a structure of inseparable elements and spaces in sound. A great musical composition is of such entity that when played it conveys the feeling that all that was heard was assembled in a cloud over us. Nothing is gone, as though time and sound have become a single image.

The corridor has no position except as a private passage. In a school, the boy walks across a hall as in his own classroom where he is his own teacher, observing others as others do. The hall asks for equal position with the library.

The society of rooms is knit together with the elements of connection which have their own characteristics.

The stair is the same for the child, the adult, and the old. It is thought of as precise in its measures, particularly for the young boy who aspires to do the floors in no time flat, both up and down. It is good also to consider the stair landing as a place to sit near a window with possibly a shelf for a few books. The old man ascending with the young boy can stop here, showing his interest in a certain book, and avoid the explanations of infirmity. The landing wants to be a room.

A bay window can be the private room within a room. A closet with a window becomes a room ready to be rearranged. The lightless corridor, never a room, aspires to the hall overlooking the garden.

The library, the work court, the rooms of study, the place of meeting want to group themselves in a composition that evokes architecture. The libraries of all university schools sit well in a court entrance available to all its students as a place of invitation. The entrance courts and their libraries and the gardens and paths knitting them together form an architecture of connection. The book is an offering of the mind.

The work court of a school of architecture is an inner space encircled by workshops available to construct building experiments. The rooms of study and criticism are of a variety of dimension and spaces in their light, small for the intimate talk and work, and large for the making of full-size drawings and group work.

Rooms must suggest their use without name. To an architect, a school of architecture would be the most honored commission.

The street is a room of agreement. The street is dedicated by each house owner to the city in exchange for common services.

Dead-end streets in cities today still retain this room character. Through-streets, since the advent of the automobile, have entirely lost their room quality. I believe that city planning can start with realization of this loss by directing the drive to reinstate the street where people live, learn, shop, and work as the room out of commonalty.

Today, we can begin by planting trees on all existing residential streets, by redefining the order of movement which would give these streets back to more intimate use which would stimulate the feelings of well-being and inspire unique street expression.

The street is a community room.

The meeting house is a community room under a roof. It seems as though one came naturally out of the other.

A long street is a succession of rooms given their distinction, room for room, by their meeting of crossing streets. The intersecting street brings from afar its own developed nature which infiltrates any opening it meets. One block in a stream of blocks can be more preferred because of its particular life. One realizes the deadliness of uninterested movement through our streets which erases all delicacy of character and blots out its sensitive nature given to it of human agreement.

Human agreement is a sense of rapport, of commonness, of all bells ringing in unison—not needing to be understood by example but felt as an undeniable inner demand for a presence. It is an inspiration with the promise of the possible.

Dissension does not stem from need but from the mad outburst of frustration, from the hopelessness of the farawayness of human agreement. Desire, not need, the forerunner of the new need, out of the yet not said and the yet not made, seems to be the roots of hope in dissension.

How inspiring would be the time when the sense of human agreement is felt as the force which brings new images. Such images reflecting inspirations and put into being by inspired technology. Basing our challenges on present-day programming and existing technologies can only bring new facets of old work.

The city from a simple settlement became the place of the assembled institutions. The settlement was the first institution. The talents found their places. The carpenter directed building. The thoughtful man became the teacher, the strong one the leader.

When one thinks of simple beginnings which inspired our present institutions, it is evident that some drastic changes must be made which will inspire the recreation of the meaning, *city*, as primarily an assembly of those places vested with the care to uphold the sense of a way of life.

Human agreement has always been and will always be. It does not belong to measurable qualities and is, therefore, eternal. The opportunities which present its nature depend on circumstances and on events from which human nature realizes itself.

A city is measured by the character of its institutions. The street is one of its first institutions. Today, these institutions are on trial. I believe it is so because they have lost the inspirations of their beginning. The institutions of learning must stem from the undeniable feeling in all of us of a desire to learn. I have often thought that this feeling came from the way we were made, that nature records in everything it makes how it was made. This record is also in man and it is this within us that urges us to seek its story involving the laws of the universe, the source of all material and means, and the psyche which is the source of all expression. Art.

266

THE ROOM, THE STREET, AND HUMAN AGREEMENT

The desire to learn made the first school room. It was of human agreement. The institution became the modus operandi. The agreement has the immediacy of rapport, the inspiring force which recognizes its commonalty and that it must be part of the human way of life supported by all people.

The institution will die when its inspirations are no longer felt and when it operates as a matter of course. Human agreement, however, once it presents itself as a realization, is indestructible. For the same reason a man is unable to work below his level of comprehension. To explain inspiration, I like to believe that it is the moment of possibility when what to do meets the means of doing it.

City planning must begin to be cognizant of the strength and character of our present institutions and be sensitive to the pulse of human relationship which senses the new inspirations which would bring about new and meaningful institutions. Traffic systems, sociological speculations, new materials, new technologies are servants to the pulse of human rapport which promises revelations yet not felt but in the very core of human desires.

New spaces will come only from a new sense of human agreements—new agreements which will affirm a promise of life and will reveal new availabilities and point to human support for their establishment.

I realized in India and Pakistan that a great majority of the people are without ambition because there is no way in which they are able to elevate themselves beyond living from hand to mouth, and what is worse, talents have no outlets. To express is the reason for living. The institution of learning, of work, of health, of recreation should be made available to all people. All realms of expression will be opened. Each singularity will express in his way. Availabilities to all can be the source of a tremendous release of the values locked in us of the unmeasurable in living: the art of living.

One city can distinguish itself from the other by just the inspirational qualities that exist in sensing natural agreements as the only true source of new realizations. In that sense the spaces where it is good to learn, to work and to live may remain unexpressed if their nature is not redefined. It is not just enough to solve the problem. To imbue the spaces with new-found self-quality is a different question entirely. Solution is a "how" design problem; the realization of "what" precedes it.

Now a word about inspired technology. The wall enclosed us for a long time until the man behind it, feeling a new freedom, wanted to look out. He hammered away to make an opening. The wall cried, "I have protected you." And the man said, "I appreciate your faithfulness but I feel time has brought change."

The wall was sad; the man realized something good. He visualized the opening as gracefully arched, glorifying the wall. The wall was pleased with its arch and carefully made jamb. The opening became part of the order of the wall

267

The world with its many people, each one a singularity, each group of different experiences revealing the nature of the human in varied aspects, is full of the possibility of more richly sensing human agreement from which new architecture will come. The world cannot be expected to come from the exercise of present technology alone to find the realms of new expression. I believe that technology should be inspired. A good plan demands it.

A word about silence and light. A building being built is not yet in servitude. It is so anxious to be that no grass can grow under its feet, so high is the spirit of wanting to be. When it is in service and finished, the building wants to say, "Look, I want to tell you about the way I was made." Nobody listens. Everybody is busy going from room to room.

But when the building is a ruin and free of servitude, the spirit emerges telling of the marvel that a building was made.

When we think of great buildings of the past that had no precedent, we always refer to the Parthenon. We say that it is a building that grew out of the wall with opening. We can say that in the Parthenon light is the space between the columns— a rhythm of light, no-light, light, no-light which tells the tremendous story of light in architecture that came from the opening in a wall.

We are simply extending what happened long ago: the beginning may be considered the most marvellous: without precedent, yet its making was as sure as life.

Light is material life. The mountains, the streams, the atmosphere are spent light.

Material, nonconscious, moving to desire; desire to express, conscious, moving to light meet at an aura threshold where the will senses the possible. The first feeling was of beauty, the first sense was of harmony, of man undefinable, unmeasurable and measurable material, the maker of all things.

At the threshold, the crossing of silence and light, lies the sanctuary of art, the only language of man. It is the treasury of the shadows. Whatever is made of light casts a shadow. Our work is of shadow; it belongs to light.

When the astronauts went through space, the earth presented itself as a marvellous ball, blue and rose, in space. Since I followed it and saw it that way, all knowledge left me as being unimportant. Truly, knowledge is an incomplete book outside of us. You take from it to know something, but knowing cannot be imparted to the next man. Knowing is private. It gives singularity the means for self-expression.

I believe that the greatest work of man is that part which does not belong to him alone. If he discovers a principle, only his design way of interpreting belongs to him alone. The discovery of oxygen does not belong to the discoverer.

I invented a story about Mozart. Somebody dropped a dish in his kitchen, and it made a hell of a noise. The servants jumped, and Mozart said, "Ah! Dissonance."

268

And immediately dissonance belonged to music, and the way Mozart wrote interpreting it belonged to him.

Architects must not accept the commercial divisions of their profession into urban design, city planning, and architecture as though they were three different professions. The architect can turn from the smallest house to the greatest complex, or the city. Specializing ruins the essence of the revelation of the form with its inseparable parts realized only as an entity.

A word about beauty. Beauty is an all-prevailing sense of harmony, giving rise to wonder; from it, revelation. Poetry. Is it in beauty? Is it in wonder? Is it revelation?

It is in the beginning, in first thought, in the first sense of the means of expression.

A poet is in thought of beauty and existence. Yet a poem is only an offering, which to the poet is less.

A work of architecture is but an offering to the spirit architecture and its poetic beginning.

"The Room, the Street, and Human Agreement," reprinted from *AIA Journal*, vol. 56, no. 3 September 1971, pp. 33–34; reproduced with the permission of The American Institute of Architects, 1735 New York Avenue, NW, Washington, DC 20006.

Louis I. Kahn at the Theater of the Performing Arts in Fort Wayne, Indiana, 1973 (Photo: Gabril R. Delobbe).

┌─────────────┐
│ 1972 │
└─────────────┘

Architecture

The John William Lawrence Memorial Lectures

This, of course, is immensely important to me because of the
(can you hear?)

AUDIENCE: "Yes." "No."
KAHN: "Can you hear now?"

I just want to say the word, John Lawrence,
means a great deal.
It means a great deal because
he could communicate without speaking.
As soon as you would meet John
you knew he was your friend.
There was a kind of rapport,
an immediacy of rapport,
the quality of which I would like to talk
about in the sense of human agreement.
He had it; the entire feeling,
the embodiment of what it means.

(I have to stay away from these lights, if you don't mind. I think I will be much
more comfortable here. I'm not in the limelight and that makes me very comfortable.
You don't have to see me you just have to hear me talk.)

It was just that he was the embodiment of the sense of human agreement

270

and I want to talk about human agreement.
I think I cannot say more for a person
than to say he has the quality,
the immediacy of the quality,
of human agreement.
The quality, which makes understanding complete, without example.
It is just this quality
which though the image of the quality
is different in each individual,
it still has the force of complete agreement. It's almost the same kind of agreement
that one would say, "It's a nice day."
And though there may have been areas of misery behind one individual,
and may mean the joy of having passed over the admirations of the other,
the agreement is quite the same.
Someone taught me that symbolism was the period between life and death—
that the man on the battlefield who had absolutely no education
and one who had many degrees,
felt the force of the cross deeply.
He felt this was symbolism;
when it was understood in terms that had nothing to do with information on others.
But it almost seems too ponderous to speak of it in those terms,
to say of a joyous character that John
—I would say is—
because I feel his presence very much, and his great eyebrows,
and his eager and joyous face,
and you can't think of anything but in terms of the great continuity,
the great continuum.
Nothing is destroyed.
I don't believe anything is destroyed in nature,
nor do I believe anything is destroyed in the way of anything living.
To me the question of why anything,
makes that quite conclusive,
that nothing is destroyed.
We wonder what is that is the great continuum,
but I sense it through the very field of expression
which John belonged to as well as myself.
Questions in class today about where is Architecture going
were very easy to answer because it is not going anywhere else

but than it ever was
and I mentioned that what it is has always been,
what will be has always been
and what is has always been.
Because it is remarkable that a field of expression comes about
because it could not have come about
unless it was in the nature of man.
And if it does come about, it is completely indestructible.
So one questions, is the field going to change—
is the profession going to change?
I would say yes.
The profession is certainly going to change;
but Architecture isn't going to change.
In other words, Architecture really has no presence.
It is a spirit, yes.
Only a work of Architecture has presence.
But Architecture itself is constantly waiting for a new aspect of it,
which by the way always is, always was, always will be, to
present itself through the singular genius of an individual
or the singular inspirations of a group.

Today I distinguished desire from need—
that need is a temporary, measurable thing.
There is no denial that need is disgraceful not to give.
But desire is insatiable,
and presents itself in many, many aspects,
always new because it is completely unmeasurable and unpredictable.
Only circumstance brings it out
and it always surprises as another aspect of the nature of man.

I had to write about a thought I had
about the inspirations, the desire to be, to express,
which is the real reason for living,
and the means to express,
and I thought of the whole area of the source from which to be was desired
as that being the aura of silence.
Silence,
the wordless,
soundless,

murmur of the desire to be, to express.
And I thought all material being spent light.
Light as a prevalence of the luminous which I cannot conceive as being material.
But entering a wild dance of flame which spent itself and became material.
So the mountains are spent light,
the air is spent light,
the streams are spent light
and we are spent light.
If we visualize a pull, or an attraction,
between the desire to be, to express,
meeting at a point of a threshold.
the means to express being nature itself,
the material means meeting at the same threshold
as silence went to light and light went to silence
and this is the moment of inspiration.
It is the place of the inspirations.
It is the place, or rather you might say the aura,
at this juncture,
of silence to light,
light to silence.
The inspirations, which merely means the desire to be, to express, meets the possible.
When I think of that, I can't think of problems.
Problems incidental now,
problems incidental yesterday,
or what will come.
Because it will all be the same.
There will always be problems.
But the guiding motivation is that anything is possible
because we were possible.
When one thinks from such an aura of the intangible came something that was tangible,
then what can't nature make?
What can't it make?
It's just impossible to think that it cannot make anything that comes from man.
Man can think of the most fantastic
and one must say because he does, it's possible.
I think the wish in the fairy tale is the beginning of science.
So what is science
if not coming from the great desires;

and what is Art,
but in that very threshold of silence and light,
the place of the inspirations,
wherein actually you can say is the sanctuary of art,
the seat of the unmeasurable,
and also the seat of the measurable.
Where both meet is Art.
Where the incredible meets the possible.

On the Board of the Bicentennial I was given a long list of particulars
which many of its members had gotten together—
had gotten up, which would cover any possible subject, or area of study, or concern.
The world now has, so the centennial can express itself fully in this trying time.
It was a very, very long list.
They asked me to look at this list,
to add to it what they may have left out about Architecture.
I said surely.
I said this is a long list,
but it's not long enough.
And I said it would never be long enough.
If you can think of such a list,
or such a statement,
which would not require a list,
maybe you would be all comprising.
And at that moment I had to answer what this is
and I thought of the three inspirations.

I said the inspiration to learn was one.
As though it were something within us that actually desired learning.
And this desire was a natural force,
an inspiring force, to learn.
And I made a little footnote to this
saying that this had nothing to do with education.

The second was the inspiration to meet.
And I said all your particulars about city planning
are only one little iota of what it means
in the inspiration to meet.
The city is only a part of the inspiration to meet.
It has nothing to do with traffic solutions,

population studies,
social predictions,
business ventures—
nothing at all.
Here are just servants to the whole sense of meeting.
I said if you realized that a store was a meeting of the customer and one who sells.
I think the first thing, probably, the storekeeper would do, is serve coffee.
And the store design would be very different.
The inspiration to meet has in it tremendous architectural attitudes.
It is the human thing—
not the technology;
but the human thing,
the human quality,
which is that inspiration to meet,
that very thing you can write thesis after thesis, after thesis,
just on the sense that it stems from a place to meet.
It's desire, it's a hunger; an insatiable hunger.
It is part of desire.
Need is just so many bananas.

And the third was the inspiration for well-being
which includes all of medicine,
which includes your desire to excel, prowess, a tremendous thing.
There isn't a boy who doesn't think in terms of prowess.
He thinks in terms of flying through the air without the aid of wings.
It's the fairy tale that is so important.
I know if I were to think of changing my profession at this moment
(and it's a pretty hard thing to think of, first of all, it's probably too late)
I would think of one thing—
that I would love to write the new fairy tales.
Because I know that it would be more inspiring
than all the technological questions that we think so much of today,
which are just servants
just another hammer and another nail
and are of very little consequence
including all the statistics in the world
because they are only based on things as they are.
And that's purely circumstantial,

everything is very, very wrong,
and we take the wrong and make some kind of a record of it,
as people take traffic counts of the purely circumstantial condition of a street,
which has nothing to do with the series of faults;
but if you think of the street as a meeting place,
if you think of a street as being really a community inn
that just doesn't have a roof.
And if you think of a meeting hall,
it is just a street with a roof on it.
If you think of it in terms of meeting.
And the walls of this meeting place called the community room,
the street,
are just the fronts of the houses,
and the streets were dedicated by the houses to the city for their use.
Today those streets are disinterested movements
not at all belonging to the houses that front them.
So you have no streets.
You have roads;
but you have no streets.
To bring back the streets;
to make redefined movement, and place movement in an order of movement,
where the street takes its rightful position
as belonging to the community of communication.
I think you can straighten out your plans very easily.
I would start with that, very simply.
You just are really defining the rightful demand of houses to bring their streets back.
I think the character of the streets would change enormously if that were done.
School is a meeting place.
It is a place good to learn.
If you would rule out corridors in a school,
and substitute halls from classroom to classroom,
the hall would become a classroom,
and probably would vie with the library for equal importance.
It's the free place,
where boy meets girl, or boy meets the other boy,
speculating on just what a man is.
Being free of the servitude of lessons and judgments,
this room could be given a course position like any other course.

In the making of rooms there is the core of Architecture.
I would say that Architecture stems from the making of a room.
A room is so sensitive
that you would not say the same thing in a small room as you would in a large one.
In fact, if you are only with one person in a room,
it might become generative
because the ventures of two people can make you say what you never said before,
because you are not in an atmosphere of performance
as you would be if another person, besides the one, were present.
The vectors would become tremendously confused
and you would turn an event which could happen with two people into a performance
in which you are just saying your lines,
calmly putting the second act third just for your own amusement.
But then the same lines with two people
are likely to be very, very different.
Wallace Stevens,
who was an insurance salesman, and poet,
and a man who aspired to be an architect,
wrote some verses, on Architecture.
He said it on having written some verses, highly imaginative.
He said to the architects:
What slice of the sun does your building have?
And one could paraphrase by saying,
what slice of the sun enters your room?
As if to say,
the sun never knew how great it was until it struck the side of a building.
Just so one must think of Architecture—
not the operational aspects of it:
how many, how much,
prefabrication,
profession.
Where is Architecture going?
You might ask yourself where are you going.
Architecture can wait
thousands of years
because its presence in this world is indestructible.
If you want to not feel the edges of its inspiration,
that's your hard luck.

A plan is a society of rooms.
The rooms talk to each other
and they make up their minds where their positions are.
And they must aspire, each room, to be as all comprising,
as all rapport, with its nature.
It must be itself without being named beforehand.
If you name a room before it becomes a room, it dies;
because it becomes just another item.
To say I'm going to make a living room, it should be here;
you don't think of the room in the proper way then.
Because if you think of it in terms of a room,
where you might have a bay window,
because it makes a room within a room,
where a person momentarily dissatisfied with himself can sort of sulk for a moment,
even in the presence of company.
And the fireplace,
not just something that you crib from a book,
but think all over again
as being a part of such a place which fulfills the nature, living room.
Think of a stairway,
think of a stairway as an inseparable part of a two-story area.
You know that each riser and tread must be as accurate as a micrometer caliper.
Because the young guy,
who wants to climb the three stories in no time flat,
must be led by the rhythm of the stair and trust it,
so he cannot fail
because he has all the powers of coordination and depends on it.
And that same stair must be good for the child,
for the young man and for the old person.
And one characteristic of the stair,
that of the landing,
must be solved with such care that the landing can rise to the point
where it itself becomes a room,
where there would be a little bookcase,
where there would be a place to sit,
and have a window.
Why?
Because the old man can then ascend the stair with a child,

and he says to the child, "You know, I always wanted to read that book
and I think I'll rest for a moment and look at it."

The young boy climbed readily up the stair
while the old man never really admitted that he couldn't quite make it.
But it must be that kind of sensitivity put to the elements of a work of Architecture.
Each inseparable part of the nature of the society of rooms
has to be regarded as not knowing its mysteries until you have,
in all freshness,
without references,
just by the simple feeling of the wonder of its first invention that you reconsider it.
You know nothing about it,
until it has become part of you.

The measure of a city,
in the sense of it being part of the inspiration of meeting,
is what results from the meeting,
and what is sought in an inseparable part
of such a meeting sensed by human agreement.
It is human agreement;
it is the inspiration which comes from human agreement,
which gives us our schools,
our places of government,
our places of health,
recreation.
Those things are not surrendered.
Or rather, the surrender to the financing of such things
would not be readily given,
unless it were really an inseparable part of human agreement.
You support it because you cannot deny it support.

Now the first spaces named to make such places available and support it
were always nothing short of being a miracle
because they had no precedents.
I believe we must start our present buildings as though there is precedent—
to discover the spaces where it is good to learn,
good to work,
good to live in.
We call these places institutions.

Maybe today we like to think of them as being establishments.
And it's true they are but establishments.
Think of the village green.
Where is the village green?
Is the city hall the village green?
Should there not be a realm of auditoria, which is the village green?
Shouldn't there be the city place,
which the mayor inherits and part of his sense of wanting to be a mayor,
is partly due to the feelings of well-being
of inheriting the city place as part of his trust,
where,
if a dignitary comes to town,
he does not send him to a commercial hotel
but he lives in the city place,
where people who want to meet as part of their civic contributions
would find a place to meet instead of meeting in sundry places
and reporting every month or so the balance in the treasury
of ninety-four dollars and sixty-four cents.
So the original sense of institution
sometimes falls by the wayside by rush of enterprise,
the excitement of all that;
but the growing of the new,
let's say,
places where the inspirations to meet express themselves as availabilities.
. . . . . .
I'll cut the sentence off by simply thinking of school as really a religious place
where such matters are thought about
because in the market place you can't think of it,
but to prepare yourself for the marketplace,
which has a very destroying . . . .
and therein also is the source of your expression,
that you stand with much to offer
because your mind is full of the vast incompletenesses around us,
of the inspirations to learn,
to meet
and that of well-being,
constantly there waiting for someone to express it
as not manifest in the present institutions of man.

280

So the institutions are really on trial
because they have lost their original inspirations
and they have simply become operational.
And very little is done to revive it with more of the qualities
that it had initially but live for the qualities which were expressed before
and then just simply ride along with the blow as time goes on.
Every one of our institutions needs reviving
and the human agreement that made them possible still exists.
It's an indestructible thing,
human agreement;
but what doesn't exist is the constant efforts to the inspirations to express,
which you should be motivated by in reviving again the three inspirations,
and I say three inspirations
because I can't find the fourth.
I don't know what it is.

The measure of a city is its institutions.
Institution merely means that you are supporting something.
You have said it is part of a way of life.
This country is the richest country of all countries in availabilities.
You can call it institutions if you like and availabilities.
When I work in India and Pakistan, there are no availabilities.
(This reminds me very much of all the Schools of Architecture.)

I really feel that the Schools of Architecture
must be devoted primarily in a program of what these inspirations can bring forth.
What truly is an availability?
It is the place of availability.
And the city is not something that is going to die.
I was told the other day that Venice,
which is certainly what you would consider an old city,
is the youngest city in Italy.
There was during the time of its heyday an undeniable force of people.
When they came there, learned from other people.
They saw themselves through others.
We must make our cities great.
I think we must take them out of the hands of (what can I call them?)
money-changers, I guess,
and to make every building count

as contributing to the connections of our spaces
which reflect the inspirations of man.
How can we build on a theory of spaces
which really should be part of a treasury of spaces—
every space being considered in their best light
as only worthy to be in a city.
So that those who offered the original space,
because they were capable,
by their minds and by their enterprise,
must in the end offer it to the city
because every important place in the city everybody else wants to be.
It cannot be as the die is cast,
nor as the dice were rolled.
An important place in town belongs to everybody.
It may be necessary that an office building surrender its first six stories
for the sake of its civic position—
your library may be below, or maybe some auditoria.
I think the idea let's say of other facilities, like even a bank;
because a bank just as much belongs to a way of life as does a school.
So we don't have these terrible artificialities of calling places cultural centers
just because it has an auditorium and an art gallery
and I don't know what else it has—a statue.
I think the bank is part of our culture.
If it is, it wouldn't take such a prissy attitude.
It's part of it, as the shop is.
I think the art gallery belongs in town—not on a podium.

Art is just the only language of man.
Because it is the one language which tries to encompass the unmeasurable.
And all language really, fundamentally, tries to do nothing but unmeasure
—so it is more encompassing.
As soon as it becomes measurable it becomes very, very limited.
Reflect on the tremendous value of the word "good,"
and then say "very good,"
and tell me which is more powerful.
"Good" is infinitely more powerful than "very good."
Already the measurable sneaks in and depicts it less.
The language of man is Art.

ARCHITECTURE

We were talking about schools
and I mentioned that I believed in the schools of talents—natural talent.
I said that a person who has a natural talent to dance beautifully
should be given the opportunity to extend this talent
and for the moment forget other requirements.
And you would soon see
because of the force of his being able to express himself in his natural talent
that he would on his own, study Latin.
I know, you see, when I went to school I studied Physics,
and when I wrote the notes of my teacher in front of me I didn't hear what he said.
All I did was to write notes.
Next to me sat a man who could listen to what was said.
and also write notes.
Now when I read my notes, after I wrote them,
I couldn't understand them,
so I copied the man's notes who could hear and also write notes.
And I passed my examination, not from what I wrote, what I read,
but from the notes of my next-door neighbor.
Because I had no talent to write notes and to listen at the same time.
Now if this teacher understood this he would have said to me,
"Now, Lou Kahn, you've got to attend your courses in Physics
because Physics is essential to the work that you are cut out to do.
But don't take notes.
Do anything, make drawings
—anything you want to.
But you will be examined
and I will ask you to draw Physics for me."
We might consider it.
There's something to it.
It's terribly exaggerated, I know,
but we're having fun, so . . . .

I have an advisor in front of me.
What do you want me to say?

MRS. KAHN: I can't hear you very well.

You can't hear me. Can you hear me? Is it difficult?
No, I didn't think so. Did you say yes?

MRS. KAHN: They can't hear in the back.

Can you hear back there?

AUDIENCE: Yes.

I simply have to straighten this out. You have no idea.

I know I wanted to talk about a lot more than this. And . . . .
I just want to mention the difference between the architect
and the profession of Architecture.
They are two different things.
I know they are different
because Michelangelo was not a professional architect.
And I know that I could never think of identifying Botticelli as a professional painter.
It's a kind of society recognizing those who have equal concerns;
but you can't expect support from such a society.
You've got to think of yourself as having;
all you have, to make the desire to express, which is the major,
or rather the only, motivation for living.
And it is that which is all important
and I think the people who are talking about committees deciding what to do
—you know the old story,
that a camel is a horse made by a committee.

It cannot be done.
The embodiment of the entire sense of something lies in the single individual,
who can with all that comes to him,
sense that quality of appropriateness without having to justify every part of it.
It just comes in a flash as being true
—and without having to prove it.
I mentioned in class today
that Einstein was that kind of designer—intuitive.
He knew it was right.
He knew that one could prove it
though he never really set out to prove it with the same finality that others tried;
in trying to destroy it, proved it to be true.
So there is great heart for the individual.
All you need is to reflect enough
and that one never learns anything that is not part of himself.

And that was certainly true in my case.
I know a few things;
but for all the courses I took I must say,
I can say truly, I know nothing.
But I did learn that it was a wonderful thing to know.
In that respect the school, I would say, is the synthesis.
But school is a great place.
I teach school because I think school is my chapel.
When I go to school,
I think my duty is to write Psalms.
And I don't know if I do or not;
but I certainly think of it that way.

I don't know; I think I've probably said enough.
Thank you very much.

"Architecture," The John William Lawrence Memorial Lectures, Tulane University School of Architecture, 1972 (New Orleans: Tulane University, 1972); reprinted with permission from The Louis I. Kahn Collection, University of Pennsylvania and Pennsylvania Historical and Museum Commission.

I Love Beginnings

Speech given at the International Design Conference, Aspen, Colorado, 1972

I love beginnings. I marvel at beginnings. I think it is beginning that confirms continuation. If it did not—nothing could be or would be. I revere learning because it is a fundamental inspiration. It isn't just something which has to do with duty; it is born into us. The will to learn, the desire to learn, is one of the greatest of inspirations. I am not that impressed by education. Learning, yes; education is something which is always on trial because no system can ever capture the real meaning of learning.

In my own search for beginnings a thought has recurred—generated by many influences—out of the realization that material is spent light. I likened the emergence of light to a manifestation of two brothers, knowing quite well that there are no two brothers, nor even One. But I saw that one is the embodiment of the desire *to be/to express;* and one (not saying "the other") is *to be/to be.* The latter is nonluminous; and "One" (prevailing) is luminous, and this prevailing luminous source can be visualized as becoming a wild dance of flame which settles and spends itself into material. Material, I believe, is spent light. The mountains, the earth, the streams, the air, and we ourselves are spent light. This is the center of our desires. The desire *to be/to express* is the real motivation for living. I believe there is no other.

I began by putting up a diagram calling the desire *to be/to express* silence; the other, light. And the movement of silence to light, light to silence, has many thresholds; many, many, many thresholds; and each threshold is actually a singularity. Each one of us has a threshold at which the meeting of light and silence lodges. And this threshold, this point of meeting, is the position (or the aura) of inspirations. Inspiration is where the desire *to be/to express* meets the possible. It is the maker of presences. Here also is the sanctuary of art, the center of the expressive urges and the means to expression.

When I first made this diagram, I made it to be read from left to right; and here it is in mirror-writing (to mystify and to evoke an even greater source than itself) and so as to put nothing in front of you that is really thoroughly readable; by this means you can strive to find something that even goes beyond this realization. Again, I am always looking for a source, a beginning. I know it's in my character to want to discover beginnings. I like English history, I have volumes of it, but I never read anything but the first volume, and even at that, only the first three or four chapters. And of course my only real purpose is to read Volume 0 (zero), you see, which has yet not been written. And it's a strange kind of mind that causes one to look for this kind of thing. I would say that such an image suggests the emergence of a mind. Your first feeling is that of beauty—(not the beautiful nor the very beautiful) just beauty itself. It is the moment, or you might say the aura, of perfect harmony. And from this aura of beauty—on its heels—comes wonder. The sense of wonder is so very important to us because it precedes knowing. It precedes knowledge. When the astronauts went into space and the earth appeared as a marble, blue and rose, I felt nothing was less important than knowing. Maybe knowledge was still important, but knowing certainly was not. Yet strangely enough Paris or Rome—the wonderful works of men, all of which came from circumstantial conditions—somehow diminish the importance of the mind as compared to the sense of wonder that seems to have prevailed at that time. I do think, however, that a toccata and fugue remained, because of the distance from measure that was kept. The immeasurable was the one thing that captivated the mind; the measurable makes very little difference. When we talk about pollution the worst part about it is that when you see a gentle stream polluted your sense of wonder about the stream leaves you. If you go to a stream where the water is still clear, you feel something ominous about being near a stream that will soon fall from its position of wonder. Never must that leave our minds and no substitutions, nothing operational, should be admitted; except matter, which should be there to help us look back and to wonder again. This relationship, to be of any worth at all, must remain constant and not be just an accumulation of so much knowing.

Let us consider the inspiration to learn. If you stop to think of other inspirations, it's pretty hard to find any. For instance, I mentioned that all city planners must be part of the inspiration to meet. But then when you think of school, it is also part of the inspiration to meet. There's another inspiration which is somehow on trial—as I prefer to express it—and that is, the inspiration to well-being. And well-being includes such things as ecology. Yet it mustn't be considered a subject like ecology, or anything else. It must be realized as something catastrophic tainting our sense of wonder, our instinct to meet to learn. You can see why the original inspirations surrounding architecture, when it first became something apparent, were unclassifiable except as a kind of inspired moment which later acquired a title. But its beginning didn't have a title. It just had an undeniable urge to be brought into being. And up to then, and I think it will always be that way, there was no such thing as Architecture; there was the spirit but no presence whatsoever. What does have presence is a *work* of architecture, which at best must be considered as an offering to Architecture itself if only because of the wonder of its beginning. So when people talk about architecture being in one niche and urban planning being in another, with "city" planning in a third, and environmental design in still another, these to me are purely marketplace divisions. And I feel it's very destructive if a man on his stationery says that he practices all these things. In the marketplace this constitutes a very great advantage. Yet a man who feels Architecture as a spirit, cannot title himself this way because he would consider it pure dissipation of his original inspirations. An architect can build a house and build a city in the same breath only if he thinks about both as part of a marvellous, expressive, and inspired realm. From the first feelings of beauty, or the first sense of it, and the wonder that follows comes realization. Realization stems from the way we were made because we had to employ all the laws of the universe in order to be. We hold within us the record of the decisions that make us particularly human. There is the psychic record; and there is the physical record together with the choices we made to satisfy this desire to be, which in turn directed itself to what we now are. I believe that this nucleus is in the leaf and in the microbe. It is in every living thing. There is consciousness, I feel, in all living things. How wonderful it would be—in order to really understand ourselves—if only we could capture what must be the consciousness of the rose. That must, perforce, have such beautiful simplicity that we would then be able, I think, to solve our problems in a kind of offertory glow as we cannot now do.

From this understanding of the process of realization comes *form*. Form is not shape. Shape is a design affair, but form is a realization of inseparable components. Design calls into being what realization—form—tells us. You could also say that form can be detected as the nature of something and design strives at a precise moment to employ the laws of nature in putting that into being, by allowing light to come into play. This resource of material that is to *make*, to call into being; this maker of presences is the element that puts the measurable into what you're doing. Until it is brought into play, everything is fundamentally and consistently unmeasurable. Whatever you leave then has both in it. At the moment a painting is made, and at that time only, can you say, "I don't like red," or "I like small canvases." Only then is existence revealed to be what thought "would be" or could give you. And thought, in turn, is revealed as having existence but no presence.

Design demands that one understand the *order*. When you are dealing, or designing in brick, you must ask brick what it wants, or what it can do. And if you ask brick what it wants, it will say, "Well, I like an arch." And then you say "But, uh, arches are difficult to make. They cost more money. I think you can use concrete across your opening equally as well." But the brick says, "Oh, I know, I know you're right, but you know, if you ask me what I like, I like an arch." And one says, "Well now, why be so stubborn, you know?" And the arch says, "May I just make one little remark? Do you realize that you are talking about a being, and a being in brick is an arch?" That's knowing the order. It's knowing it's nature. It's knowing what it can do. Respect that tremendously. If you're dealing with brick, don't use it as just a secondary choice, or because it's cheaper. No, you have got to put it into absolute glory, and that is the only position that it deserves. If you're dealing with concrete, you must know the order of nature, you must know the nature of concrete, what concrete really strives to be. Concrete really wants to be granite but can't quite manage. Reinforcing rods are the play of a marvellous secret worker that makes this so-called molten stone appear wonderfully capable—a product of the mind. Steel wants to tell you that it can be an insect in strength and the stone bridge that it is built like an elephant; but you know the beauty of both, harmony due to the extension of the material to its fullest capability. If you just cover a wall with stone, you feel that you've done something inferior, though that can be said for the very best of us. To get things right in your mind and then to act in the purest manner can isolate you very much. However, it is terribly important to make the move downward; it's made cautiously and in full knowledge that you're doing it.

288

Now, a group of architects were chosen to collaborate in the bicentennial plans for Philadelphia. Though it now seems like something that is not to be, I still want to tell you about it. It was pretty difficult to get all these so-called *prima donnas*, you know, to work in unison. But it was the way I had trained myself to think in terms of silence and light which made it possible for me to propose the scheme that finally everyone did select as representative of what we were trying to do. The original concept, before any of us got on the scene, was that of making a street (which I concur with absolutely and was the first to praise). A street is really a community room. It already has a tremendously binding character, and offers an immediate starting point instead of requiring you to think of the items you might say you see, like what should be in an exposition. We drew a building—looks pretty angry—but that is a building. It was a series of three buildings a little like this, it doesn't matter what the shapes are. This building was the court of expression and wants to be programmed by the great expressors (those who are interested in movies, printing, painting, sculpture, architecture—all the expressive urges). Another court was to be programmed by the great scientists who would be able to convey manifestations of light, air, water, and land. So we called this the "natural resources," or the court of natural sources. Here was the "forum of availabilities" connected by a great street with a canal in the center of it as well as other transportation. Near the street were alcoves which I'll draw quickly. They flanked the street with availabilities—auditoriums and various places that were the results of the meeting, you might say, of light and silence. The functions themselves played a minor role because the real participation was the offerings made on the street of these availabilities. The theory was to invite all people who are learning (and this doesn't stop with your college work). The offer was to anyone interested and it was particularly directed to those who have no notion of what availability is. The Indians, the Pakistanis—I would say, the Chinese—nationals of many African countries, in fact, the greater part of the world by far, do not share in the immediacy of availabilities. The availabilities were there to make possible the fulfillment of the expressive urges or instincts.

This brings us to city planning. I think a city is measured by the character of its availabilities. School provides one form of availability. I believe in talent schools for the development of natural talent; I believe if a boy, no matter how young, shows aptitudes toward dance, he should, before all else, be sent to dancing school. He will then avidly look for other schooling, but the center of his interest should be focused on whatever he naturally does well. One never learns anything that is not part of oneself, part of that "*One.*" Everything else you learn is just attached, just glued on, unless it has real substance in you. I believe that if one follows one's natural predilections, he will eventually learn even the most difficult of subjects merely because he has had the necessary freedom, given to him immediately. And school, above all other places, should be the center of freedom. There should be no judgment, no comparing one person with another. I believe that if you have a classroom of 30 students in which freedom reigns, you would have 30 teachers. Think of a corridorless school; instead of a passage, which a corridor is, you have a hall oriented to the garden, a hall that vies with the library for equal importance. Two fireplaces mark the ends of the hall, and there are window niches that allow for places one can go in the very midst of the meeting place which this student schoolroom (free of obligation) is. You would not find it in any ordinary program. It should be something which the architect, in his first reaction to being offered the opportunity to express a realm of space where it is good to learn, must begin all over again. Disregarding the program given to him, he must rediscover the nature of rooms where it is good to learn. He would never present a series of rooms called seminar rooms (1, 2, 3, 4, 5, 6, and so on) but would consider a seminar room as a discovery in itself. Such rooms would probably not be named for anything that appears on a plan. Instead, they would offer possible orientations from which one could choose the environment where it's good to talk about what you're talking about based on the number present. So with classrooms, so with the library which today has the disdainful title of "Information Center." How far that is from the original inspiration is unbelievable. The place has become "operational," as though information were that important. A book is tremendously important. Nobody ever paid for the price of a book, they only pay for the printing. But a book is actually an offering and must be regarded as such. If you give honor to the man who writes it, there is something in that which further induces the expressive powers of writing.

And while we are on the subject of "*natures*" . . . I am building a theater in Fort Wayne, Indiana, and having therefore observed theaters, I came to the conclusion that one must regard the auditorium and the stage as a violin, a sensitive instrument where one should be able to hear, even a whisper, without any amplification. The lobbies and all other adjunct spaces may be compared to the violin case. The violin and its case are completely different. Then going backstage, in many theaters I found nothing more than the inside of a wastebasket. As the actor emerges from this wastebasket, he seems pretty calm, as though nothing had happened, but behind stage the mop is right next to him. That is just hell. I decided then to think of it all as the actor's house and to design his house half a mile away from the theater, regarding the "Green Room" as the living room with its fireplace, the practice rooms, the dressing rooms, as if it were all a function of that house . . . I even installed a little chapel where a man could think of his lines alone without being prodded. Then outside this house I built a porch which faced the street, then wheeled that backstage and presented the porch of the house as what you see when the curtains open.

I was trying to discover the "nature" around which design was possible. This can also be thought of as what one does in building a house when one considers the bedroom as being in a field, with no roof so you can see the stars. The windows may be limited because the window is really above you. Then you discover that the room isn't just a sleeping room, but becomes a sick room; and when you need a cup of tea you long for the kitchen. Slowly, stealthily, the bedroom creeps to the kitchen, maybe even begs for forgiveness. The living room does the same, despite its freedom; so does the kitchen. But the house recombines in a loving way, an understanding way. Somehow it gathers strength not by looking into how things are made now, but how they could be made. The city must also be considered in the light of how it could be made, not in how to correct what is already there.

I think the most inspirational point from which we might try to understand architecture is to regard the room, the simple room, as the beginning of architecture. You know, when you enter your room, how you know it like no one else knows it. Maybe it is the windows of the room that are the most marvelous thing. Wallace Stevens, the American poet, said something for architects. (He aspired to be a one.) He asked, "What slice of the sun enters your room?" As if to say that the sun never knew how great it was until it struck the side of a building. Can you put that in a Univac machine?

I think that a plan is a society of rooms. A real plan is one in which rooms have talked to each other. In another sense, the plan may be said to be the "structure of the spaces in their light." If you consider that structure is the maker of light, because structure releases the spaces between and that is light giving. It could be a matter of an entrance or a window or even a little building with windows in it, because the distances between columns are so resourceful that you cannot cope with the generosity of such a construction using concrete (which has such tremendous power and need have very little material). The disciplines of the column provide an endless study. Its elements are, as we said before, in the sense of form that a building has. The form of a school could have something to do with the conversation of the various rooms, their nature, and how they complement each other and enrich the environment with the feeling of a "good place to learn." Consider elements in a house, for instance, in which the living room contains a bay window where a boy admonished can sit and feel that he is away or in his own little room. Or consider a stairway that goes from one level to another as being in a sense "measured" by the agility of a boy with all his coordinating faculties who wants to run up the four flights in no time flat. In such a case, when an architect draws a plan that involves a stairway, he cannot exert enough accuracy. Where he can draw the walls with a certain abandon, the stair must be drawn as if he were making a ruler or a measuring stick. Such is the sense of importance that must be felt. And the stair must have a landing-well—a number of landings. And the landing must want to be a room really. The landing is quite a wonderful thing because the stair, the same stair, is used by a child, a young man, and an old man. And when the old man ascends the stair with the young boy and reaches the landing there must be there a window, possibly a window seat, and maybe a bookcase. So as he ascends he says to the boy, "You know, I always wanted to read this book."

The roof, the floor, the ceiling, are really all elements and they deserve, of course, to be dealt with as such. But there is a great tendency to resort, you know, to *Graphic Standards*, where you find out everything you have to know. It'll tell you everything. It'll tell you what kind of stair is all right, but it'll never tell it as you (as an architect) must feel it.

This sensitivity is beautifully exemplified by Gertrude Jekyll, who was a famous landscape architect and did many gardens for Lutyens in England. Explaining sensitivity in the making of her gardens, she said she was ascending a stairway one morning in one of them. A little boy whom she knew was running down the stairway as she was coming up, and she said, "Oh, Johnny, you're up so early." But he replied, "Aw, Miss Jekyll, I'm supposed to be invisible."

Speaking of the "orders"; the order of movement, the order of light, the order of wind, of water, of whatever surrounds us . . . I had an assignment, which could not be carried out, to build a city that was eventually to contain 500,000 people—the capital of Gujarat State in India to be known as Ghandi Nagar. There the river Sevarmarti is dry, except when the monsoon comes and torrents of water sweep down its channel to the sea. I conceived bridges that straddle the riverbed, whose sole duty was to cross to the other side, but that might at the same time capture and store the water that runs down at the time of the monsoon, the clear rainwater [sic] that is wasted. And from there would be aqueducts running to places in the future city, such as the fire station, the police stations, the maintenance center, the air-conditioning center, and of course, the water supply centers. The mango trees, which are sacred, would stay just where they were, yielding a point of departure for residential quarters. The streets were oriented in accordance with the wind. Other utilities also followed the water lines. Thus "natural" features, especially the water stations (water means a tremendous amount in a town in India) were the basis of the plan. There was no other physical planning theory in back of it but the "orders," that were to be the starting point. Yet I was also looking for ways of introducing what I think is a much more important starting point, and these were to comprise the availabilities. The immeasurable availabilities, that must be held answerable to the urge in us *to be/to express*.

"I Love Beginnings," reprinted from *Architecture and Urbanism*, Special Issue on Louis I. Kahn, 1975, pp. 278–86.

An Architect Speaks his Mind

An interview with Beverly Russell

"Structure is the Giver of Light"

"Talk to a brick and it will tell you it likes an arch," says architect Louis Kahn. Arches, tower 40 feet in the students' housing at the School of Business Management, Ahmedabad, India. And more soaring arches are contained inside walls pierced with great circular vents designed to withstand earthquakes. Brand-new building in this country, the library of Phillips Exeter Academy, where circles carved out of concrete open up layers of book-filled floors to light. Walls bear the marks of the plywood forms in which the concrete was poured, typical of Kahn's insistence that "how the walls are made be evident." The Kimbell Art Museum, at Fort Worth, Texas, just completed, a grouping of concrete shells, massive (each is 100 feet long) yet fragile looking (the concrete is four inches thick). Inside, white oak floors, travertine, and "a silvery light."

On The Colonial House

The Colonial house is a marvellous house. It has an eternal plan in my opinion. No matter how much variation you put into it, it's still an eternal plan. It has a hall and a stairway that goes up to the bedrooms. A landing that is a room, for the old man to stop and rest on the way up. You can get in the front and you can also get in the back. The dining room is separate and when you really have this separation, it means independence, independence even for the mother who is setting the table. Today, we put the dining room in the living room and when guests come they see the table. The hostess is constantly rushing in and out. She may go gracefully from place to place, be charming and all that, but the charisma of the house is disturbed. I say today you can still use the Colonial house, the room separations make responsive places. One can become the place where you go away while somebody else is doing something else. If you blend spaces in the Colonial way, you have a society of rooms in which each one has its character, allowing delicate differences to express themselves. In a way, people meeting in them are different people from those who live in divisionless spaces.

On The Room

The room is the beginning of architecture. You do not say the same thing in one room as you say in another, that's how sensitive a room is. A room is a marvellous thing, a world within a world. It's yours and offers a measure of yourself. What slice of the sun enters your room? You feel the privacy of it, you feel *that* sun belongs to you, coming through the window, playing along the sills and the jambs and the walls. If you watch it, it belongs to you, really. It's just your particular place, your particular room.

On The House

A house can be made in many ways. I would say a house is a society of spaces talking to each other, expressing a way of life. I wouldn't think of it, to begin with, as known rooms: kitchen, living room, that sort of thing. They become such places without naming them. One of the most devastating faults today that destroys the ultimate creative instinct is to give something a name before it earns one. A house must be made so that any person, not necessarily the one who ordered it, must feel he can make there a home. An architect can design the most wonderful house for one owner that can become immediately nothing when somebody else moves in. That person, who ordered the house to reflect a collection of fragmentary ideas, prevents the house from being what I call part of the treasury of spaces. What you must think of, when building, is that you're adding to the treasury of spaces. Those wonderful Georgian houses in Dublin! You can't call them anything else but a treasury of spaces. It's as though the house was ordered for your purpose, but it's all there, to be used by other people in their own way. The house that is made with the feeling that Home is as possible to many as it is to you, has the power to become a treasury.

On Craftsmanship

A craftsman never wants to cover his work. In a good drawer the dovetailing is not hidden, the joint is the beginning of ornament. The joint is where ornament begins. The less the craftsman enters into something, the more there is a modification of the craft. I have reached a time where I realize I have my own way of expressing myself, an approach, an attitude toward building that is so tied up with the integrity of the building that I could not disguise a joint, nor could I disguise the material itself. So I couldn't apply anything to it. I could use decoration in a sense that things that are put there are themselves something—a sculpture or a painting. But you know, I go into houses where what I do is not—and I love the houses. There's a unity that I don't try for because it isn't in my nature. I insist the way the walls are made be completely evident. And it's exactly what a craftsman looks for.

On Color And Light

I have no color applied on the walls in my home. I wouldn't want to disturb the wonder of natural light. The light really does make the room. The changing light according to the time of day and the seasons of the year gives color. Then there are reflections from the floors, the furniture, the materials, all contributing to make my space made by the light, mine. Light is mood. The color of light is very pronounced. We know that a red light will cast a green shadow and a green light will cast a red shadow. A blue light will cast a yellow shadow and a yellow light will cast a blue. It's surprising when a sunset is truly a prevailing red, not confused; you will see an inky green shadow. Ever since I knew that to be true, I grew away from painting and depended on the light. The color you get that way is not applied, but simply a surprise.

On Man's Inspirations

There are three drives; man is motivated by three things, his reasons for living: the inspiration to learn, the inspiration to meet, the inspiration to well-being. The living room is of the inspiration to meet, but so is also the city. Just think what a city could become if we kept in mind that its initial will-to-be is the answer to the inspiration to meet. Our educational institutions should revel in the inspiration to learn, sensed through commonality. Today the school system is not of commonality, it's a different thing entirely and reflects little the inspiration to learn, which is in everyone. We can illustrate this so easily, how the school can become something it was a long time ago, by simply taking a plan of a school and deciding that the most important room, besides the classrooms and the library, is the Hall. Because the Hall can become the classroom of the children with no obligations, no lessons to be prepared, no study periods, no judgments. In the program, there must be this room, which is really the place of commonality, too, and a place that expresses human agreement so beautifully. You see, how important that is, to review the spaces that are true to a certain institution?

On Brick

If you talk to a brick and ask it what it likes, it'll say it likes an arch. And you say to it, look arches are expensive and you can always use a concrete lintel to take the place of an arch. And the brick says, I know it's expensive and I'm afraid it probably cannot be built these days, but if you ask me what I *like* it's still an arch.

On Wood

I am in the midst of designing two houses. Wood is on the inside and out. I like wood, I think wood's wonderful, very pliable, and a beautiful material. It's warm and very friendly, too. Wood is not like plaster, which can sweep across a surface: it's very precise.

On The Fireplace

The fireplace plays a strong part in my houses. I feel it represents the presence of a man and therefore is of home. I'm designing a fireplace that is really a little house, a clump that sits there and has all its own architecture, and the rest of the house just sort of rambles around it. It's done in stone, rather large limestone blocks. It's as though the fireplace room were brought in from outside. Wonderful, because you can go there and be alone.

On The Street

The street is a community room; its walls are the buildings, sky is its ceiling, but it truly is a room. And you might say, the meeting room or meeting house really stems from the sense of street. It has to do with a fundamental feeling of needing human agreement. We need to feel the generative force of human agreement. It is beautiful as a source of inspiration of the creative. You know, you see in a street, which doesn't know its neighbors, a feeling of commonality. And it's a powerful thing that—commonality is a force that makes rapport possible. Most cities now don't have little streets, they have great dividers that erase the street quality. When you see little streets in cities that are dead-ended, they still look like community rooms. And those that go straight for great distance have lost their character as rooms. We should redefine the street for people in our cities. Streets must be given back to the residences as their community rooms, to the shopping areas as their community rooms. They are meeting places in full meaning of the city. Roads are not streets. City planning could make such distinctions by reconsidering the order of movement.

How'm I Doing, Corbusier?

Interview with Patricia McLaughlin

McLAUGHLIN: Maybe you could start by telling me something about the way you see architecture?

KAHN: It's a difficult question you ask, just the way you have it, because it's like asking a dentist how he sees dentistry—how I *see* it—because every day I see it differently.

McLAUGHLIN: But the interesting thing is that a dentist probably has a different view of your mouth than you do . . .

KAHN: (laughing) Yes, he seems to be interested in it!
    You see, I was to be a painter, won prizes in drawing since I was eight years old. In my last year in high school, everybody expected me to become a painter. I'd made drawings since I was three years old, and they were thought to be interesting—not in any exaggerated way, because a three-year-old shows no real evidence of talent.
    In high school, I had my teacher of art, William F. Gray, a tall, wonderful-looking man with a blonde-gray goatee—I don't know whether you want to listen to all this—I'd just say he supported me always . . . he supported me always and was

conscious of my talent.

No, don't put it that way, just put it this way: he gave a course in architecture, acquainting us with Gothic, Renaissance, Greek, Roman, and Egyptian architecture.

We had no obligation but to listen for a half year to his slide talks. He gave us five drawings to make; they were five drawings which were to be copies of five plates already prepared. Most of the students struggled through these drawings—everyone was obliged to take it—most of the students struggled, were unable to make these plates, and I found ways of helping them, and making their drawings in disguised methods so they could not be detected as my drawings. That doesn't say much for my character, does it? But it's true. I'd finish them off with inkblots and other disturbing things . . . At that—how do you say "getting off the track?"—I was . . . I was trying to get them off the track, trying to get them off the track so they won't know who did it. They were truly difficult to make . . . But this is only a little thing of the memory— things that stay in the memory . . .

McLAUGHLIN: They were difficult drawings, or they were difficult to disguise?

KAHN: Oh, difficult for anyone, difficult for anyone to make them—I'm sure that my own drawings were full of faults.

But it was those talks that just made my almost . . . well . . . my desire, my really strong desire to be a painter fade. Architecture struck me between the eye and the eyeball, let's put it that way, it's pretty close.

I was—it was a discovery of a natural tendency—you see?—a natural tendency to be able—no, not "to be able," because I wasn't able at the time—to have . . . to be struck . . . I was struck by the *offering* aspects of this art, something . . . an art that is . . . that *reaches* . . . An art you can *walk around* and *be in*, walk around and be in. And life-size.

McLAUGHLIN: Do you mean in that sense an offering? Offering itself to people?

KAHN: Yes, in that sense an offering, that it . . .

Every work of art is an offering, every work. I would say that *now*, I know, you see, that the greatest work of an artist is his in-touchness with commonalty, *in-touchness with commonalty*—his sense of the eternal quality, the eternal quality in . . . in *humans* which . . . who . . . humans who *respond* to the yet-not-said and the yet-not-made— right?—without previous example . . . without previous example, and *sense*, if not immediately then eventually, a new avenue of response to these . . . to the . . . the eternal qualities revealed. It's not maybe a full sentence, but the idea is there.

The greatest offering, the greatest work, the greatest *part*, the most *wonderful* part of an artist's work does not really belong to him. He is a catalyst of this eternal quality, and he can only claim the way he himself interprets it.

Picasso opened new avenues. His paintings belong to him, but the new avenues do not. *Things* belong to him, but the new avenues do not. In that way you explain the catalyst—he was just there, he senses it . . . It is these qualities which the next painter—or the painter next to him, put it this way—recognizes as an opening to his *own* talent. That's why Picasso has many followers. But if they imitate him, they're no one—you see? To write like Mozart is meaningless, right? To be influenced by Mozart's eternal quality—*eternal quality*—is the seed which stimulates the true artist.

Architecture came to me through the examples of the great work, true. But I now know that—because I can still see those examples after so many years as the most resounding influence—let's say, the most resounding *reflections*—of powerful commonality, *powerful commonality* . . . truenesses—you know?—just think of it, *truenesses*, it's a word, never mind, I invented it, something which deals with man's facts—not with facts out of the laws of nature—not facts out of the *orders* of nature, but *man's* facts.

May I just put a note down? I believe that truth is anything that happens, whether you like it or not. It is an unmeasureable quality, an unmeasureable quality; facts dealing with natural phenomena lend themselves to measurement.

We cannot seek the truth. Truth is just revealed, just revealed through our course . . . our course . . . through our courses in living—I don't know whether that strikes you as being true or not? You can't seek the truth—it is always newly revealed, it's a living thing. You don't know the truth except through living. It cannot be written down as being the truth, because even the same event is recorded differently, responds differently, *records itself* differently in every singularity. The truth is really *your* truth, your personal truth.

I feel the same way about knowledge and knowing, I feel the same . . .

McLAUGHLIN: As about truth?

KAHN: Yes. You have a very sequential mind—you can put together what has been said before with what is said after it. I cannot. I rather think cryptically, and not this way. You help me a great deal by asking this question. I tend to relate things that are not really immediate, that are way back there somewhere (and I think it's continuous!), which is why I'm very hard to follow.

The difference between knowledge and knowing, yes, knowledge and knowing—when knowledge comes to a person it becomes personal. As the person receives it, it cannot be conveyed . . . cannot be conveyed . . . —or, rather, as it becomes personal, its greatest value is in what way this personal aura can . . . can . . . can . . . is . . . is conveyed to others—right? What you see in the way of knowledge . . . knowledge becomes *your* knowledge, and the way you reveal it . . . the way . . . the way your singularity *can* be conveyed to others.

Knowledge comes through attitude, somehow . . . or maybe not attitude, maybe that is not the way it is, but attitude is really a singularity, too—you take an attitude because of your singularity, you're pulled to it, and this is the teacher. The singularity is the teacher. The teacher is *there*, it isn't in the imparting of knowledge—what is already printed and what is available can be gotten without the help of someone else. It is available. But what is immeasurably valuable is *how the singularity is revealed*— how the singularity is put before us—you see?—put before us. Because this is completely unique, every singularity being unique—yes? Every person is different, and as you get to know it, if you can convey . . . if you can convey the aura . . . the aura of your singularity—aura of your singularity, put it this way—there is a uniqueness which . . . which ah . . . which is *stimulating* to another singularity, because it puts *trust* in the singularity, it makes one conscious of one's *own* singularity, *that's* the value of it.

A teacher in a way *fights* specific knowledge because he knows how changed this knowledge is, what change this knowledge goes through in himself. Oxygen to one scientist is different—even *oxygen* is not the same oxygen in one or the other person.

Knowledge remains an incomplete book, remains always an incomplete book, is always *in* an incomplete book, gathering always more and more pages, more and more pages in its quest for the totality of order itself. Laws of nature are extracted . . . extracted . . . as fragments of order. The good mind always places this fragment in relation to his speculations on order.

It doesn't sound much like a personal interview. But you ask me what I think of architecture: it lies, you see, in the thoughts which you put down. I can't answer it as if it were just a professional question. If I worked always conscious of my profession, I think I would lose . . . I would be . . . would be . . . would be *soothed* into thinking that my profession is holding me up. I'd be leaning on the profession—if I were absorbed in my feeling that I am in a profession, the profession of architecture. Whereas I don't think about it, I think only of what gave beginning to my . . . what responded so naturally to . . . —at the time of Mr. Gray's talks, right? Mr. Gray's talks—the beginning it made in me.

I believe so much in the power of beginning . . . *beginning.* I love English history . . . I love English history . . . I have many volumes of English history. I must say I do glance through—broadly through—all the books, never really absorbing very much . . . absorbing very much . . . *But* the first chapter I read very thoroughly, and I turned to the first chapter every time I open the book, reading it thoroughly and finding, since I have so poor a memory, new things in it all the time.

I *know* what it is: it is my desire to sense Volume Zero. Volume Minus One. A search for the *sense* of beginning, because I know if man . . . —no—I know that the beginning is an . . . is an eternal confirmation. I say eternal because I distinguish it from, let's say, universal. *Universal* deals with the laws of nature and *eternal* deals with the nature of man. If man's nature would not approve, a beginning would be impossible. So beginning is a revelation which reveals what is natural to man—it never would have happened. What the human approves—human as a larger term for man, instead of man simply as the species—is natural to all humans. I would say the beginning, then, is natural to all humans. The beginning reveals the *nature* of the human, right? Right!

You can say that the first school was an approval of something within us, in our desires, revealed by circumstance. The circumstance *primes* the giving of man's approval. I put it this way: a man was under a tree—who did not know he was a teacher— talking to a few little ones, who did not know they were pupils. They approved of each other, and the first classroom was built. It was the beginning of "school."

I've used these examples so often, I hate to hear it written about. Maybe you can do it so much better, because it sounds so much quotelike, and it shouldn't really be—understand it, and write it as an understanding, almost better than a quote. Often I am very hard to understand, because I have images in my mind, not fully examples either, not part of my experience, just a sense . . .

McLAUGHLIN: Have you always been conscious of thinking this way?

KAHN: Yes.

McLAUGHLIN: Is it something that's developed through thinking in terms of . . . thinking about space?

KAHN: No, space came out of it. The predilection to think this way is where space comes from . . . It wasn't space, because space would be nothing, only a word, and repeated as a word. It is often used in a way that I've never used space, as it's talked . . . even as space. I've heard people talk about space, and they all seem completely wrong to me. We never know what space is, and what is talked about as space . . .

I think it must be some preparation, some eternal preparation, or attitude, or tendency, what may be called a talent, you see, a natural talent—it seems awfully august to call it natural talent, to accuse yourself of having natural talent; I wouldn't like that conveyed at all. It would be a wrong way of putting it. It would be just to say your tendency would make it be . . . your singularity is what brings it on, just how singular you are. And anyone is singular, and it must be said so.

That's why I believe in schools of natural talent—that one should not just teach what somebody thinks is good for everybody. It *isn't* good for everybody, because you don't really learn what's not part of yourself. You don't apply it, it doesn't become part of your tools immediately, because they are tools that belong to someone else.

A guy like me should be taught physics by having me listen to the lecture, but never having to be examined in it. That should be left for the physicists, the future physicists. But I must listen; I need to listen because the seeds of so much are in this wonderful science. It's important to listen because in physics lie the seeds of many priming forces in a man. But it does not mean that he will eventually know the founding, the meanings . . . meanings and messages . . . meanings and messages of so marvellous a subject as physics. That really belongs to the man who has natural tendencies, because almost after the first two talks—already he is a competitor of the teacher, the natural physicist is. A man who is just taking the course because it is required is one who loses: he only gains what is part of him, that's all, and everything else is completely lost.

I believe, though, that universities can learn much by thinking in terms of the freedom of each individual in what he learns—that freedom be given, that he not be judged, but that he *be*, however, allowed to enter any field that he seems to want to know about. And this would be a fine atmosphere of the great free place of the mind, you know, called the university. You see my point? I want you to see this point, I think it could mean something to somebody else.

As a teacher—after I have listened to the courses in physics—without taking notes, mind you, because that's distracting to a man who doesn't have it, his ear for it, or, you might say, his *predilection* . . .

McLAUGHLIN: Yes, I find that taking notes myself—that I have to wait until after I have it written down to think about whether I understand it . . .

KAHN: That's a great revelation . . . You see, I love physics, but when I had to listen with the idea of taking notes in order to pass examinations in it, I didn't hear what was said, I didn't know what I wrote down in my notebook, and I couldn't even understand the questions when the questions came up. I also had to copy a friend's notes who was next to me, who seemed to understand *everything* that was said, who could write notes also to make him remember what was said, and he did excellently in all the examinations, and to this day that friend has that kind of mind, I notice. He has the same kind of mind.

There's a distinction between a brain and a mind. A brain is an instrument, but the mind is the soul of the brain. And that really is where the singularity comes in.

McLAUGHLIN: Did you find that when you were a small child you were expected to learn things that were not part of you?

KAHN: Yes, all along. There isn't a subject I had difficulty with that I don't today love. I do love them—I love mathematics, I love physics, I'm fascinated by all avenues of learning.

But I cannot say I remember *any* of it specifically, and could not be trusted in *any* way to teach such subjects. But I would say I absorbed only one thing, a kind of aura of the subject, without any sense of knowing anything about it, of knowing *specifically*, that is. If I were questioned as to what it really is, I would just have to think of the wholeness of it, but I cannot think of anything specific. And it is because I cannot absorb what is not part of me—in the end, it all gets lost, because its receptivity is not part of you. I must think of other ways of saying it . . .

In other words, I would say, if I were told by a physics teacher, "Now, Louis Kahn, we think you should know, be exposed to, physics. But you needn't take notes, just listen. You'll be examined in physics, but I'd like you to answer by *drawing* physics for me"—how I see it through drawing, which was just so natural to me, from the very beginning, with all those prizes in drawing that came to me almost every year— it was my natural way of expressing. I think I would have surprised the teacher with my interpretations—they certainly would not have anything to do specifically with physics. My mind would be free, it would be respected for what it *is*, and I would surprise myself and also the teacher with what would come out of it.

It is this freedom I talk about, this freedom which I think would be full of happiness, you know. I believe that a person who has a predilection to dance beautifully should be really given all the opportunity to exercise this natural talent. His development would be startling—unhampered, and therefore startling. I think eventually he would learn Latin on his own, to make his talent more expressive.

You understand? Today, for instance, I read physics, I read physics now, and when I read it I know much more, because I deal with physical phenomena.

McLAUGHLIN: Do you mean, once the dancer has been given every opportunity to dance, he will develop other aspects?

KAHN: To enrich his expression, yes. I think it's absolutely true. I do it all the time. I read poetry, I read all the things that were difficult at the time; now I read about what I went through in high school and college, all examinations which I passed, but they were not presented to me in such a way that I could absorb them. Had I been given more drawing, more philosophy, subjects which I had a natural predilection

303

for . . .

McLaughlin: You had an . . . an "attitude" toward philosophy?

Kahn: No, I wouldn't say that, because I didn't know what that was, and I don't know what it is now. I don't think it's really a subject anyway—I think it's, again, something which, if you spit out as you find it in a book—again I think it's the kind of thing which I don't think you can. But you can be influenced by in what way it *constructs you.*

You're not a philosopher by having read philosophy, not at all. I think you are a philosopher because you are just *naturally* one. And if you call yourself a philosophy major, you are calling yourself almost nothing—just about as much value as a multitude of doctors of philosophy theses, which I really believe is really a false title. It's a false title to be given a doctor of philosophy in a subject—because he went through the mill, you see. I think a person who seeks this title as a stamp of approval in the eyes of those who mete out jobs is in the marketplace, is really in the marketplace. So if you get your Ph.D. so you get a better job or you can teach, I think it's a marketplace idea, that should not be fostered by the University.

I note with a great deal of respect the music department at the University of Pennsylvania which has abandoned the Ph.D. dissertation—and how true . . . how true—how true the mind is to have thought . . . to *see* the competitive aspects of universities . . . to sense that art . . . that philosophy . . . that a doctor of philosophy in the arts is just a big lie. You can't put it in the arts at all. Or, I would not put "a big lie"—I think I would say, it's an ostentation. Can you put it that way? It's an ostentation.

Everybody lies, by the way, in one form or another. It's not a good word. Lies many times protect us. It's rather a mystical thing—it could be the way you want it, and not the way it happened. You know, there's something wonderful about that aspect. I don't think *lie* is a good word to apply.

I don't know why you're writing it down, it's just a personal comment.

McLaughlin: It's a nice idea.

Kahn: I many times, in that sense, lie—it's only because I have so damned much fairy tale in me. I never lose sight of the thing. I believe the wish and the fairy tale is the beginning of science. I think if I were to trade my work for something equally as strong in me—as impelling in me, rather than strong (strong is a self-evaluation, and that isn't good, isn't a good idea at all, not good to write about—I hate that, by the way, anything that you may write about which seems as though I have put myself on a pedestal, this is something that I really hate to read—but *impelling* is something else,

304

is something that drives you—) is to write, is to be the writer of the new fairy tales. And maybe to use whatever talent I have in drawing to illustrate them.

Recently I acquired a book printed by the Nonesuch Press of the *Divine Comedy*, printed in English and Italian, *but* the big thing, the big thing is that it is illustrated by Botticelli. What a book it is! It's so marvellous! It's so modest—the illustrations are conceived . . . are line—just simply line—are line drawings—the thinnest and most daring, thinnest and most daring accents of line, but they're still lines—but the most daring thinness and, and—how to say?—*thickness* of lines. They *look* like allegory! Every figure has an internal life, every figure, though flat on the page, has internal life. I saw but two or three, but two or three illustrations and I decided categorically that this book must be mine. I have had it now for a year and I have not yet seen all the illustrations: just so much I want to believe that there are not 40 illustrations, but 40 *million* illustrations.

These drawings *must* have had a profound influence on Blake, on Flaxman. I'll show you—you know Blake's work?—here: much stiffer, but must have been an influence. The most beautiful is the formality he uses—see the shading here, this is foreground, this is background—it's a formula, but it is a beautiful one. There's sweetness in it. Of course, Dante himself—what a beautiful mind! In the last canto in *Paradiso*, he introduces . . . he says, "Oh, Virgin Mother, sister of thy Son . . ."— just that simple phrase could take the place of the New Testament—just sweetness, belief in what is not the usual course, unmitigated faith! The power of poetry which seeks to unclothe itself of words . . . a matchless combination of Botticelli's white sweetness, his sense of *primavera* . . . —I say that only because it's such a beautiful word . . . and it has a sense of beginning.

This is all in answer to your question—a rambling answer—"how do you see architecture?" I see it as a sense, an expression of all eternal qualities. The poet, the painter must also see it that way. So must the lawyer, the physician, the engineer.

So respecting this, your work . . . work that's worthy is always considered by the artist as a kind of offering, an offering to the spirit of the art. For instance, architecture really has no presence: it really is a spirit. It comes . . . it comes almost . . . from the human who responds to the first, let's say, evidence of it, or presence of it. Existence can be in the mind, and have no presence. Presence must employ the laws of nature to make it evident. Because everything that's made is made by nature, even your body is a product of nature. The motivation, however, is not. The motivation has a lodging place in what nature makes. It lodges in you and makes it possible to sense it through what nature gives you as an instrument of expression—yes?

McLaughlin: Yes . . .

KAHN: And architecture *emerges* from that instinct to express because we actually live for what I think is the only purpose, that is, to express. We live to express.

McLAUGHLIN: To make what exists present?

KAHN: To make what exists present is the urge of the artist, of the maker. It's true of everyone, even in speaking or dancing or walking beautifully—there is evidence, always, of everyone . . . of everyone . . . of this will to express, even those who express in violence.

So architecture has no presence, but it has existence—you see? Because architecture is a spirit as painting is a spirit.

McLAUGHLIN: You mean "architecture" as an abstraction?

KAHN: Yes—as a sense, as an emergence, as an *evidence* of spirit. And a *work* of architecture is what has presence. And the best of this presence is . . . is . . . is *made* as an *offering*, an offering to architecture—and, may I add, in all joy and humiliation—and humility, not "humiliation"—"and humility"—I can throw words around, and sometimes just the wrong ones.

I remarked before, you know, that the most *telling* quality of a man's work is to what extent he cannot claim ownership to what he does—to what extent he can desert what truly does not belong to him. I've said it before—that which has these qualities of human *acceptance*, human *response* and acceptance—it may take hundreds of years to accomplish—no, not to accomplish, to be *felt*.

The artist suffers only in what way he expresses his own powers of commonality, right? "He suffers" means "he must accept for himself," you see, the way *suffers* is an old word . . .

McLAUGHLIN: Do you mean, in the old sense of the word *suffers*, that he's passive to it, it comes to him?

KAHN: No, he's not passive to it, maybe *suffers* is the wrong word if it means passive to you—I mean, "he must be *satisfied* with"—he can only *claim* his . . . his inventiveness of expression . . . his inventiveness of expression which is his work, and how he is personally identified with his work, let's put it that way. That's what I meant to say when I said there's no point in composing like Mozart, but it's the making of the other man through Mozart's work—it's the quality of commonality in the work which makes the other man. I said it before, but I just want to reiterate it, because—it has something to do with the story I invented about Mozart.

I just invented it—I say, "A dish fell in Mozart's kitchen, and the floor was of stone—the kitchen maids shrieked with surprise—right?—and Mozart said, 'Ah, dissonance!' " He discovered an eternal quality in music, something indestructible, belonging to the human, and to all musicians—or to *music*, not to all musicians, "to music," I would say: it's much stronger, more specific, "belongs to music." And as he composed, as he composed using dissonance, *that* belonged to him.

So must the engineer have in mind Freyssinet, who is a very great engineer—you know how to spell Freyssinet?

MCLAUGHLIN: *F-R-A-I-S-S-O-N-N-E?*

KAHN: Ah, you are guessing very beautifully! I don't know how to spell it myself, but I have a book here . . . Here, here it is.

Freyssinet—many engineers understand such things, stressing, building of bridges and buildings, and very unusual constructions, all very true to nature. It's the discovery of nature's powers, that's all—that's what anyone does who's a *real* engineer.

Or the painter—you might say, Leonardo. Or the physician—who would you point out as a great physician?

MCLAUGHLIN: Osler?

KAHN: Yes, a good University example—somebody who has made a path, possibly—how many little Oslers were made through him, you see?

Every man has . . . has a figure in his work who he feels answerable to. I often say, often say to myself, "How'm I doing, Corbusier?" You see, Corbusier was my teacher. I say, Paul Cret was my teacher and Corbusier was my teacher.

And . . . and I have learned not to *do* as they did, not to . . . not to *imitate*. I would say—imitate?—but to derive out of their spirit, to derive out of their spirit. I don't want to say *what* was derived, because it hurts; *derive*—it's very strong, *derive* is powerful if not . . .

They invent, what would that be?— *derive* is a verb?—and *derived* too is a verb—English is not my subject.

But what I've told you, isn't really written very much anywhere—I mean, some of this is, but the more personal things, which I have not . . . I just told you, Cret, Corbusier . . .

MCLAUGHLIN: You were talking about how, with Cret and Corbusier, you learned not how to do *what* they did, not to imitate them, but to derive *from* their work . . .

KAHN: Derive from . . . *derive* is not the word, really—but *sense their spirit*.

MCLAUGHLIN: I'm wondering if you think they had a special art in making it possible for you to do that . . .

KAHN: Yes . . .

McLAUGHLIN: . . . and if there's a way that you try to make it possible for *your* students to do the same thing—to sense your spirit?

KAHN: Oh, yes—in the student work, it's constantly—no, that's a horrible way of putting it, so categorical—I make so many mistakes, I can't say it's constant.

The work of students is not pointed . . . is not pointed to the solution of problems. Primarily, it is to sense the nature . . . not of a school, but *school*, the *nature* of *school*, the nature of the place . . .

But you don't know what it is really, without getting it out of your guts—you won't know what it is until you *sense* what it is, and *then* you look up what other people *think* it is.

But first you must sense it through this powerful instrument, this beautiful instrument, *intuition*. This sense of trueness . . . this sense of trueness is only a sense of the inheritance, built-in inheritance of the sympathetic experiences in your own making in which all the laws of the universe were involved, and all the sense . . . all the, you might say, the spirit sense of the *will to live to express*. It is . . . it is a nuclear source of this . . . of this record—would you say, "odyssey?"—of the way you were made. I think that all of learning . . . all of learning—I mean, all of the *will* to learn— stems from a desire to recall how we were made. I think that is the intuitive sense. I think if we put this intuitive sense into play . . .

It may sound pedantic to say it, as if you were trying to make everybody adhere to *your* sense of how to learn, you see, and that is not good, that is the trouble with education, that it tries to install a system, where it should be a *free* society of learning, which should, in a way, change every day with the personalities that are present and the cross stimulation of singularities. Of course, I don't want in any way to exclude the course studies which . . . which activate the mind . . . well, maybe I'm getting a little off the track.

I keep thinking always of this free society . . . I was thinking of you coming from the University, and I was thinking in terms of the University, which I speak so much about because I really envision one of the most beautiful places to be in, that is a university. It is without question a *prime* necessity in life.

I would say the three greatest inspirations in man are the inspirations to *learn*, the inspiration to *meet*, and the inspirations of well-being. They all serve, really, the *will to be to express*. This is, you might say, the reason for living.

(Kahn turns to his essay on "Silence and Light.") The will to be to learn, to be to express is expressed by silence. By silence I don't mean quiet—but in the sense that Malraux calls his book *Silence*—I think it's *The Voices of Silence*—he means only the feeling you get when you pass the pyramids, you feel that they want to tell you how they were made. Not *how* they were made, but what made them *be*, which means what was the force that *caused* them to be made, right? These are the voices of silence, right?

And I believe that all material is spent light. I say, "Light to Silence, Silence to Light." It is the desire to express, meeting the means to express—all of nature's . . . material.

At this point of meeting (which to everyone is a different threshold—to some, silence is so great, and it can go a great distance before it meets the means to express, and to some it goes a short distance to find the means to express, so in each form there is a different kind, which I don't explain anywhere)—and this is the inspirations, at the point where . . . the threshold where the urges to express meet the possible.

This [published essay] attempts to explain things which I have written. Naturally, though I call it "Silence and Light," I speak very little about it, because I don't know how to extend things, because I don't have any historical knowledge, nor any research tendencies. I can't look up and find other literature, I just can't do it. And so it's left, in a way, in a very undeveloped state, as though it were just an offering for someone else, you know, to extend. It doesn't happen, because I really say too little to make it completely understandable. That's why I like to talk about it, because I talk about it more freely, because writing is very difficult for me, though I've done some . . .

Here's the Fort Worth Museum, and here's a natural light fixture—all the light here is natural. It's a lighting fixture which takes the light from the garden and spreads it over the entire museum—no unnatural light. This is just a photograph taken of the thing when it wasn't quite finished, and some trees put in. And the whole thing is done with this lunette—the light source is here, the light fixture is here, which spreads the light over these cycloids, and the injurious rays are filtered at this point. So the amount of light you get inside is no more injurious to whatever is there than electric light is. So you don't have to shut a museum off, as it usually is because natural light is injurious. But it doesn't have to be.

So this is a kind of invention that comes out of the desire to have natural light. Because it is the light the *painter* used to paint his painting. And artificial light is a static light—you see?—where natural light is a light of mood. And sometimes the room gets dark—why not?—and sometimes you must get close to look at it, and come another day, you see, to see it in another mood—a different time, you see, to see the mood natural light gives, or the seasons of the year, which have other moods.

And the painting must reveal itself in different aspects if the moods of light are included in its viewing, in its *seeing*. This is another example of what one sets in his mind as being a *nature* of something. I think that's the nature, really, of a place where you see paintings. And research would *never* have given it to me, because all I could find were ways of doing it completely contrary to the ways I think a museum might be. So it must be derived out of your own sense of its nature, of its service, of the *nature* of a school, of the *rooms* of a school, or the rooms of a museum.

From it one finds himself, and also finds the avenues of his own expression, which is the best offering a man can make, because it derives out of his singularity, yes? It ties together. That's how men are taught: men are taught to find themselves in the nature of their own expressions coming from their own personal nature. This, coupled with experience and the making of things, could bring about a wealth of interpretations of the nature of the places which architecture offers—where one can learn, one can bring up his family, one can meet with others . . .

I would say, if I were to teach city planning, I would abandon all statistical knowledge of cities, because a city is a different place every day. It is made from the play of multiple interests. The rules of man are meant to be changed; the laws of nature cannot be changed. To think of new rules and attitudes to supplant the ones that are in play is much more important than to have your head crowded with the rules that prevail.

To think of new rules is much more important than to think of remembering, or working with, the rules that are now in play, right? A rule—did I say?—is meant to be changed because when it *is* changed, it is because of the weakness of the rule as revealed in the course of its *filtering*—you see?—through human nature. To discover a new rule is to discover new avenues of expression, right?

The laws of nature tell us that the pebble on the beach is the absolutely right color, the right weight, the right position—instead of saying "right," I would say "undeniable"—because it is placed there by the interplay of the laws of nature: placed there not by any consciousness, no: placed there nonconsciously, where a *rule* is a conscious act needing circumstances to prove its validity or the need for change.

This is all to do with teaching, really, that one *knows* these things. The important thing is to, first of all, give credence to the thought that a man should not be judged, but he desperately needs criticism. Criticism, in its true light, is always constructive. Often, so-called critics are really just judges, based on personal opinion. A critic need not be in the field of his criticism. He must be a sensor of validities and the nature of a field of expression. An architect criticizing another architect could fall out of the role of criticism when he thinks in terms of comparison—his work and the other man's work. The teacher of architecture must in the same way exclude his own ways in favor of the qualities of commonality in architecture.

McLAUGHLIN: Do you think a lot of people who have studied with you have been able to sense your spirit?

KAHN: (laughing) Well, first of all, I don't think they're old enough.

No, I think many do feel this, but I think this is a dangerous thing to talk about, because you don't know in what way—*when*—a man develops. It would certainly be difficult to detect . . .

I would say that those who imitate the way I do things have not learned anything. Many of them do it. But many express themselves in *their* ways, which does not necessarily reflect with utter clarity the teachings which I take as being good. Those who use the words which I use to explain their own work—even with greater clarity, you see, than I myself could convey—do work which I don't sense as being important.

It must be so much that's *you*, so much of the individual, that the words of teaching must not be in any way in evidence, so completely has it been transformed into the singularity, you see.

So, you see, it's contrary . . . it's a question which is so difficult to answer directly because their work is sometimes—that which students do—is not anything like yours, and they are the best. Those that even repeat your words are not good.

And it must be also considered that people don't develop—an architect does not develop—*easily*, because there is so much—*so* much—traffic that a talent must go through: his ability to get a client, you see—or the *fortune*, the *fortune* of getting a client, not "ability"—the development of a talent through a succession of work cannot be just done suddenly—and the personal sense of perfection, interpretation and perfection. I believe it takes a long time to be an architect, it takes a long time to be an architect of one's aspirations. Right? To become an architect professionally takes just overnight; I would say you could be an architect professionally overnight. But to feel the spirit of architecture from which one makes his offerings may take *much* longer.

I've said so many things I haven't said to anybody before—I feel rather well about it.

I always—when I read tapes back, I modify, not to be something that sounds like it's coming from Olympus. It must not sound this way because, actually, there's a natural kind of urge to express in more succinct terms, but not too many words. It could sound like an attempt at poetry, or something like that, which is really not my intention.

The intention is to really be seen in what is my truer nature—and that is not to like anything that I've done, and I trust really only that which could emerge, what was primed by the work that preceded. It is only this: if you want to ask me what my best work is, I couldn't really tell you. It would be, as many people express, what is yet not made, what is yet not expressed. I have the feeling that the greatest men died—terrible word—thinking that they have done nothing, judging from what lodges in them as the yet unexpressed.

McLaughlin: You mean that, even though you work hard at expressing things, the balance is always off-balance, the unexpressed is so much heavier?

Kahn: It is also true that in the work completed is the mass of qualities unexpressed in this work which waits for the opportunity of release. I would never feel bored to be given a commission similar to the one I just did—just executed? just satisfied? or maybe "just did" is better—for that reason, without any sense whatsoever that I would become a specialist in that field of expression—it tells you how meager it must be to be a specialist. I think you can make sense out of that?

McLaughlin: Is that the most difficult thing about being an architect, the heaviness of the unexpressed—or is it not difficult because it's necessary?

Kahn: No, it's not—I think "the heaviness" is not so much as "the emptiness." There's a kind of unfilled emptiness; it's not fulfilled. In other words, what you've *done* does not fulfill. Your example of heaviness is a matter of scale—it isn't scale. It lodges in what may be the essence of silence, which really has no weight whatsoever—it's completely devoid of anything material, anything that's measured, so *weight* has a measurement quality that—it's really not true. It's an unfulfillment of the spirit which is completely insatiable.

Your will to express, that is to say, your desire to live to express, is where it touches. That's a very beautiful tie-up—I think it's beautiful—between the measurable and the unmeasurable . . . could there be put in the *qualities* of the unmeasurable? . . . which never can be actually measured, nor fulfilled, nor predicted. It ties in with such qualities as eternal, of what is meant by eternal, because it is the seat of the unmeasurable from which the desire to be to express comes, which hammered at the door of nature and said, "Make me an instrument of expression." And we, in our presence, are instruments of expression.

There is so much sense of it when you are in the presence of a person of beauty, and I don't really mean necessarily a physical beauty—the beauty of a very old person in which is traceable, you see, the will to live, the will to live *forever* because of the light, you see, of . . . of . . . of the promises of expression, you know. That's what I see in a beautiful person.

"How'm I Doing, Corbusier?," reprinted from *The Pennsylvania Gazette*, vol. 71, no. 3, December 1972, pp. 19–26.

Thoughts

Man and Nature

'Man is only concerned with true. Nature is not concerned with true, and of course I mean the physical nature as compared to human Nature.'

'Nature is unconscious, but the psyche is conscious, demands life. Nature makes the instruments which make life possible, it will not make the instrument unless the desire for life is there.'

'Nature is the giver of all presence, we need Nature but Nature does not need us.'

Silence and Light

'Architecture has no presence, music has no presence, I mean, of course, the spirit of architecture and the spirit of music. Music, in this sense as in Architecture, favors no style, no method, no technology: this spirit is recognized as Truth. What does exist is a work of architecture or work of music which the artist offers to his art in the sanctuary of all expression, which I like to call the Treasury of the Shadows, lying in that ambience, light to silence, silence to light. Light, the giver of presence, casts its shadow which belongs to light. What is made belongs to light and to desire. . . . '

Order of Space

'In structure you have physical order, in the space, however, the order is more psychological, but if you say physical order in space is the space served and the spaces that do the serving, that is purely a physical order, because there is no character, except the realization that one space is different from any other space, that is different. So there is physical order also in space. You will say the psyche order is the realization of the nature of spaces in their character, like a place to learn certainly cannot be in the corridor, because people go by, the noises are made, there must be within the space. Therefore you will say, in the order of space this space must be away from circulation. . . .'

Form and Design

'Form encompasses a harmony of systems, a sense of order, and that which characterizes one existence from another.

Form has no shape or dimensions.

Form what

Design how.

Form, as the realization of nature, is made up of inseparable elements. Form has no presence. Its existence is in the mind. Form, when realized, does not belong to its realizer. Only its Interpretation belongs to the artist. *Form is like order.*'

Served Space and Servant Space

'I have no method of work, I only have principle around which I work, there is no method, there is no system. There is nothing systematic about the servant space and the space it serves, because it is only a realization of a kind of nature that is the realization of what I think is true of Architecture. In the plan there was ancient plan, and modern plan is different from the attitude between the servant area and the area served.'

Structure is the Giver of Light

'The structure is a design in light. The vault, the dome, the arch, the column, are structures related to the character of light. Natural light gives mood to space by nuances of light in the time of the day and the seasons of the year as it enters and modifies the space.'

'For the making of a room, it is there the room in its light, the light has much to do with what you are. You bring the room with glare, with too much light, with too little light, with light it does not have somehow definable. It seems to be contrary to the room's dimension where it oriented it all, influencing what will happen in this room in the course of the day, the course of the month, the course of the year.'

The Connectors

Not having a separate connector comes from my understanding of structures, which make themselves as they do in nature, nonconsciously, and the connector is the conscious thing.

A soft growing thing, it comes from the finest step of the nature growing way, now well built to construct something nonconsciously, it does not make connectors. It is in the shape itself where the connector is, this is the same thing, only it is surprisingly supplied by our practicality, our conscious practicality. And so all, in the very intricate and turning, are meant to devise connectors which are not required. They were just in the nature of how to place the building, the connector was made by the building to building.

The Room, the Street and Human Agreement

'The room is the beginning of Architecture.'

'A street is a room, a community room by agreement. It changes its character from intersection to intersection changes and may be regarded as a number of rooms.'

'The city stems from the inspiration to meet. It is very important, there shall be places to meet, meeting is the most important part of a city plan.'

"Thoughts," reprinted from *Architecture + Urbanism*, vol. 3, no. 1, January 1973, pp. 23–40.

Clearing

An interview

I was relating my experience with the Art Commission, where architects present plans of schools on land available in neighborhoods, often too small to have a playground big enough for the pupils to come and at least meet each other at that moment as the whole school in play. School therefore has to assume several yard periods. And that you related to your own time in school, when the assembly was really in a sense the classroom. And the yard certainly was one. And now you get the order to have a classroom which will assemble a half or even a quarter of the school, and the yard is cut down to just what is barely necessary to have only a period, a small period, of meeting outside; you get some fresh air, that's what you do, natural air. And all these seem like the beginning of a paring down of even that, you see, smaller rooms and smaller playfields—once the idea of the total assembly doesn't become an important part of school. So I wondered whether you couldn't just eliminate the playground altogether, and really consider that it has no more power. I don't want to say it quite categorically. My mind switched to thinking in terms of a large piece of land, which would take the place of what?—of the small, inadequate playgrounds which are distributed around neighborhoods. This, I know, would meet with a great deal of disfavor, but when you look at the plans submitted, of meted-out places for swings and for sandboxes and for any other hard-surface play, and everything is measured to *Graphic Standards* proportions, of just minimums, you realize that the architect is bound hand and foot. His imagination can't span—cannot suggest even the elimination of some relatively unimportant, let's say, elements of play, and make even a superior playground by not offering the usual standards but simply a clearing itself, and let the imagination do everything else, the imagination of the child, I mean to say. And from this I thought of the idea that after all if you did nothing else, but had as a premise to assemble land, even if you do not build on it right away, in reservation—that the act of the clearing itself, knowing that the open land is an asset without even knowing its purpose . . . That's what I meant about the power of a location being a beginning, already a beginning when the land is an asserted piece of land, waiting for the most agreed upon use. The recognition that the size of the land gives a sense of orientation to a neighborhood, a section of the city, if they were larger patches of land. Immediately you are in keeping with a sense of associated uses, similar to the anticipated associations that William Penn thought of, when he allocated even in the forests surrounding the initial development of Philadelphia five locations upon which one should not build. It's the sense of having or, let's say, employing the natural feelings of such a force, of simply a clearing, and is greater than all "standard" planning, or all the good that's expected from what has been directed through planning.

A large location, one large location of land—you see, I feel it is very true and the other is not true. The small piece of land associated with the school, where everything is measured out, is wrong because that measurement is a kind of standard established, and possibly repeated and repeated. You say that a swing requires four feet on one side and eight feet on another, but the spirit of a swing isn't there. And also, you might say, do you need a swing? Maybe a clear piece of land in which you have no swings would make the device for swings, or the device for other play to come out, merely because it is a large piece of land. And the other, which had everything accounted for, is a deadly thing. The spirit of play cannot be found with these little piddling postage stamps. Why give any play, you see, if you cannot give it in full? Because the spirit of play is not just meting out so many square feet so you can just sort of stretch your legs. You either give it or you don't. Therefore abandon the idea of a playground entirely from a school and just simply make a clearing somewhere *worthy* to play in, and that is then a recognition of part of man's desires. There it's expressed. It's not expressed in the others, that mete it out like spoonfed—token ideas of what play is. Play is wild! Play goes in all directions.

Large piece of land. Now if you can't afford to build anything, the act of making the recognition that there must be a large piece of land is a better act than fitting it out. The fitting it out will come. Not only that, but you will be able to sense what you cannot sense as an appropriate space today. Maybe the first act on that piece of land is to build a kind of shelter, not unlike that of a stoa, which is unpartitioned, and it's there as a kind of shelter which is secure in shelter because the trees won't shelter you during the rain; so this is built as a kind of first thing. You wait, you go under this thing when it's raining, you wait for the rain to be over, and you go back to play again, or you go home, or wait for a bus. But this gives you a sense of the validity, you see, of the establishment of play, and this is what you're supporting. When you're establishing that, your act can be very, very primitive and be truer than giving free notebooks and that kind of thing—that doesn't mean anything! You don't give any notebooks, but you simply are there in class without anything at all. Believe me, you'll learn a tremendous amount, if you don't have that classbook. If you can't give it in the spirit, you see, which means beginning over again sometimes rather than thinking that it is just a continuation in better and better and more and more . . . Rather not that, but strip yourself of the accumulation of established means and begin again in those primitive ways to catch the spirit of learning—where you *don't* have so many availabilities.

But you still can feel the raw desire that's in back of the agreement to have such a place. The word *agreement* is a wonderful word, because it's a simple, down-to-earth, bread-and-butter word, and we need it very desperately. And the word *institution* has bad repute, because it sounds like it's shackled, and confined, and running in one direction only. And that's what I mean really. Look how much spirit there is—you can see the open space. Would you have any hesitation to say that you have made a good act? Not a bit. If you can establish that as being truer in spirit to play. Or even if not play, just a clearing in the light of many houses—that a clearing is part of many houses. Just that. On that a school can be, and also maybe a meetinghouse could be, just simply that. Or a place of shelter. And the freedom of this area where things can be for play.

The garden. It has to do with, not nature in the broadest sense, but nature as it applies to a place which has been chosen by man and is developed for man's use in a certain way. And the architect is called in as the advocate of nature, and makes everything in the deepest respect for nature by not imitating it at all, and not allowing himself to think that he's a designer if he imitates how, let's say, the bird plants the tree. But he must plant the tree as he is man, a choosing individual, and as man conscious, nature not being conscious, makes. And then how he thinks, in the garden, as the interpreter of a personal thing—the garden belongs to a person—that it is not a place of invitation; if it is an invitation, it's a very intimate one. And that he must make a drawing for the garden with the idea that things will grow and that his drawing is really only an instruction for something that starts. And that even every balustrade or every fountain or the choice of stone is something that belongs so much to this garden that the next garden must begin over again. So therefore he *must* destroy his drawings of the garden once it is instructed to be built, and put it into the fireplace. All details, all ideas of the garden must go into the fireplace, because it really belongs to no other garden. Therefore he keeps no record of it; he must begin again as though it were the most intimate act.

You might say that nature is the workshop of God, that it is the saws and the hammers and all the means of instrumentation. But the desire to be something, if it strikes this instrumentation, if, let's say, nature makes a nod and says, "I can make it"—the desire is somehow in back of it, and is a tremendous thing. It is really the incredible. It is the part which is completely unmeasurable. It says to nature something which is not invalid, and nature makes that which it could never make had it not been for the spirit that wants it to be made. Because if nature would go on making what it makes, there would only be the matter of the sun shining and the rain falling and everything just really being right in its place because that's the way gravity wants it, that's the way the winds want it, and that's the way everything that is measurable wants it.

"Clearing: Interviews with Louis I. Kahn," reprinted with permission from *VIA*, vol. 2, 1973, pp. 158–61.

Poetics

I have taught self rewarded.
School is my chapel.
I write Psalms.
When I teach well, what I have
done is never mentioned.
Teaching is to present the yet
not said the yet not made.
It is self inspiring. The inspired
finds only himself.
Singularity to Singularity.
Human agreement without example.
To make present is an offering to criticism.
Not to judgment.
A man is greater than his works.
To judge or be judged is to
presume Eternity.
Eternity the prevailing Spirit.
Art aspires to Eternity.
Religion is its Art.

Reprinted with permission from Hideki Shimizi, "Context of Man: Louis I. Kahn," *Utah Architect*, no. 53, Summer 1973, p. 1.

1973: Brooklyn, New York

A lecture at Pratt University, Fall 1973

I discovered something one day. I was in Maryland getting another sort of honorary degree, and I had some prepared speech, which of course I wasn't going to read. I knew what I was going to say. They had a new building, the architects did. They had built a new building and it was there—I think the room was in the center—where the celebration, the degree giving, was held. The room was about a hundred and twenty feet or so long and maybe fifty feet wide and had a balcony. On two ends of the balcony there were musicians—brass instrument musicians on either end—and they played some baroque music of Venetian origin, and it was absolutely wonderful. Nobody played excellently. I heard little sounds that weren't really too good; but altogether in the way it occupied the hall, this thing made me think of something to say which was not what I had intended, and I think that seeing you all puts me in the same frame of mind.

I was going to show slides, but I'm not going to show any slides because I am bored with them, you see, myself. Maybe this is because I really don't think that telling you how I do things means very much.

I believe that a man's greatest worth is in the area where he can claim no ownership. The way I do things is private really, and when you copy you really die twenty deaths because you know that you wouldn't even go so far as to copy yourself, you see, because anything you do is quite incomplete. But the part that you do which doesn't belong to you is the most precious for you and it's the kind of thing that you really can offer, because it is a better part of you, actually. The premises anyone can use. Though you may be someone who thinks about them, you only think about them because they are part of a general commonality which really belongs to everybody.

And in getting up to speak, I had to say—after the music had been played, this great music—that it told me something that was terribly important to me. I felt of all, very joyous. I felt that which joy is made of. And I began to realize that joy itself must have been the impelling force that was there before we were there. That somehow joy was in every ingredient of our making. That which was the ooze, you see, without any kind of shape or direction. There must have been this force of joy, which prevailed everywhere within the context, that was reaching out to express. Somehow that word joy became the most unmeasurable word. It was the essence of creativity, the force of creativity. I realize that, if I were a painter and I were to paint a canvas of a great catastrophe. I couldn't put the first stroke on the canvas without thinking first of joy in doing it. You cannot make a drawing unless you are joyously engaged. And somehow, when I thought that art was a kind of oracle, a kind of aura, which had to be satisfied by the artist, and that the artist made something and he dedicated it to the art, an offering to the art as though it were something that preceded the work, I began to realize that art cannot be art unless it is a work, and not something absolutely there that is in the blue somewhere.

I thought then that the first feeling must have been touch. When you think of it, it probably is the first feeling. Our whole sense of procreation has to do with touch. Touch desired to be so much in touch that eyesight came from touch. To see was only to touch more accurately. And then I thought that these forces within us are beautiful things, which you still can feel although they come from the most primordial, unformed kind of existence. It still is retained in you.

I was writing a statement of appreciation for someone who helped me in doing work on the Roosevelt Memorial in New York, which I am now engaged in doing. I had this thought that a memorial should be a room and a garden. That's all I had. Why did I want a room and a garden? I just chose it to be the point of departure. The garden is somehow a personal nature, a personal kind of control of nature, a gathering of nature. And the room was the beginning of architecture. I had this sense, you see, and the room wasn't just architecture, but was an extension of self. I'll explain this because I think it has qualities that don't belong to me at all. It has qualities which bring architecture to you. It has nothing to do with the practice of architecture, which is a different thing entirely. Architecture really has nothing to do with practice. That's the operational aspect of it. But there is something about the emergence of architecture as an expression of man which is tremendously important because we actually live to express. It is the reason for living.

So there is then this striving, you might say, from touch to "touch," and not just touch. In this sense there is the development of what could be sight. When sight came, the first moment of sight was the realization of beauty. I don't mean beautiful or very beautiful or extremely beautiful—just beauty, which is stronger than any of the adjectives you may put to it. It is the total harmony that you feel without knowing, without choice—just simply beauty itself, the feeling of total harmony. It is like meeting your maker, in a way, because nature, the maker, is the maker of all that is made. You cannot design anything without nature helping you. And there is a great difference between the design and form and shape. And that's what we'll talk about.

This sight then came about, and sight immediately felt the total harmony—beauty—without reservation, without criticism, without choice. And art, which was immediately felt, was the first word. One can say the first line, but I think it was the first word. The first utterance could have been "Ah"—just that. What a powerful word that is; it expresses so much, you see, with just a few letters. Now from beauty came wonder. Wonder has nothing to do with knowledge. It's just a kind of first response to the intuitive being the odyssey or the record of the odyssey of our making through the billions, the untold billions, of years in making. I don't believe one thing started at one time, another thing at another time. Everything was started in one way at the same time. It was at no time, either; it just simply was there. Then came wonder. This is the same feeling that the astronauts must have felt when they saw the earth at a great distance. Of course I followed them, and I felt what they felt: this great ball in space, pink or rose and blue and white. Somehow all the things on it—even the great achievements like, let us say, Paris, a great achievement, or London—they all sort of disappeared and became circumstantial work. Yet, somehow the toccata and fugue did not disappear, because they are the most unmeasurable and therefore the closest to that which cannot disappear.

The more deeply a thing is engaged in the unmeasurable, the more deeply lasting is its value. So the toccata and fugue you could not deny. You couldn't deny some of the great works of art, because they are really born out of the unmeasurable. And so I think that what you felt was, again, just wonder, not knowledge or knowing. You felt that knowledge was really not as important as your sense of wonder, which was a great feeling—without reservation, without obligation, without accounting for yourself, just the closest in-touchness with your intuitive wonder. From wonder must come realization, because in the record of your making you have gone through every law of nature. It is part of you. Recorded in your intuitive are all the great steps and momentous decisions of the making. Intuition is your most exacting sense. It is the most reliable sense. It is the most personal sense that a singularity has, and it, not knowledge, must be considered your greatest gift. If it isn't in wonder you needn't bother about it.

This must be considered when knowledge, which is a tremendously valuable thing, comes to you. It is valuable because from knowledge, you get knowing, which is private. The only thing valuable to you is knowing, and knowing must never be imparted because it is very singular, very impure: it has to do with you. But knowing can give you in-touchness with your intuitive, and therefore the life of knowing is very real, but personal. Just think how much the schools must learn before they can honor the mind of a person. Within lodges the spirit: in the brain, it doesn't lodge. The brain is simply a mechanism. So the mind is different from the brain. The mind is the seat of the intuitive and brain is an instrument; you get them pot luck from nature. That's why each one is a singularity.

The instrument can bring to the fore that which, if it is a good instrument, would bring the spirit within you out and put it in touch: the brain makes the mind the mind. The singularity, however, is the mind, not the brain. So, with the sense of wonder comes realization—realization, somehow born out of the intuitive, that something must be so. It has definite existence though you can't see it. Nobody can see your mind, but in it lies existence. You strive because existence makes you think of what you want to express because the expression is a drive: to express is to drive. You then make the distinction between existence and presence, and when you want to give something presence you have to consult nature.

This is where design comes in. The realization is realization in form, which means nature. You realize that something has a certain nature. When you think of the making of a school, the school has a certain nature. In making it you must consult the laws of nature, and the consultation and approval of nature are absolutely necessary. There you will find, discover, the order of water, the order of wind, the order of light, the order of certain materials. If you think of brick, for instance, and you consult the orders, you consider the nature of brick. This is a natural thing. You say to brick. "What do you want, brick?" And brick says to you, "I like an arch." And you say to brick, "Look, I want one too, but arches are expensive and I can use a concrete lintel over you, over an opening." And then you say, "What do you think of that, brick?" Brick says, "I like an arch."

It's important, you see, that you honor the material that you use. You don't bandy it around as though to say, "Well, we have a lot of material around. We can do it one way. We can do it another way." It's not true. You can only do it if you honor the brick and glorify the brick instead of just shortchanging it or giving it an inferior job to do, where it loses its character. When you use it as infill material, for instance—which I have done, you have done—the brick feels like a servant. Brick is a beautiful material and it has done beautiful work in many places; it still does because it's a completely live material. In three-quarters of the world the brick is the only logical material to use because concrete is a highly sophisticated material and not as readily available as you think. And so you can talk to nature about many other things.

When I talk to students, the one feeling I always have is that everyone can surpass me in my work. They don't, but that's my attitude. I feel that being in school is like being in a chapel, and my duty is to write psalms. I come much more refreshed and challenged from the classes. I learn more from the students than I probably teach. This is not an idle thing; it is only learning, but I learn it in my own way. It isn't what they teach me, but what I teach myself in the presence of those who I think are singularities. Therefore, teaching is the art of singularity to singularity. It is not talking to a group; a group is just a matter of so many and so many singularities. They teach you your own singularity because only a singularity can teach a singularity.

Design from form is a realization of the nature of something which is in here. It's completely inaudible, unseeable, and you turn to nature to make it actually present from existence in the mind. I turn to what I said before about a room. And I would not like to feel that I have forgotten, nor you as I speak to you, about the stream of joy which must be felt. Otherwise you don't really feel anything. If what I say somehow activates it I'd be, of course, terribly pleased and honored. But back to the room as the beginning of architecture.

If you think about it, you realize that you don't say the same thing in a small room as you do in a large room. If I were to speak in the Sheraton Hotel I would have to pick one person who smiles at me in order to be able to speak at all, especially extemporaneously, without notes in front of me. It's an event and you treat it as an event, and therefore the room is different. Three people can make you say your lines that you've always said before because already you're somehow performing and not just thinking in terms of them.

Also, what's marvellous about a room is that the light that comes through the windows of that room belongs to the room. And the sun somehow doesn't realize how wonderful it is until after a room is made. So somehow man's creation, the making of a room, is nothing short of the making of a miracle. To think that a man can claim a slice of the sun. Now when you get an order from the school board which says: "We have a great idea! We should not put windows in schools because, after all, the darlings, you see, in the class need wall space for their paintings. And after all, also, a window could distract the teacher." But what teacher deserves that much attention? I'd like to know. After all, the bird outside, the person scurrying for shelter, the rain and you inside, the leaves falling from the tree, the clouds passing by, the sun penetrating, are all great things. They're lessons in themselves. The windows are essential to the school. You were made from light and therefore you must live with the sense that light is important. It isn't just a direction from a school board, an educator, so to speak, telling you what life is all about. This must be resisted. Without light there is no architecture.

Then the room is a terribly important thing. And if you realize also that a plan is a society of rooms, then the large room and the small room become a kind of great thing that you can employ. The tall room, the low room, the one with the fireplace, and the one without, become a great event in your mind and you begin to think, not of the requirements but of the nature of the architectural elements that you can employ to make the environment a place where it is good to learn or good to live or good to work. Then you are really in the midst of architecture and not in the operational atmosphere of the professional man.

You're highly protected as a professional man. There isn't a person who can even

324

say he's not as good a professional as the other fellow. You can't. Especially if you join A.I.A. Everybody's completely equal. That is not so: they're not equal. They're marvellous, yes, but not equal. And not everybody is equally talented. There's no question that talent prevails anywhere. There's no person without talent. That's ridiculous. They all have talent. It's only a question, you see, of which way your singularity can blossom, because you cannot learn anything that's not part of yourself. It's impossible.

You've learned physics, I'm sure, many of you, and you don't know a word of it, yet you passed the examination. That happened to me. I copied the notes of the guy next to me, who could listen and write. If I listened, I couldn't write: if I wrote, I didn't listen. And so I had to copy his notes because he could do both things. He knew what the professor was talking about before he said it, and I had to listen to every word. Now if the teacher had said to me, "Louie Kahn, it's important for you to learn physics because you're going to be an architect," I knew that a long time, so he was right. But he says, "I know what you are. You'll be examined but I'll ask you to *draw* physics for me. That's all. Don't just write what I said." And I would surprise him. It would be my forte, my way, and therefore must not be disturbed. You lose the sense of your worth by putting yourself in—crowding yourself—with that which doesn't belong to you at all. You'll just forget it. It will never be with you. I don't know any more than one or two principles of physics.

The plan is a society of rooms. When you realize that you don't say the same thing in a small room that you do in a large room you realize that a school should be a kind of environment of rooms which would be ready for, would be offerings to school. And in doing this you become inventive in the way that is applicable to school. You would eliminate every corridor, I'm sure, and turn the corridors into halls. The halls would be the pupils' spaces that belong to them as the classroom of the students. There, the little boy can speak to the other little boys and say, "What did the teacher say?" The other boy listens and records. When the boy gets the lesson from a person of the same age, somehow the lesson becomes understandable.

How many things must happen and where does the architect sit? He sits right there. He is the man who conveys the beauty of space, which is the very meaning of spaces, of meaningful spaces. They're all meaningful. You invent an environment, and it can be your own invention. It doesn't have to be a prototype. It simply has to be the way you see the environment for learning, and not taken from all the directions that may be gotten from your books of standards. Therein lies the architect. He is not defined by being able, let's say, to gather sufficient information to operate as a professional. Now these can be harsh words and they don't seem to be applicable to everybody. But I think it is true. I think it is applicable. That's putting up an argument and solving it yourself, right?

Now then, the society of rooms is plan. You can say it is the structure of the spaces in light. And you can relate it also to an assignment that I gave myself to draw, a picture that demonstrated light. Now if you assign yourself a theme like that, the first thing you do is to escape somewhere, because it is impossible to do this, you say. The white piece of paper is the illustration. If I illustrate light, I have a white paper, and that is light. What else can I do? I thought that was the only thing to do. But I realized that I wasn't right at all. When I put a stroke on the paper, a couple of strokes in ink, I realized that the black was where the light was not. And then I really could make a drawing. I would only be discerning as to where I put the black, where the light is not, and this made the picture come out.

I have some drawings and some slides with me, which I'll show to you some other time, which indicate this very clearly. The drawing is by Cruikshank, you know, an English illustrator of great importance to everyone. He made a drawing of a man sitting by a fire with a swaying female sort of next to him. Through a doorway in the night was a horse. The walls were receiving the light from the fire. A fireplace, out of the picture, radiated light, which caught on the folds of the undulating female and on the man sitting on his chair; the horse behind did not receive the light, but just little sparks of it. Every pen was subservient to the sense that where the stroke was, the light was not. And the thing became absolutely luminous. Closer to the fire it was practically white paper, and then it shaded away. It was a beautiful illustration of the realizations of the expressor to find the means of making evident this fact.

Now this came from the realizations I had about light and I said that all material in nature—it being, as I said before, the mountains and the streams and the air we—are made of light which has been spent. And all material is light which has become exhausted. And this crumpled mass called material casts a shadow. And the shadow belongs to light. So light is really the source of all being. And I said to myself, the existence will be to express in the ooze, which you might say was just completely infiltrated with joy. To be, from touch to sight to hearing that one becomes manifest and the experience of this has become ingrained. And the will, the desire, was somehow a solid front to make sight possible.

Now, you say, where is the significance in all this? It is the movement from silence, which is somewhat the seat of the measurable, which is the will to express, moving toward the means to express, which is material made of light. And light comes to you because actually it is not divided. It is simply something that's become manifest and that which desires to be manifest coming together. And that movement to light and the movement from light to a desire to be, to express, which meet at a point which may be called your singularity. There are as many meetings as there are people, and there must, in a way, almost be as many meetings as there are leaves on a tree, because I believe that sense must be in a tree or in a microbe equally as much as it is in every living creature. And this meeting spells your singularity.

So where's the scientist and where's the poet? The poet is one who goes from the seat of the unmeasurable and travels toward the measurable but keeps the force of the unmeasurable with him all the time, disdaining almost to write a word, which is the means. Art, the first word. And he goes toward the measurable but holds the unmeasurable and at the last moment he must write a word because, although he desires not to say anything, words propel his poetry. He has to succumb to the word after all. But he's traveled a great distance before he used any of the means. Just a smidgeon, if you will, you see. And it was enough. The scientist, who has the unmeasurable qualities, which after all are all he has as a man, holds his line, does not go away or travel with the unmeasurable because he's interested in knowing. He's interested in the laws of nature. He allows nature to come to him. Which means he has so many degrees, you know. And it comes to him. And he at that point must grab it because it's as long as he can stand the difficulty of holding back. And so he receives knowledge in full. And he works with this and you call that being objective. But Einstein traveled with the poet. He holds the unmeasurable because he's a fiddle player. And so he holds the unmeasurable for a long, long time. And he also reaches nature or light at the very, very doorstep, because he only needs a smidgeon of knowledge, because from that smidgeon he can reconstruct the universe, because he deals with order and not knowing.

No piece of knowing, you see, which is always fragmentary, is enough for a man who is truly visionary like Einstein. And he would not accept knowledge unless it belonged to all knowledge. Therefore he can so easily write his beautiful formula of relativity. It was just the way in which he just simply gave you that which can lead you to a greater sense of awe of order which all knowledge is really answerable to. One does not consider knowledge as belonging to anything human. Knowledge belongs only to that which has to do with nature. It belongs to the universe, but doesn't it belong to eternity? And there's a big difference.

When you're making something you must consult nature, like the conversation with the brick. And you can make the same conversation with concrete. And you can make the same conversation with paper, or with papier maché, or with plastic, or with marble, or any material that has its nature. And it's the beauty of what you create that you honor—the material for what it really is. And never say that you use it in a kind of subsidiary way which makes the material itself wonder when the next man will come who will honor its character, you see.

327

How much can be learned, and it's not how much you learn, but it is really how much you honor, you see, the position of learning in connection with what you're doing. Because you must really . . . you must know to feed your intuitive, but you must not trust the knowing as being something that may be imparted to someone else. You translate it into the work you do, and that is your best character because your singularity will make that which is unfamiliar if you will just trust it for what it is. It will be unfamiliar in your own way. And the various expensive arts will be, will bring forward, something which had you in it as a kind of offering to the art which you are in the middle of.

So, now turning, let's say—so far I think I haven't talked about architecture at all—we talk simply about, let's say, the plan, and what is a room, and a plan being a society of rooms. You can do the same thing when you're dealing see with plans, with city plans. There's no difference to a person who sees this in the light of its nature. What is the nature of what you are doing? Then, a plan as big as a whole city is no more complex than a house. Not at all. It's just realizing that it isn't a bag of tricks or something to do with a traffic system or things like that, because a traffic system and all the other operational systems of a city are merely operational problems. You can get people with different singularities to help you with this.

The great symphony of all forces which make a city, I think, belongs to the mind of the architect. He is the best trained to bring it all into some symphonic character. And that has nothing to do with making a kind of beautiful-looking plan. Not at all. It must be very true to its nature. So when you're dealing with a traffic problem, and you forget the helicopters, you forget the planes, you forget the parking, you forget all these things, you're only dealing with little things. Now the force of a road is one whose objective is to come somewhere. And this coming somewhere must be considered an event which serves you very well. If at that point you spend hours trying to find a parking space you have no plan. So you consider the movement as being rewarded, you consider the tall building on the street must surrender the six stories on the street for the street's purpose, and you have an elevator reach the sixth story, which exactly is what the person living in the tall building wants. He doesn't want to live on the first level. And you just consider everything as though it had its nature.

Most of all we mustn't forget that in a city the street must be supreme. It is actually the first institution of the city. It is a decision out of commonality that you choose a place out of all places to build a place where others can settle. It's a very important decision. It's of the same importance as the positioning of the Greek temple in Greek days amongst the hills. Of all the hills, this hill is chosen for the temple. And then all the other hills sort of beckon to it as though bowing to this decision, because you do not see the hills. No, you see them as only respecting the decision of the placing of this eulogizing kind of building which, you might say, is remarkable in that it has never been there before.

I honor beginnings. Of all things, I honor beginnings. I believe that what was has always been, and what is has always been, and what will be has always been. I don't think the circumstantial play from year to year and era to era means anything, but what has become available to you from time to time as expressive instinct does. The man of old had the same brilliance of mind as we assume we have only now. And that which made a thing become manifest for the first time is our great, great moment of creative happening. I have books in my place. I like English history. I like the bloodiness of it somehow—you know it's horribly bloody—but out of it came something. It's really just a miscuing of how things are made, and if you were to write a history of fear, I think you would write the most true of history books. And I have one of eight volumes, and I only read the first volume and only the first chapter, because every time I read it I also read something else into it. And the reason is that I'm really interested in reading Volume Zero. And maybe, when I get through with that, Volume Minus-One. History could not have started at those places. History was much, much preceded. It just isn't recorded.

And that is the beauty of our work in that it deals with the recesses of the mind from which what is not yet said and what is not yet made comes. And I think it's important to everybody, because desire is infinitely more important than need. And it's disgraceful not to be able to supply the needs. It mustn't be considered an achievement if the country gives us our needs. It must be something that is a foregone conclusion if you're brought upon this world. But desire, to stymie that, to stymie the qualities of the not-yet-said and the not-yet-made, desire is the very reason for living. It is the core of the expressive instinct that has to be given play.

In cities, probably the measure of a city is the degree or the quality of the availabilities. We are living in a country which is the richest of all in availabilities, if we were to speak up. And I'm glad we don't, because as soon as we become conscious of it, it'll be just as ruinous as McCarthy, who spoiled our true consciousness, our sense of democracy. He tried to define it and called for sides to be held, to be counted, and therefore destroyed the beauty of what democracy could be. And we're suffering to this day because of the attempt to isolate, you know, the qualities of democracy. I believe that the availabilities are really in this country. And we don't really appreciate them because they are there to be had. We want more of it because it's the very nature of us. It's possible to avail yourself of something. And so availability is the hallmark of America. And it's been bandied around, it's been kept from certain people, but I think it's just there. You're about to assert yourself, and you find that it also comes your way. And I think that in the city, if I were to say, if I were to make a city plan,

I think I would say, "In what way can I make the architecture of connection which would enliven the mind as to how the availabilities can be even more enriched than they are?" Put them into focus. They lost their character in the course of the operations because the original inspirations are gone. Other people take over and you do not sense, you see, those inspirational moments which made those intuitions possible. And there are many still that are, in the air, completely possible.

The architect's job, in my opinion, and I must close on this, is to find those spaces, those areas of study, where the availabilities, not yet here, and those that are already here, can have better environments for their maturing into those which talk and say things to you and really make evident that the spaces that you make are the seat of a certain offering of man to next man. It is not an operational thing. You can leave that to the builders and to the operators. They already build eighty-five percent of the architecture, so give them another five percent if they're so stingy, so very selfish about it, and take only ten percent or five percent and be really an architect and not just a professional. A professional will bury you. You'll become so comfortable. You'll become so praised, equally to someone else, that you'll never recognize yourself after awhile. You get yourself a good business character, you can really play golf all day and your buildings will be built anyway. But what the devil is that? What joy is there if joy is buried? I think joy is the key word in our work. It must be felt. If you don't feel joy in what you're doing, then you're not really operating. And there are miserable moments which you've got to live through. But really, joy will prevail. And thank you very much.

"1973: Brooklyn, New York," reprinted from *Perspecta 19: The Yale Architectural Journal*, 1982, pp. 89–100.

Louis I. Kahn with Balkrishna Doshi, 1974.

1974

Foreword

In the work of Carlo Scarpa
'Beauty'
the first sense
Art
the first word
Then Wonder
Then the inner realization of 'Form'
the sense of the wholeness of inseparable elements.
Design consults Nature
to give presence to the elements.
A work of art makes manifest the wholeness of 'Form'
the symphony of the selected shapes of the elements.

In the elements
the joint inspires ornament, its celebration.
The detail is the adoration of Nature.

Foreword reprinted from *Carlo Scarpa Architetto Poeta* (London: Royal Institute of British Architects, 1974), unnumbered pages.

Harmony Between Man
and Architecture

A lecture in Paris

I want to talk to you about architecture and human agreement and when I look at the tall building which is going up at Montparnasse, I have the feeling that man and architecture are not in agreement. I thought that in many respects it was no good: one absolutely obvious one is that it fails to demonstrate, in any kind of way, the genius of French engineering. When one thinks of a high-rise structure one thinks of columns down below, at street level, supporting the weight and lending their strength to carry the columns above. Down below, the columns give the impression of groaning under the load, whilst those on top should give the impression of dancing like fairies, liberated from their load, very light, doing the smallest possible share of hard work.

If you look at the building, all the columns are alike. What has happened to the genius of French engineering? Think of the wind, that important factor in the construction of high-rise buildings; resistance against the wind is such an important discovery that one might expect it to be reflected in the external aspect of the building. But this one stands up as if nothing were happening, as if natural forces were not involved, as if man alone were involved, an autocrat talking to himself and to no one else.

This is why I felt so very sad to see that the genius of French engineers and architects had not been used, and that all that had been done was to copy existing American works, designed without much care in the absence of ingenious and thoughtful engineers.

I think that a building should show how it was made, should give some idea of the struggle involved in building it. Buildings dating from other periods, which bear witness to this struggle, do exist. A few days ago I was in Bruges; I was very touched by the way man has mixed bricks and stones . . . the marriage of these two materials resembles a dialogue between human beings and the natural world; because we ourselves are made of natural materials and we possess, in our sensory perception, in our consciousness, solutions to all problems, provided that circumstances are favorable to their manifesting themselves.

Our intuition is always ready to spring into action, to grasp information because it bears the imprint of millions of years of experience, ever since the world began; for

I do not believe that man began at a given moment, he began at the same time as everything else.

To come back to the buildings we were discussing, we could say that they bear no relation to these ideas, they are related only to money; our buildings in the United States are also related only to money. I am sorry to have to say this but I must, because Paris is not only your city, it belongs to the whole world.

This morning I went for a walk along your marvellous river Seine; in amongst the other buildings I noticed Mansart's roofs. They really were the skyscrapers of the architecture of their day, for relatively speaking they are higher than our high-rise buildings; but they seem high in a human sense, whereas ours seem high in a financial sense. The latter are "anarchitectural," they are just heaps of masonry, which is not necessarily architecture.

Then what is architecture . . . ?

I should not really be speaking to you about this when others are more qualified than I am to do it. In fact, only a poet could talk about it, until the architect reaches the stage when he possesses the secret silent qualities of the poet. A poet tries to say nothing, but has to say something because verbal expression is his only tool; he will therefore write, trying to put something immaterial, through which feelings can flow, on paper, choosing from amongst the materials that are in his mind. I don't know of any greater compliment to an architect than to tell him that he is a poet.

What of construction, then? The constructional aspect will only appear on condition that these buildings are put into the hands of capable engineers who can work in collaboration with the architects. Architects should have to listen to what engineers have to say, and learn from it, just as engineers should listen to and try and understand the aspirations of those who design high-rise buildings.

Nowadays the Eiffel Tower is like a toy; it has been humiliated. At one time the Eiffel Tower was the expression of the engineering genius of France: it is not a building so it does not matter if it is so high. It is a structure, or a sort of engineer's sculpture. But as soon as we are concerned with a place where people are going to live it is a different matter, how can one compare their heights?

When people take a look at these high-rise buildings they realize that they have completely destroyed Paris. In my opinion the first thing to be done is to demolish them, because all Paris's magic has disappeared: to me it is cruel and insensitive.

As I have just flown in from Philadelphia you must be thinking that I should not be speaking to you, French people, in this way, because it is your country and not mine. But I feel the same way as you do when you see a polluted river which has lost its magic. When you see a mountain stream which has not yet been polluted you can feel sorry for it. You know what will be its fate when it gets into the bad company of the rivers downstream.

If the magic is lost, the most precious instinct that we possess goes with it.

The capacity for wonder is a primitive instinct: with no knowledge, no study, by wonder alone one can get really close to beauty which is total harmony, which has nothing to do with the Beautiful with a capital B. This is something outstanding: beauty is the most potent of the senses that man must have been aware of when he became conscious of his own instincts for the first time. We know in a spontaneous and innate fashion when things are beautiful: the Beautiful is quite different. Beauty is in itself a potent sense and when harmony is not there it disappears. One notices this immediately: in front of an ugly building some detail may "please," but when the building is bad in itself it is as wounding as a polluted river.

Man's agreement with architecture is an example of something that stems from intuition, and what else is intuition but a record of the psychical and physical decisions we have made, particularly at our most dramatic moments. Intuition is the sum of the whole universe; when the universe is in question what happens to the laws of the universe is of little importance—I utilize them all without isolating any of them, because basically we know by intuition everything that is to be known.

To my mind intuition is one of the most precise of all our senses. We must, somehow or other, integrate it with our sensibility, along with knowledge and the things we have to learn. To me, knowledge is an unfinished book: and knowledge is itself aware of being unfinished. The elements of knowledge have been assembled by men, since knowledge did not come out of the skies; our knowledge applies only to the physical world, the biological world defies description. The only things that can be described as a part of the human organism are those parts that nature has given us as tools. From henceforth we are machines for finding out, capable of enlarging the potentialities of the brain, but never reaching as far as the mind, for the mind is the soul of the brain.

Our brain is not always consistent, being very diversified; but the soul itself is always the same. Thus the mind is responsible for the individuality which causes one person to be different from another.

Let us consider now the fact that our knowledge is something to respect. Knowledge gives impetus to our intuition and makes it function. Knowledge pushes forward the marvels of intuition, but the comprehension of each individual's knowledge is a personal matter. Comprehension cannot be shared with anyone. I do not believe that psychology or sociology has anything to do with man's knowledge of mankind. These are statistics, speculations, at best very inadequate. One man may know everything about sociology and another will not achieve this knowledge even if he reads 20,000 volumes. The first has it in him because it springs from the deepest part of his being,

335

from his intuition; consequently one should not speak of it as a science. There is nothing scientific about it, it is rather in the realm of the exploration of matter.

Man's agreement is in a real sense the gift of his intuition. I maintain that architecture is very closely associated with it, engineering also, because it is a profession involving "design," and I am using this word in the sense in which the French understand it, that is to say "the process of executing some plan." We call the instructions given for making something "design"; you use the laws of nature for this, and initially sense of form, or sense of inseparable parts. Concept is very close to form, but concept and idea are also closely linked; thus to conceive is to know everything about the thing one wants to create.

When one has a concept one cannot fail. A client may show you the door, of course, but in the execution of your idea you cannot fail. It is the same with an idea: an idea is only real if it can be used to produce something. The phrase "I have an idea, but it did not come off" does not exist. I maintain that form has nothing to do with outward appearance; in "design" we are concerned with appearance, we choose an aspect and anyone can do as much. Form is the area in which the architect can give the best of himself because of his knowledge of the inseparable elements. If a construction possesses this quality of inseparable elements, the project has a chance of being legible.

With regard to office blocks, they do not possess form; the inseparable elements are made homogeneous and do not demonstrate the association of separate parts. One can see the inseparable elements in a high-rise building very clearly; in a low building it is different, since then there is no struggle against the wind and no anti-wind adaptation to be made. The dimension of the colonnades is different, but they must be expressive because man lives by self-expression. His mind is obsessed by attempts to make his building available to children, or to grown-ups as well for that matter. You go into a building, a child must see it and say "Look how they have done that!" "What is it for? Oh! it's against the wind," and the child understands and has learned a lesson that he will not forget.

Sense of beauty comes first and may have nothing to do with the critical faculty, it may simply consist of a general feeling that everything is harmonious.

If a man loses his sense of humor he becomes old; at the same time one should never forget fairy stories. I believe that fairy stories are the forerunners of science and if I had to change my profession, which is hard to imagine at my age, it would be to write new fairy stories. I would like to have done it in Paris (before they built the buildings I was talking about just now).

With regard to execution, it is the interpretation of form and is very close to form. For instance, take away the hydrogen from H_2O and you are left without water.

If you think of an axe, you have one sharp edge, a big heavy end, and a handle; take away one of these elements and you are left without an axe. That is what I call tangible form, and it is the same notion as inseparable elements. Your plan will be bad if you don't make the blade sharp enough because you have used bad materials, if it is not heavy enough because you have used plastic, or if you have made the handle so short that you cannot cut down trees with it. The concept that there must be a heavy end, a sharp blade, and a handle is what I mean by form; it comes out of your head and has nothing to do with the creation of outward appearance. Outward appearance comes later and I want to insist once again on the importance of form.

Well then, you will say, a form-school, a form-house, a form-factory and so on, these are all intuitive things drawn from your experience, from your sense of order or your sense of what is right, to the extent that the agreement of man is involved. You know that you will have to reach this agreement because in it resides the confirmation of what you do. Your intuition, fraudulent and impetuous faculty that it is, tells you that even if your work is not accepted now, it will be later.

Thus when you think for example of a school there are only two inspirations: to learn and to direct, and I think that they are very close one to the other.

If I had to give lectures on town planning I should not want to call them that, but rather "architecture of high intention." Architecture is not really divided into town planning, urbanism, or a number of other departments such as programming or the study of the environment; an architect has no need of all these titles—or maybe he does need them to protect himself. Some architects seek them for their market value; when they have them they get the biggest business.

The title of architect in fact embraces all the others.

Architecture is an ancient profession, though perhaps not the most ancient, and as such does not need anyone to intervene on its behalf. But it does need to be accepted wholeheartedly, in such a way that when you think of a school you must think of it as a place where it is agreeable to learn.

When you are faced with a building program you should not feel too tied to definitions such as classroom no. 1, classroom no. 2, classroom no. 3—particularly if this indicates that all your rooms should be the same. What you should do is discover new kinds of spaces: here a little room with an open fire, there a room where three or four students can meet and chat quietly. Don't call these classrooms, call them rooms, rooms without labels.

Why small and large rooms? Because one does not speak in the same way in a small room as in a large one. Even the teacher is transformed by the place he is teaching in.

Now let us look at the areas which are not on the school program: you must not

337

accept the program offered by the chief of works because it will simply be based on what people have done before. The architect must always ask himself: to what "dominion" does this construction belong? In this case it is in the dominion where it is agreeable to learn. This is all that he needs to know, the how and the why are not important. The architect knows that he must start from scratch and recreate the miracle which we knew in our first school, when the child is not aware of being a pupil and the teacher is not aware of being a master.

Inspiration is to be found right there, in the origin of schools; this is a lesson that should never be forgotten, if it is forgotten then human agreement can never be reached.

But this human agreement must be constantly lived, it should stem not from a higher authority but from the individual nature of each person as the most precious gift it has to bestow: why should we redo what others have done? There is a richness in the expression of each personality which no other man possesses; because he has not got the same brain, because he is another person. For each one of us the size of our sense of eternity depends on the quality of our brain, and I use the word "eternity" to distinguish it from the universal.

The universal relates only to the physical, whereas the eternal relates to everything which concerns man. This to my mind gives a marked predominance to the universal and it also defines order. Order envelopes all natural laws, and not only those few that we have today; these laws will be revealed one day and their discovery will change existing physical laws (as happened when relativity was defined); the same will happen with all measurable things that we are able to investigate.

No one can explore eternity. Eternity has to be revealed: I believe that it is revealed by circumstances, but I also believe that one cannot search for truth. Truth appears and you recognize it simultaneously, but it is always changing.

Man makes rules, the law is universal in character, but a rule has something in common with eternity; rules can change and the greatest joy belongs to the person who finds a new rule, because he knows that this will put mankind in closer contact with the feelings of the community—this feeling must be shared by all those who write or paint or design.

Within the community of all men, I want to include microbes, and leaves and branches and all living things because I truly think that they have a consciousness; it is too arrogant to think that we are the only people to possess consciousness.

There is another question: the question of silence and light, and this relates to what I was saying just now. Silence is the force out of which grows the will and the desire to express oneself. I should like to say that this will is a progressive uneasiness, whilst desire is related to the words which have not yet been spoken and action which has not yet taken place. The desire for expression is without words, without a name, without weight, and I think of it as something that can be explained passively because, since it has no weight, since it is immaterial, anything concerning its quantity or quality is unacceptable. But whilst I think of that I think at the same time of "light," of "material" because I know that to make anything one has to use materials.

Then what, we should say to ourselves, are materials? I have come to the conclusion that materials are utilized light; (it is better to say that than to say used up light because this strongly evokes the idea that it is time to go to bed); I mean to say that the light has burnt itself out in order to become a material. If you keep that in mind, you will comprehend that everything is utilized light—mountains, air, water, even ourselves who are part of nature. But the desire to be, to express oneself must have come from some marvellous impulses, which were weightless and influenced the natural world to make possible the creation of a living being.

The movement of silence in light and of light in silence crosses a threshold, and this is the moment when the desire to be, to express oneself encounters the possible: the natural world is the possible, and this moment is different for each one of us.

The desire to be and to express oneself is found in scientists, too: we should not dismiss the scientists, but he does have to be more objective, and objectivity is something directly concerned with the natural world. When one has relationships with people one cannot be objective; one can only be objective in relationships with things attached to the natural world.

The moment of inspiration is the moment when what you want to express intersects with what is possible. There also is art's sanctuary, the point at which all art arrives in the end. Basically man's only language is art, which gives words a terrifying strength: art says "it's good," non-art says "it's very good"; the latter modifies the former so that what was good seems less good than before. Adjectives are really nothing but big impostors when they deal with nonmeasurable qualities. Everything is fine when you say "one, two, three," but that all changes when you say "good," or especially "very good," because these are nonmeasurable words, the most nonmeasurable words that exist.

All around us there are buildings and the men who were inspired to build them deserve to be generously praised; even if they are dead one should really ask their permission to build something else beside their buildings. They will be understanding enough to say "one can demolish." Who else has the right to say it?

These testimonials to the past are important, they are tradition; but tradition is like the product of distillation, the essence that remains. Tradition is only valid when it can be everywhere, here and now as well as in the past.

Can you say that Mozart's works are traditional? They are wonders of the human mind, of its sense of eternity; did he retrieve them from eternity? Where were they before? Where can you buy them? You can't buy them! These are the qualities that the great musicians bestowed on music and the great architects bestowed on architecture.

An architect must be able really to love someone, someone whom he truly cares about. I often say to myself "How am I doing, Le Corbusier?" I don't mean that I copy Le Corbusier's works, but this is the way I feel toward the man who had something to bestow, whose perception of architecture was different than that of other architects.

As I said earlier, man's agreement rests also in his response to light and silence; you have to work through the natural world if you want to achieve something. Consequently, when you make a plan, you must know the laws of nature, not in an academic fashion, but you have to respect them.

For example, if you are dealing with concrete, what you have to do is to keep in mind that it is not brick or stone or anything else. You are dealing with a material which is marvellous in itself. It is a cross between steel and melted stone, and you can make it do things which no other material can do.

Therefore concrete forms should not bear any resemblance to structures made of any other material. The way you have used it and the way it looks must let people see that this is the material you have been using and nothing else.

Steel is also a great material, but as soon as your steel leaves the ground you are obliged to take precautions against fire, and the steel shapes are then lost under fire-protective cladding.

There is another point to which I must draw your attention: this is that our towns are becoming infested by streets. The streets are nothing but roads, though they are still called streets, so invaded are they by motor cars. The cars turn them into canals, one could almost fill them with water and the effect would be the same. You cannot cross them, it is too risky. The only streets one can still cross are those in which cars have trouble in moving about, like small streets which discourage the motorist. It is becoming imperative to change our present definitions and to decide which are still streets and which are roads, and to work accordingly. This does not mean that cars will be entirely excluded, but it means that traffic will cease to inspire the same anguish as it now inspires when one has to cross a road. Cars have to go to certain predetermined places, that is the individual motorist's problem, but there are also those who go on foot to take into consideration.

Those who go on foot are the pedestrians; before there was the horse. This friendly creature only went slowly, it was even possible to run faster than a horse. Now we have a machine which, if it is not going fast, is not really doing what it was designed to do, and which also has difficulty attempting to maneuver in small streets, just as people do.

Going shopping is a problem because a one-way street takes you far away from the shop, because it's the wrong moment to cross the road, because you have passed the place you wanted to go and now you can't find the shop.

In fact the street is a common room, and the most vital human institution in a city. The facades and buildings along this street belong to it, they are the walls of the street, the roofless room.

The first time man built a street in a forest he encouraged others to do likewise. In a sense the street is like the forerunner of all human institutions.

I think if one distinguished between streets and roads in towns things would change; I think it is important to zone streets rather than pieces of building land. If streets were zoned in terms of traffic I believe that constructions would find their right place in the space left available. Shopping streets would tend to become busier and a block attracting a lot of motor traffic (which a shopping street does not) would become less busy.

One could group buildings which are just temporary garages or offices in certain areas and then they would not clutter up the center, the small streets and small squares where it is pleasant to live; land values would not be pushed up and people would no longer be forced to move out of the town. One could find a place for them, creating a sector where cars could be adequately maintained and where the architecture would be such that the problems of motor cars and buildings would be resolved. One can build office blocks over basements running to four or five levels when access involves a great many cars. One might initially develop a street architecture above which there would be lifts, liberating space and not causing more overcrowding in streets not built for heavy traffic. A total plan is necessary, therefore, and not just a business arrangement which only poses greater and greater problems to the town council; a plan which would include provision for access and services to the buildings so that they can really make their contribution.

Whilst the astronauts travel farther and farther from the earth everything shrinks and disappears, yet Beethoven's Fifth Symphony does not disappear for it is something incommensurable and as such lives in the mind, never to be rejected. Everything that is commensurable will not last very long. Thus ultimately everything that is made should possess qualities which defy measurement. These qualities can be found in ancient buildings. There are always people who prefer to live in old houses because they find the quality of life better there; this began only in the early days of building when methods were in their infancy and new circumstances arose. A sense of life, a sense of work had been rekindled and from them the buildings took their lasting qualities.

I do not think that you would learn this in the sociology courses or psychology courses given to architects: curious methods, already distorted by the attempt to make a kind of box; someone says do this, do that and so on, this is like this, that is like that: in fact I don't think that man can learn anything which is not already within him.

There is a difference between what and how: how are you going to learn since we are not born knowing how to make things? But of course we have predilections, that is, we know "what": the roots of this intuition, about which I was talking to you a little while ago, must be nourished.

Let us take the example of the Parthenon. You can see in the sunshine the walls are broken; the columns ruined the walls, which protected man from danger. When man realized that all was calm outside he pierced a hole in the wall and said "I have made an opening." The wall wept and said "What are you doing to me?" And man said "I felt that all was well and that I had to make this opening." Man realized the need for an opening, he decorated it and made the top half into an arch; the wall liked that and agreed that it was beautiful. One never considers if it is noble or not to have an opening because in the order of the wall the window was included.

If we now think about the column, we should see it in terms of a wall which has admitted more and more openings until it has all become concentrated on one upright, called a column. This achievement, which is a miracle of reflection, has been capable of defining its different parts, and of realizing that the forces in play at the top are different from those at the bottom, and how these forces are going to reach the ground.

Now let us take a look at a column in a text book. Just another column, you say; no, we must think: "It's a miracle," until we feel that we must reinvent the column.

If you put one column on top of another, something is created which is beautiful to look at; now we have total harmony, now we have a visible manifestation of man's mind interpreting the natural world, in its pristine state, now we have a renewal of man's original sense of wonder.

It was thus when the first styles appeared and the whole world rallied. People did not then take off in all directions: they kept in line, realizing that they were working with certain inseparable elements. So the Greeks were satisfied with playing around with a few simple elements.

On the subject of elements when you think of the plan of a house, the staircase, the walls, the ceiling, these are elements which must be thought about very carefully; for instance the staircase is a very interesting element and when you design it you must draw it as accurately as you have ever drawn anything. You must spend as much time designing the staircase as you will designing the whole house because the measure of the staircase is a rhythmic measure of the whole: it will be measured by the sense of rhythm of that boy who is going to climb four stories in no time, provided that all the steps are the same height. If the rhythm is broken the boy breaks his neck, so be guided by him. The procedure is the same if the staircase is used by a child, a young man, or an old person.

If there is a landing this can be a focal point on the staircase. You will need a window, a seat or a little bookcase so that the old person climbing the stairs with a young man can say "You know, son, I've always wanted to read that book."

It is structure which gives light. Think of the rhythm of the columns of the Parthenon, light, shade: the columns are shade, between the columns is light.

I wanted to talk to you about rooms: these are the basis of architecture and we have already seen that people do not express themselves in the same way in a small room as in a large one. The structure of a room must be obvious in the room itself. The lighting of a room must stem from its very structure, and, as the American poet says, speaking of light: "The sun never knows how large it is until it hits the side of a building or shines inside a room."

It must be a surprise for the sun when a building starts to go up; it was not there before and the sun does things it never thought it could do with this strange man-made object; nature could not have created it. Man depends on nature for everything he does, but nature alone can do nothing: nature cannot build a house or a railway engine, or make an airplane.

"Harmony Between Man and Architecture," reprinted from *Design Incorporating Indian Builder*, vol. 18, no. 3, March 1974, pp. 23–28.

The Samuel S. Fleisher Art Memorial

The city is essentially a meeting place. It is valued by the character of its availabilities. Our way of life is born of freedom which has inspired availabilities the like of which no nation has. The character of this freedom is so great that even a law must adjust to its unmeasurable qualities.

When I was in my early teens, I went to the Graphic Sketch Club. I walked from 7th and Poplar to 8th and Catherine. I was given an easel, paper, and charcoal in the life class. All I could hear was the swishing of the strokes and the soft and privately directed voice of the critic. It was a meeting availability, a place full of offerings.

One Saturday morning I came early. No one seemed to be around. The room to the right of the entrance was open. I walked in to see the work of the masters of the school on the walls. Someday, I hoped I would be selected too. I noticed that the piano in the room was open. I had been playing at home on an ancient, large piano given to me, which was also my bed. My instrument had the sound of little bells. When I touched the keys of the school piano, angels filled the room. I sat down to play the Second Hungarian Rhapsody, not the way it was written since I could not read. When I left the room, I found several people had been listening. They asked that I play the next day at a concert which the Symphony Club was giving in this room. I tried everything to refuse but had to agree. Sunday I played the same piece but faintly as I had played it the day before. (Luckily, I was the first to play.) Mr. Fleisher offered me a scholarship to study composition (not piano). When I told the good news to J. Liberty Todd, a Quaker and Director of the School of Industrial Art, he was flabbergasted, "no, you must not accept . . . nothing but Art!" he said. My mother was heartbroken. My father agreed with him.

At Central High School, William Gray, teacher of Art, gave talks on Architecture. I was to be a painter but he touched the very core of my expressive desires. How circumstantial, but how wonderful is the light thrown upon the threshold when the door is opened.

A city should be a place where a little boy walking through its streets can sense what he someday would like to be. I have designed buildings in India, in Bangladesh. In these countries where commonality is rarely expressed in the institutions available, I might not have had such aspirations.

I have presented the idea that the Bicentennial be the "Congress of the Institutions" (Availabilities) designed to present to all visitors those beliefs that inspired our Declaration of Independence, spoke to the heart of human harmony in feeling, and inspired our people to create such richness of availabilities. Such inspiration has been so deeply woven into our way of life that citizens thought in terms of what offerings they could give to honor its beauty of conception.

"The Samuel S. Fleisher Art Memorial," reprinted from *Bulletin of the Philadelphia Museum of Art*, vol. LXIII, no. 309, Spring 1974, pp. 56–57.

Louis I. Kahn in Ahmedabad, 1974.

Selected Bibliography

The following is a partial listing of Louis I. Kahn's published writings, lectures, and interviews. All of the works reprinted in this volume are listed, along with other publications of interest.

1931

"Pencil Drawings." *Architecture* LXIII, no. 1 (January 1931): 15–17.

"The Value and Aim in Sketching." *T-Square Club Journal* I, no. 6 (May 1930): 4, 18–21.

1942

Howe, George, Louis I. Kahn, and Oscar Stonorov. "Standards' Versus Essential Space: Comments on Unit Plans for War Housing." *Architectural Forum* 76, no. 5 (May 1942): 307–311.

1943

Stonorov, Oscar, and Louis I. Kahn. *Why City Planning is Your Responsibility*. New York: Revere Copper and Brass, 1943.

1944

"Monumentality." *Architecture and City Planning: A Symposium*, 77–88. New York: Philosophical Library, 1944, 77–88.

"War Plants After the War." *Journal of the American Institute of Architects* II, no. 2 (August 1944): 59–62.

You and Your Neighborhood . . . A Primer for Neighborhood Planning. New York: Revere Copper and Brass, 1944.

1949

"A Dairy Farm." *Beaux-Arts Institute of Design Bulletin* XXV (March 1949): 2–5.

1953

"On the Responsibility of the Architect." *Perspecta* 2 (1953): 45–47.

"Toward a Plan for Midtown Philadelphia." *Perspecta* 2 (1953): 10–27.

1954

Architecture and the University. Princeton: The School of Architecture, Princeton University, 1954.

"How to Develop New Methods of Construction." *Architectural Forum* (November 1954): 157.

346

1955

"A Synagogue: Adath Jeshurun of Philadelphia." *Perspecta* 3 (1955): 62–63.

"Order and Design." *Perspecta* 3 (1955): 59.

"This Business of Architecture." *The Student Publication of the School of Architecture of Tulane University.* New Orleans, 1955.

"Two Houses." *Perspecta* 3 (1955): 60–61.

1956

"An Approach to Architectural Education." *Pennsylvania Triangle* 42, no. 3 (January 1956), 28–32.

"Space, Form, Use: A Library." *Pennsylvania Triangle* 43, no. 2 (December 1956): 43–47.

1957

A City Tower: A Concept of Natural Growth. University Atlas Cement Company, United States Steel Corporation Publication No. ADUAC-707-57 (5BM-WP), 1957.

"Architecture is the Thoughtful Making of Spaces: The Continual Renewal of Architecture Comes from Changing Concepts of Space." *Perspecta* 4 (1957): 23.

"Order in Architecture." *Perspecta* 4 (1957): 58–65.

"Spaces, Order and Architecture." *Royal Architectural Institute of Canada Journal* 34, no. 10 (October 1957): 375–377.

"The Entrance to a Theater." The Emerson Prize, Fall Term, 1956–1957. *National Institute for Architectural Education Bulletin* XXXIII (January 1957): 10–11.

1959

"Concluding Remarks to the CIAM Congress, Otterlo, 1959." In *New Frontiers in Architecture: CIAM in Otterlo 1959*, by Oscar Newman. New York: Universe Books, 1961.

1960

"Marin City Redevelopment." *Progressive Architecture* XLI, no. 11 (November 1960): 149–153.

"On Form and Design." Speech at the 46th meeting of the Association of Collegiate Schools of Architecture, University of California, Berkeley, April 22–23, 1960. Reprinted in *Journal of Architectural Education* XV, no. 3 (Fall 1960).

"On Philosophical Horizons." *American Institute of Architects Journal* XXXIII, no. 6 (June 1960): 99–100.

"World Design Conference." Statement by Louis I. Kahn, reprinted in *Industrial Design* 7, no. 7 (July 1960): 46–49.

1961

"The Sixties: A P/A Symposium on the State of Architecture: Part I." *Progressive Architecture* (January/March 1961).

"Louis I. Kahn." Discussion recorded in Louis I. Kahn's office in Philadelphia, February 1961. *Perspecta* 7 (1961): 9–28.

"A Statement." *Arts and Architecture* 78, no. 2 (February 1961): 14–15, 28–30.

"Form and Design." *Architectural Design* XXXI, no. 4 (April 1961): 145–154.

"Wanting to Be: The Philadelphia School." Interview with J. C. Rowan, in *Progressive Architecture* (April 1961): 130–149.

"Architecture—Fitting and Befitting." *Architectural Forum* 114, no. 3 (June 1961): 88.

"The Nature of Nature." *Journal of Architectural Education* XVI, no. 3 (Autumn 1961): 85–104.

"Order Is." *Zodiac* 8 (1961): 14–25.

"Design with the Automobile: The Animal World." Excerpts from an interview by H.P. Daniel Van Ginkel, in *Canadian Art* XIX, no. 1 (January/February 1962): 50–55.

1962

Dixon, Rose. "Coffee Break with Louis I. Kahn: A Very Modern Architect." *The Philadelphia Sunday Bulletin Magazine* (January 28, 1961): 12.

"The Architect and the Building." *Bryn Mawr Alumnae Bulletin* XLIII, no. 1 (Summer 1962).

"Form and Design." In *Louis I. Kahn*, by Vincent Scully, 113–121. New York: George Braziller, 1962.

Wurman, Richard Saul, and Eugene Feldman. *The Notebooks and Drawings of Louis I. Kahn*. Philadelphia: Falcon Press, 1962.

1963

"Ordine nel movimento." *Edilizia Moderna* 80 (September 1963): 7, 106–107.

1964

"A Statement." *Arts and Architecture* 81, no. 5 (1964): 18–19, 33.

"Louis I. Kahn sull'architettura." Excerpts in Italian from address delivered at International Design Conference, Aspen, Colorado, in *L'Architettura* X, no. 7 (November 1964): 480–481.

"Our Changing Environment." The First World Congress of Craftsman, June 1964.

"Talks with Students." *Architecture at Rice* 26 (1969).

1965

"Remarks." *Perspecta* 9/10 (1965): 303–335.

"Structure and Form." *Royal Architectural Institute of Canada Journal* 42, no.11 (November 1965): 26–28, 32.

1966

"Address by Louis I. Kahn—April 5, 1966." *Boston Society of Architects Journal* 1 (1967): 5–20.

1967

"Louis Kahn: Statements on Architecture." Lecture given at the Politecnico in Milan, January 1967, in *Zodiac* 17 (1967): 54–57.

"Space and Inspirations." Lecture at the New England Conservatory for the symposium "The Conservatory Redefined," in *L'Architecture d'Aujourd'hui* 142 (February/March 1969): 20–35.

"Twelve Lines." Exhibition statement on Boullée, Ledoux, and Lequeu, in *Visionary Architects: Boullée, Ledoux, Lequeu*. Houston: The University of St. Thomas, 1968.

1968

Foreword to *Pioneer Texas Buildings: A Geometry Lesson*, by Clovis Heimsath. Austin: The University of Texas Press, 1968.

"Revolutionary Champions." *American Institute of Architects Journal* (January 1968).

"Silence." *Via* 1 (1968): 88–89.

1969

Foreword to *Villages in the Sun*, by Myron Goldfinger. New York: Praeger, 1969.

"Silence." *L'Architecture d'Aujourd'hui* 142 (February/March 1969): 6–7.

1970

"Architecture: Silence and Light." In *On the Future of Art*, by Arnold Toynbee. New York: Viking, 1970.

1971

"Not for the Fainthearted." *AIA Journal* 55, no. 6 (June 1971): 25–31.

"The Room, the Street, and Human Agreement." *American Institute of Architects Journal* 56, no. 3 (September 1971): 33–34.

1972

"An Architect Speaks his Mind." Interview in *House and Garden* 142, no. 4 (October 1972).

"Architecture." The John William Lawrence Memorial Lectures, Tulane University, School of Architecture, New Orleans, 1972.

"How'm I Doing, Corbusier?" Interview with Patricia McLaughlin, in *The Pennsylvania Gazette* 71, no. 3 (December 1972): 18–26.

"The Invisible City: International Design Conference in Aspen." *Design Quarterly 86/87* (1972).

"The Wonder of the Natural Thing." Interview with Marshall D. Meyers, Philadelphia, August 11, 1972, in *Louis I. Kahn: l'uomo, il maestro*, by Alessandra Latour. Rome: Edizioni Kappa, 1985.

1973

"Clearing." Interview with Louis I. Kahn, in *Via* 2 (1973): 158–161.

"Louis I. Kahn." In *Conversations with Architects*, by John W. Cook and Heinrich Klotz, 178–217. New York: Praeger, 1973.

"1973: Brooklyn, New York." Lecture given at Pratt Institute, Fall 1973, in *Perspecta* 19 (1982): 89–100.

"Room, Window, and Sun." *Canadian Architect* 18, no. 6 (June 1973): 52–55.

"Thoughts." *Architecture and Urbanism* 3, no. 1 (January 1973).

1974

"Poetics." *Journal of American Education* XXVII, no.1 (February 1974).

Foreword to *Carlo Scarpa architetto poeta* (London: Royal Institute of British Architects, 1974). Exhibition catalogue.

"Harmony between Man and Architecture." *Design* 18, no. 3 (March 1974): 23–38.

"The Samuel L. Fleisher Art Memorial." *Philadelphia Museum of Art Bulletin* LXVIII, no. 309 (Spring 1974): 56–57.

1975

"I Love Beginnings." *Architecture and Urbanism* (1975): 278–286.

Johnson, Neil E. *Light is the Theme: Louis I. Kahn and the Kimbell Art Museum.* Fort Worth: Kimbell Art Foundation, 1975.

1977

Ronner, Heinz, Sharad Jhaveri, and Alessandro Vasella. *Louis I. Kahn: Complete Work, 1935–1974.* Stuttgart and Basel: Birkhë user Verlag for the Institute for the History and Theory of Architecture, and The Swiss Federal Institute of Technology, Zurich, 1977; and Boulder, Colorado: Westview Press, 1977.

1979

Lobell, John. *Between Silence and Light.* Boulder, Colorado: Shambhala, 1979.

1984

Tyng, Alexandra. *Beginnings: Louis I. Kahn's Philosophy of Architecture.* New York: John Wiley & Sons, 1984.

1986

Wurman, Richard Saul, ed. *What Will Be Has Always Been: The Words of Louis I. Kahn.* New York: Access Press and Rizzoli, 1986.